ESSAYS

Literary, Moral
and
Philosophical

BENJAMIN RUSH

EDITED, WITH AN INTRODUCTORY ESSAY,
BY MICHAEL MERANZE

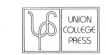

Union College Press
Schenectady, NY 12308

INTRODUCTION

From the observations that have been made it is plain, that I consider it possible to convert men into republican machines. This must be done, if we expect them to perform their parts properly, in the great machine of the government of the state. That republic is sophisticated with monarchy or aristocracy that does not revolve upon the wills of the people, and these must be fitted to each other by means of education before they can be made to produce regularity and unison in government.—OF THE MODE OF EDUCATION PROPER IN A REPUBLIC

THE American Revolution was a highly utopian and a highly contentious process that, beyond the struggle for home rule, promised new possibilities for humanity. "We have it in our power to begin the world over again"—Thomas Paine's bold assertion—was only a concentrated expression of a widely-held revolutionary faith.[1] But the revolution was neither smooth nor consensual. The conflict between radicals and tories on the question of independence was only the first of a series of bitter struggles: over the proper way to conduct the war for independence, over the degree of popular control over government, and over the proper organization of government itself (and indeed over whose interests the government should serve). The Revolution may have opened a new future for Americans, but what form it would take remained very much an open question.

Few individuals immersed themselves more deeply in that task of shaping America's future than Benjamin Rush. This signer of the Declaration of Independence was a prolific writer on political and social questions, a founder of several colleges, and an aggressive promotor of social reforms. The fact that he was also revolutionary America's leading physician and medical teacher and theorist profoundly affected his vision of the emergent order; he believed that the new age should be based not only upon the precepts of an enlightened religion but upon scientific principles as well.

His collection of literary, moral, and philosophical essays articulated and justified this vision. Although earlier versions of many of the essays had appeared as articles or pamphlets during the late

---

[1] "Common Sense," in Philip S. Foner, ed., *The Life and Major Writings of Thomas Paine* (Secaucus, N.J., 1948), I, 45.

1780s and early 1790s, they were first gathered into a volume in 1798. Taken singly, each essay seems guided by a clear intent. But what, besides having one author, holds together a collection of essays which range from education to punishment to manners to history to biography? What is the purpose of, say, a "Eulogium upon Dr. William Cullen"? Or of the "Thoughts on Common Sense"? What are their contexts? And how might we best read them?

I

"Most of the *distresses* of our country, and of the *mistakes* which Europeans have formed of us," Rush wrote Richard Price in May of 1786, "have arisen from a belief that the American Revolution is over." Rush thought different: "we have only finished the first act of the great drama. We have changed our forms of government, but it remains yet to effect a revolution in our principles, opinions, and manners so as to accommodate them to the forms of government we have adopted."[2]

Without a correct understanding of the revolution and a reorientation of the way people thought of their relationship to their institutions, the republican experiment was doomed to fail. Just this danger, he argued, had been demonstrated by the conflicts marking politics and society during the 1780s. In "An Account of the Influence of the Military and Political Events of the American Revolution Upon the Human Body," Rush suggested that Americans did not understand what responsibilities independence entailed: "The minds of the citizens of the United States were wholly unprepared for their new situation. The excess of the passion for liberty, inflamed by the successful issue of the war, produced, in many people, opinions and conduct which could not be removed by reason nor restrained by government." The result, in his eyes, was that many had gone mad over liberty. "The extensive influence which these opinions had upon the understandings, passions, and morals of many of the citizens of the United States, constituted a

---

[2] Benjamin Rush to Richard Price, May 25, 1786, in Lyman Butterfield, ed., *Letters of Benjamin Rush* (Princeton, N.J., 1951), I, 388.

form of insanity, which I shall take the liberty of distinguishing by the name of *anarchia*."[3]

Rush's fear of disorder reflected more than just his reaction to conditions in the young republic. Raised in an evangelical Presbyterian family, he had been educated by proponents of Great Awakening New Light philosophy, first at school and later at Princeton. Then, following college and an apprenticeship as a physician, he pursued advanced medical studies in Edinburgh, the home of the Scottish Enlightenment. His experiences in Britain bolstered attitudes acquired in America. Long before he attained prominence as a public figure the dominant patterns of his thought and personality had been set: a sense of the obligation of social activism; the belief that individual discipline and public order were dual necessities; a conviction that Christian love and republicanism were interconnected; and the assurance that the teachings of the Enlightenment and of revealed Christianity were inextricably bound.[4]

The Revolution reinforced these basic beliefs. When the struggle between Great Britain and her North American colonies culminated in the mid-1770s, Rush was one of Philadelphia's most ardent proponents of independence (as the fact that he shepherded Tom Paine's *Common Sense* into print attests). Yet, despite his radicalism on the question of independence, he recoiled from many of the effects of the Revolution in Pennsylvania. Pennsylvania's had been the most radical of the internal revolutions of the 1770s; it was the state in which the popular movement had gone furthest to empower the lower classes. Rush had forged close ties to the city's radicals; even so, he helped lead the fight against the democratization of political responsibility. Pennsylvania's democratic constitution of 1776 was a major target of his ire; publicly and privately he attacked the document as an instrument of "mobocracy." The same propensities were evident in his efforts as a founding member of the conservative Republican Society (a group opposed to the more egalitarian Constitutionalists on issues of public policy and

---

[3] Benjamin Rush, *Medical Inquiries and Observations* (Philadelphia, 1805), I, 293.

[4] The fullest treatment of Rush's intellectual development and mature philosophy, to which I am indebted throughout, is Donald D'Elia, *Benjamin Rush: Philosopher of the American Revolution* (Philadelphia, 1974).

dedicated to undermining and overthrowing the Constitution of 1776). Indeed, Rush opposed virtually all efforts of the lower classes and their allies during the war to control the price of the necessities of life, and he became a vigorous defender of Robert Morris's economic policies in the early 1780s. Rush consistently allied himself with those who strove to stem the "excessive" democracy that they viewed as a growing menace to the state and the nation.

Finally, in the late 1780s, he eagerly supported both the Federal Constitution of 1787 and Pennsylvania's more conservative Constitution of 1790. This latter document, like the Federal Constitution, established a tripartite system of government to restrain the "passions" of the majority. Rush, in fact, was a federalist before there were Federalists. His criticism of Pennsylvania's 1776 Constitution— that its unicameral legislature and weak plural executive would lead to chaos—anticipated the attack on the Articles of Confederation as well as the Federalist disdain for the state legislatures of the 1780s. In addition, Rush's assertion that power must be delegated to representative authorities anticipated Madison's theory of representation in *Federalist* X. "It has been said often," Rush wrote in 1777, "and I wish the saying was engraven over the doors of every statehouse on the Continent, that 'all power is derived from the people,' but it has never yet been said that all power is seated in the people. Government supposes and requires a delegation of power: It cannot exist without it."[5] His project was the reconstruction of relations of authority; his goal, the fashioning of proper systems of representation.

Although firmly committed to these political reforms, Rush believed that they were only part of the solution to what he thought ailed the nation. Nothing less than a thoroughgoing social and psychological re-ordering would be required for the republic's survival. Moreover, at least during the 1780s and 1790s, he had no doubt that such social reconstruction was possible. Turning philosophy into practice, he joined many of the social reform organizations that emerged during the period, including the Society for Political Inquiries, the Pennsylvania Society for Promoting the Abolition of Slavery, and the Philadelphia Society for Alleviating

---

[5] Benjamin Rush, "Observations on the Government of Pennsylvania," (1777), in Dagobert D. Runes, ed., *The Selected Writings of Benjamin Rush* (New York, 1947), 71.

the Miseries of Public Prisons. These societies had diverse purposes, yet they arose from a common belief in the need to redefine American conceptions of community and the institutions that helped shape social life. Rush also evinced his faith in the possibility of self-transformation, as his long-standing advocacy of temperance indicates. Finally, like many of his fellow late eighteenth- and early nineteenth-century social reformers, Rush set great store in education as a tool of social advancement and order. Dickinson College, Franklin College (later the College of Franklin and Marshall), and the Philadelphia College of Physicians all owe their existence in some part to his direct efforts.

Rush's social vision reflected a combination of Scottish moral philosophy and Anglo-American sentimentalism. Within "human sensibility," he believed there existed a psychological basis for Christian love, an innate capacity for "sympathy" which made possible all human bonds. "Sympathy" connoted the ability to comprehend and, through imagination, to empathize with the experience of others. By "feeling" the pain or sorrow of others in this manner, people could overcome their isolation, associate, and aid each other. "Sympathy" was thus the psychological basis not only of charity but also of the rules of virtue and propriety.

The capacity for "sympathy," however, meant that individual psychology was inherently unstable; the sympathetic character was eminently corruptible. The same route that led to good effects also made individuals vulnerable to corruption if they were not taught to discriminate in their sympathies, of if the objects available to them for emulation were not controlled. The epistemological and pedagogical doctrine of the association of ideas reinforced the importance of sympathy. Following David Hartley, Rush believed knowledge (and virtue) develop through the mind's correlation of different ideas into larger truths. Faulty or undeveloped association of these ideas, however, could lead an individual or a society into error, and thus into vice. Consequently, it was not only permissible but necessary to control the association of ideas in education, criminal justice, and society in order to avoid a future of "anarchia."

Rush's *Essays* (and the concurrent political activities with which they were connected) can be read as a program for a post-Revolutionary life built upon discipline and the reconstruction of authority. For Rush, a return to monarchy or autocracy was not an

acceptable corrective for the "excesses" of liberty. His preferred alternative was transformation of the habits and mentalities of the
citizenry. The *Essays* offered both prescription and justification for
his particular vision of a post-Revolutionary society which would
create and employ disciplined, productive subjects who would, in
turn, construct and maintain a republic that joined agriculture,
commerce, and manufacturing. Rush's vision was of an America
shaped by the values of restraint, sobriety, deference, and industry.
If Americans followed his teachings, they would achieve both
expansion and order. If not, they would slide into chaos.

Rush sought to secure republican virtue in the context of a
democracy. Classical republican theory suggested that "virtue," the
disinterested pursuit of the public good, developed among landed
gentlemen who were secure both in their property and in their
access to arms. These twin sources of social power ensured the
independence of judgment which, in turn, would enable virtue to
triumph over passion. But, although this philosophy denied the
possibility of virtue to those without property or access to arms (as
well as to women and all dependents) from the possession of virtue
and, thereby, worked to exclude them from politics, practice had
already moved beyond theory. The post-Revolutionary Pennsylvania on which Rush was writing did not limit access to the political
process to landed gentry and their professional and mercantile
peers. Despite some restrictions on the male franchise (and total
exclusion of women), in general the "lower" classes had access to the
polls. Furthermore, these recent entrants into the political process
had demonstrated their capacity to organize for their own political
and social aims during the Revolution. Rush's project was to ensure
that these groups exercised their power in what he considered a
virtuous fashion. If the traditional social bases of "virtue" did not
exist, new social bases must be established. Institutions would have
to be created, and habits instilled, which would remake the
psychology and behavior of the lower classes. Education and—
where it failed—punishment would be the keys. Through them he
hoped to extend and control the experience of the Revolution—and
thereby secure republican virtue—in a new society.

II

Rush's strategy for reconstructing representational authority centered on knowledge. Clearly, Rush viewed education and punishment as functions of authority, and since the monarchy had been removed as the symbolic and actual basis of authority, a new ground for it had to be developed. That ground, in Rush's republic, was the combination of scientific and Christian truths. Men of knowledge (and the gender limitation is appropriate for Rush's vision), not aristocrats or populist politicians, would assume the authority to guide the future through their adherence to the principles of enlightened science and Christian precepts. America's new political situation mandated a new fusion of knowledge and social practices.

In order to liberate practice from custom, men of truth needed to point the way. Progress occurred only as social policy was entrusted to those well versed in social thought. "It has been remarked, that the profession of arms owes its present rank, as a science, to its having been rescued, since the revival of letters, from the hands of mere soldiers, and cultivated by men acquainted with other branches of literature."[6] Rush believed the techniques for the discovery of truth to be uniform, no matter the field of knowledge. "The reason of this is plain. Truth is an unit. It is the same thing in war—philosophy—medicine—morals—religion and government; and in proportion as we arrive at it in one science, we shall discover it in others" (80). Enlightenment endowed one with the capability not only of being, for instance, a doctor but of instructing the community on morals and government as well.

Rush's reformation of thought and practice began with an attack on common sense. In "Thoughts on Common Sense," he refuted the notion that "common sense" is a faculty of the mind or a type of reason. Instead, it consists merely of mental custom, inherited ways of thinking which bear no necessary relationship to truth. Instead of representing truth, common sense is "the perception of things as they appear to the greatest part of mankind. It has no relation to their being true or false, right or wrong, proper or improper.

---

[6] Below, this edition, 97. Hereafter, all references to this edition will be noted parenthetically in the text.

For the sake of perspicuity, I shall define it to be, Opinions and Feelings in unison with the Opinions and Feelings of the bulk of mankind" (147).

True wisdom, in contrast, meant thinking critically about custom and common sense. "To think and act with the majority of mankind, when they are right, and differently from them, when they are wrong, constitutes . . . the perfection of human wisdom and conduct." The task of the philosopher, more often than not, is to criticize general beliefs and perceptions. "In matters addressed to our reason," Rush suggested, "the principle business of reason is to correct the evidence of our senses. Indeed, the perception of truth, in philosophy, seems to consist in little else than in the refutation of the ideas acquired from the testimony of our senses" (149). Reason is counter-intuitive, and the task of social leaders was to restructure the systems of common perception and thought.

Ultimately, the growth of knowledge would overcome the distinction between reason and sense perception. "[W]hen the exact connection between the senses and reason is perfectly understood, it is probable that the senses and reason will be in unison with each other, and that mankind will as suddenly connect the evidence of all the senses with the decisions of reason, as they now connect, with certainty, the distance of objects with the evidence of the eyes." So, too, the alignment of reason with common sense. "In the perfection of knowledge, common sense and truth will be in unison with each other. Unfortunately, it is now more related to error than to truth . . . " (149).

In part, Rush's campaign against common sense extended from his conviction that enlightenment was already at work within the historical process. Throughout, the *Essays* refers to agriculture, industry, warfare, and morality as areas in which science and religion were banishing ignorance. His faith in intellectual progress is clearest in the attack on the worship of the ancients and the opposition to the teaching of classical languages. Rush was convinced that to continue to insist that students learn the classics would be to ignore the potential benefit of a present neither bound by confining and antiquated ideas nor enslaved by the tyranny of mere habit. "It has been said that the Latin language has become a necessary part of liberal knowledge, inasmuch as the European nations have by common consent made it the vehicle of their discoveries. This argument had some weight while science consisted only [in] learning what was known; but since the enquiries of philosophers have been directed to new objects of observation and experiment, the Latin language has not been able to keep pace with the number and rapidity of their discoveries." It was possible, and indeed necessary, to look at the world afresh. Technology, too, he believed had altered the relationship of the moderns to the ancients: "we live in an age in which knowledge has been drawn from its dead repositories, and diffused by the art of printing, in living languages, through every part of the world" (21, 22).

But Rush did not equate freedom from custom with intellectual anarchy. The liberation of reason would lead to the acceptance of Christian Truth, he presumed, because the contradictions between science and religion were only apparent and derived from the immature state of human understanding: "There are many things in scripture above, but nothing contrary to, reason" (96). God had provided humanity with three sources of truth: observation of nature and the study of natural history, introspection, and the study of the Bible. Only the lack of skill or the limits of will and intellect prevented humanity from perceiving the links among these three sources (64). Presupposing that nature, humanity, and the Bible all had one divine author, Rush was convinced that knowledge would tend to unity. Thinking, instead of being confined within custom, would be constrained within truth.

Herein lies the strategy of the *Essays*. In its entirety, the book represents a systematic attempt to overturn custom and replace it with ideas and practices based upon Rush's notion of truth. This effort is most visible in the programmatic character of many of the essays (the proposals for an expansion and restructuring of schooling; the transformation of the aims and practices of punishment; the revaluation of social character and values in the historical essays; the proposals for social and political reforms scattered throughout), but it is equally evident in Rush's rhetoric and argumentation. In proposing to restructure social institutions and values, Rush also attempted to control the grounds of the discussion.

In a manner typical of the Enlightenment, Rush endeavored to win his readers to the method of "truth" by demonstrating the variety of custom and common sense. In a series of issues (including slavery, capital punishment, republicanism, dancing, and medicine), he either juxtaposed the common sense of the past with the common sense of the present or compared the various customs of different countries or societies at the same time (147–149). Exposure of these inconsistencies was designed to undermine any claim to universality. If custom and common sense were inadequate justifications for particular beliefs or institutional arrangements, he believed, they should be displaced by religion and science.

Having freed his readers from custom, Rush then aimed to bind them to a new vision of truth, in part through the rhetoric of flattery. In the "Thoughts Upon the Amusements and Punishments Which Are Proper for Schools," for instance, his strategy for mollifying George Clymer (and the general reader of the volume) is quite clear: "I am sure you will not reject my opinions because they are contrary to received practices, for I know that you are accustomed to thinking for yourself, and that every proposition that has for its objects the interests of humanity and your country, will by treated by you with attention and candor" (34). Only those warped by passion and interest would fail to join with him.

Rush fully appreciated the importance of rhetoric. Eloquence he stated, is "the first accomplishment in a republic, and often sets the whole machine of government in motion . . . We do not extol it too highly when we attribute as much to the power of eloquence as to the sword, in bringing about the American revolution" (10). No leader of an enfranchised polity could afford to ignore the art of public speaking and public writing. That man of science and religion who was Rush's intellectual would almost literally inscribe his vision of society upon society. This emphasis on the training of verbal sensibilities is especially evident in his justification of the Bible as a central text in teaching the young. By "obliging children to read it as a school book . . . we insensibly *engrave*, as it were, its contents upon their minds . . . " (63). This common text, by providing a common means of valuing all texts would help unify society and furnish the avenues of discourse within it. Or, put another way, Rush was proposing to bind his reader (and the schoolchildren reading the Bible) within his vision of a reconstructed society, much as a book's binding sews its pages into a larger whole.

In the programmatic sections of the *Essays*, this process typically operates through either or both of two strategies. The first asserts several principles as self-evident premises, from which the author then reasons deductively. One instance of this approach occurs midway through the "Enquiry into the Effects of Public Punishments upon the Criminal, and Upon Society," where, after laying down six principles of the human mind, Rush announces: "These axioms being admitted (for they cannot be controverted) I shall proceed next to apply them, by suggesting a plan for the punishment of crimes, which, I flatter myself, will answer all the ends that have been proposed by them" (86–87). Since his axioms "cannot be controverted," Rush, the voice of truth and humanity, has effectively defined the terms of the debate. The second strategy takes the form of the critique. For example, in "Thoughts on Common Sense," he begins by describing an inherited belief; then, having acknowledged the popularity of the idea he is criticising, he dismisses it as "mere custom" and counters with a set of "self-evident" contrary premises. Whether the argument proceeds in an assertive or a critical mode, the end result is a new policy position grounded in a previously hidden truth. Rush may leave open the possibility of disagreement on the truth of an interpretation—truth, after all, is progressive—yet the form of the argument precludes anything other than science or religion from guiding social policy.

Rush's special deployment of truth, however, relies not only on the reader's assent to the premise and to the claims of reason as the guide for social policy but also on the credentials of the framer of the argument. Thus, while establishing the authority of his propositions, Rush also labors to establish his authority—as his frequent entrances, and intrusions, in the guise of the heroic critic of inherited ignorance attests. In addition, and in accord with the eighteenth-century's predilection for moral exemplars, Rush offers his readers two other models of enlightened intellectuals—William Cullen and David Rittenhouse—who combined piety, knowledge, and patriotism. These were the symbols of the new citizen who would emerge from an enlightened society and lead in the cultivation of a republican future. In extolling Cullen and Rittenhouse—intellectuals, like himself, who manifested his desired values and qualities—Rush is in effect reinforcing his own authority as preceptor.

III

The correlates of a new citizen were the new social institutions they would create and be created by in turn, and to no institution did Rush assign a more pivotal place than the school. "Freedom," he wrote, "can exist only in the society of knowledge"; learning is "friendly to religion" and "favourable to liberty." A proper education would combine morality and utility, the love of liberty with the love of discipline and duty. Moreover, in addition to spreading "just ideas" about law and government while improving manners, it would furnish keys to the enrichment of agriculture and manufacturing (1). By combining and meshing the retooled components of society, education would produce "republican machines."

A reformed education, Rush thought, needed to be guided by more than just the desire to disperse knowledge. Rush insisted that the schools inculcate a mutually reinforcing love of God, of the state, and the republic. If the allegiances of individuals were interwoven in this manner, there would be no abuse of freedom by citizen-subjects simultaneously endowed with rights and the obligation—ensured by their recognition of truth—to uphold republican and Christian duties and laws.

To create these citizen-subjects, Rush advocated expanding the educational system. Addressing Pennsylvania lawmakers, he suggested the creation of free schools in each township or area containing one hundred families. Above these free schools he proposed four colleges—one each at Philadelphia, Carlisle, Lancaster, and, sometime in the future, Pittsburgh—crowned by one University.

Rush envisioned this educational system as a unified and unifying structure. "The university will in time furnish masters for the colleges, and the colleges will furnish masters for the free schools, while the free schools, in their turns, will supply the colleges and the university with scholars, students and pupils." From the unification of education would come the unification of culture. "The same systems of grammar, oratory, and philosophy" would be taught everywhere and, as a result, "the literary features of Pennsylvania will thus designate one great, and equally enlightened family" (2). A shared culture—not a shared descent—would make Pennsylvania a family.

Christianity stood at the center of this cultural integration.

A devout Christian who, unlike many of his more skeptical peers, never lost his faith in revelation, Rush believed in the unity between religious teachings and scientific truths. Even more importantly, he remained firmly convinced that Christianity and republicanism were mutually reinforcing—indeed, that they were in "truth" the same system. Christian "truths"—the equality of humanity, the importance of love, the interconnectedness of individuals, self-denial—were, according to him, intrinsically linked to republicanism. "A Christian," he argued in one of his least empirical statements, "cannot fail of being a republican" (6).

Christianity, he believed, was the basis of all public spiritedness and, consequently, a crucial component of plans for education. "I beg leave to remark, that the only foundation for a useful education in a republic is to be laid in Religion. Without this there can be no virtue, and without virtue there can be no liberty, and liberty is the object and life of all republican governments." Although he professed that he would prefer the teaching of any religion, even "the opinions of Confucius or Mohomed," to the teaching of no religion, it was Christianity that he sought to include in the schools. Christian "doctrines and precepts," he declared, were "calculated to promote the happiness of society, and the safety and well being of civil government" (6). He attacked those who opposed the teaching of religion because it would prejudice the minds of students. He encouraged both the use of the Bible as a school book and the active proselytizing of schoolmasters. For him, Christianity formed the basis of virtue and truth—and it should be taught as such.

In a sense, one's relationship to God and Jesus formed the basis for Rush's vision of reformed human relationships. Human beings are all equal before God—hence his opposition to monarchy and slavery. Love, he argued, was the essential Christian attribute, just as love of humanity is the central Christian teaching, because it points to the human equality and individual liberty which he saw at the base of republicanism. But this human equality occurs within the context of the inequality in the relationship between the human and the divine. Human beings are bound to love by divine will; the separation between the human and the divine means that loving is *commanded*. Human beings are equal because they are equally subject to the law—and they achieve their fullest humanity through submission to the law. Since, as Rush saw it, Christian love thus simultaneously empowers and constrains, he concluded that Christian citizens would be both free and obedient.

But Rush's notion of Christian love did not mean that individuals should love all people equally. The student "must be taught to love his fellow creatures in every part of the world, but he must cherish with a more intense and peculiar affection, the citizens of Pennsylvania and of the United States" (7). Despite his own experiences in Edinburgh, Rush wished to prevent Americans youths from becoming attached to foreign countries or customs. "The principle of patriotism stands in need of the reinforcement of prejudice, and it is well known that our strongest prejudices in favour of our country are formed in the first one and twenty years of our lives" (5). An education at home would help to strengthen ties to the state.

Moreover, a proper education in patriotism would reinforce the lesson of obedient freedom. Rush never rejected the classical republican belief that the public realm took precedence over the private. "Our country includes family, friends, and property, and should be preferred to them all. Let our pupil be taught that he does not belong to himself, but that he is public property. Let him be taught to love his family, but let him be taught at the same time, that he must forsake, and even forget them, when the welfare of his country requires it" (7). Like Christian love, political independence brought both opportunity and obligation; liberty includes the sacrifice of private desire for public good.

Finally, the hearts and minds of students must be bound to the principles of republicanism and the perpetuation of the republic. Rush wished to see students taught that "there can be no durable liberty but in a republic, and that government, like all other sciences, is of a progressive nature." Students could—indeed must—work to preserve and improve the republic, "not only to increase the happiness but to promote the duration of republican forms of government far beyond the terms limited for them by history, or the common opinions of mankind" (8). Republican machines would reform and improve, not overthrow or undermine, the republic.

Rush offered more than general educational principles, however. To turn students into citizens he authored a precise curriculum combining utility and morality as well. His curriculum, it is impor-

tant to note, has the same doubled structure as the general educational principles. Much of the program—for instance, Rush's
rejection of teaching ancient languages and his advocacy of the
modern, his commitment to teaching reading and writing, and his
insistence on the importance of science and agriculture—points
towards the liberation of the individual from the past and from
ignorance. But equally important are those areas—the teaching of
Christian principles, the history of earlier republics, knowledge of
the laws—designed to direct and control the individual's participation in society. Rush regarded the very process of obtaining
knowledge as simultaneously liberating and constraining; individuals freed from the constraint of custom would be subjected to the
demands of truth.

This same pattern appears in Rush's proposals for the punishment of students. In "Thoughts upon the amusements and
punishments, which are proper for Schools," he decried corporal
punishments as inappropriate means to control children (at least
those above the age of four). Instead, he suggested a careful,
disciplined exercise of authority to bind the students affectionately
to their master. Were this to fail, schoolmasters should adopt
punishments designed to shame the conscience: "private admonition," confinement after school, public shaming before classmates.
These punishments were to lead to the internalization of discipline.
Rush's strategy here corresponds to the intentions evident in his
educational proposals: to free children from inherited practice in
order to bind them more closely to authority.

Nowhere is this simultaneously liberating and constraining
purpose clearer than in "Thoughts Upon Female Education,
Accommodated to the Present State of Society, Manners, and
Government, in the United States of America." Rush urged that
women, for several reasons, must be educated to fulfill their "duties
of social and domestic life" (54). Committed to female education on
philosophical grounds, he was convinced that the attempt to deny
women learning was nothing more than a male prejudice. But there
were practical reasons for this support as well. Given American
realities, wives needed to be prepared to assist their husbands in the
handling of business and the government of servants (the class
dimension of Rush's educational program should be noted in
reading this essay). Moreover, he believed women should play a

critical role in educating their sons and husbands to assume their proper place in public life. As Linda Kerber, Rush Bloch, and others have shown, a regendering of virtue occurred in the years following the revolution, leading to that complex of ideas which historians call "republican motherhood."[7] In this reconstructed notion of virtue, women were given the role of moral arbiters for their males—to teach their sons' moral values, and to restrain the behavior of the men around them. Rush strongly advocated both. Nothing less than the survival of the republic was at stake in these efforts.

But, in order to reshape men, women themselves needed to be reshaped through education. As in the case of males, educating women implied training them in the rules of truth and virtue to ensure that they fulfilled their social duties in a disciplined fashion. The better educated the woman was, the more governable she would be. "If men believe that ignorance is favourable to the government of the female sex, they are certainly deceived; for a weak and ignorant woman will always be governed with the greatest difficulty . . . It will be in your power, LADIES, to correct the mistakes and practice of our sex upon these subjects, by demonstrating, that the female temper can only be governed by reason, and that the cultivation of reason in women, is alike friendly to the order of nature, and to private as well as public happiness" (54). In freeing women from unreasonable authority, education would tie them to the authority of reason.

As his views on female education indicate, however, Rush's commitment to universal education should not be confused with a social egalitarianism. He expected that women would receive a "peculiar" education, i.e., one fitting them for their particular social role (44). Education was to be differentiated along gender lines to meet what he took to be the fixed and separate social duties assigned each sex. Similarly, among males, Rush's educational proposals implicitly reinforced class distinctions. Although he advocated free schools for everyone regardless of social standing, attendance at a college or at the university depended on parental willingness and

---

7 Cf. Linda K. Kerber, *Women of the Republic: Intellect and Ideology in Revolutionary America* Chapel Hill, 1980); Ruth H. Bloch, "The Gendered Meanings of Virtue in Revolutionary America," in *Signs: Journal of Women in Culture and Society* 1987, xiii, 1, 37–58.

ability to assume the costs of advanced education (2). Aside from the question of whether a working class family could really spare the children's time (and hence their labor) to allow them to attend school, these costs effectively excluded the less wealthy from more advanced education. Hence Rush's frequent defense of his educational proposals as effective training for someone entering the professions or commerce, for it was the middle and upper classes whose character and behavior he was most concerned to shape (at least through education). Instead of curbing the influence of wealth he sought to discipline it and root it in knowledge.

Rush's educational plan was simultaneously democratic and hierarchical. Mass education would create a common culture, but, within that common culture, it would reinforce social distinctions based upon class and gender. It would enable individuals to participate in the life of the republic, but it would direct and curtail their understanding of what that participation entailed. It would serve to make individuals aware of their rights and liberties, but it would discipline their exercise of those liberties by subordinating desire to the truth of Christian republicanism. And it would make citizens both rulers and ruled. This doubleness should not be understood primarily in a political or social sense—as in the ancient Greek idea of the alternation of political office-holding (Rush was an opponent of forced rotation in office). Rather, it was a condition within individuals as they exercised their freedom only in terms of the obligations of truth and virtue.

IV

Rush's writing displays a social optimism arising from his confidence in reason; nonetheless, there is a fear at the center (both literal and figurative) of the *Essays*. His educational program, after all, remained to be implemented; in the meantime, not all citizens recognized "truth." What should be done with those who remained uneducated and trapped in misunderstanding and custom? How could his values be inculcated in those who would not read—and hence not be transformed by—the *Essays*? The answer lay in punishment and social discipline. Because of the centrality of this problem for Rush's program, and because the essays on punishment offer fine examples of Rush's rhetoric, it is worthwhile to follow their arguments at length.

Early versions of "An Enquiry into the Effects of Public Punishments upon Criminals, and upon Society" were first presented in 1787 as a critique of Pennsylvania's new system of public penal labor. In the autumn of 1786, the state had seriously reduced the number of crimes subject to capital punishment, and it had ended corporal punishment for larceny. Under the new law, convicts were subjected to terms of servitude at hard, public, penal labor. Known as the "Wheelbarrow Law" because convicts were chained to wheelbarrows while at their public works, the statute was hailed by its proponents as an enlightened, republican penal system. Not only would the convicts be spared so that their characters could be reformed, but they would also serve the community as reminders of the price exacted for failure to obey the law.

In practice, however, the "wheelbarrow law" quickly generated its own contradictions. Onlookers, instead of soberly observing the convicts from a distance, chatted with them, taunted them, provided them with alms or liquor, and even helped them to escape. The convicts themselves proved difficult to control: they were reluctant workers, and having been brought together on the city streets and (at night) in the jail, they acted collectively, sometimes violently, against the authorities. Crime in the city increased—or at least so commentators believed. Although many argued that the solution to these problems lay in a more rigorous enforcement of the law, an opposition movement dedicated to replacing the law developed and worked to make its weight felt. Rush was one of its leaders.

In the "Enquiry," he aimed to demonstrate the insufficiency of only reforming the application of the law; nothing less than a reconceptualization of the means to meet the aims of penal law would do. The essay posits that inherent connections exist between, on the one hand, corruption and the public display of criminals, and, on the other, reformation and the segregation and concealment of criminals. Although Rush did argue that public punishments are harmful to the character of those subjected to them, his attack on public punishment focuses upon the symbolic or communicative function of punishment and its effect on the community. It is the spectators' ability to interpret the meaning of public punishments "correctly" that concerned him; the public display of criminals, he argued, is too susceptible to misrecognition and miscommunication.

Despite the specific and local nature of the "wheelbarrow law," the essay, in a manner typical of Rush, couches the argument in terms of a general truth. "The design of punishment is said to be," (NB: not "*I would like to argue that*"), "1st, to reform the person who suffers it,—2dly, to prevent the perpetration of crimes, by exciting terror in the minds of spectators; and—3rdly, to remove those persons from society, who have manifested by their tempers and crimes, that they are unfit to live in it." Ever since "the first institution of government," Rush admitted, both social practice and received opinion had agreed that punishments needed to take place in public (79). But he rejected this traditional wisdom. Temporary exclusion from society, taking the form of imprisonment, he insisted, could better achieve reformation and terror than placing criminals on public display.

On this question, as on others, Rush thought unexamined tradition the enemy to be overcome. He believed the idea of public punishments sprang not from reason but from erroneous "first thoughts" which "long and general prejudice" had legitimated. But reason, "the only just sovereign of the human mind," Rush contended, must prevail (79). Just as the knowledge of truth had been extended in morals, medicine, philosophy, religion, and government, so it must be extended into the understanding of punishment.

The "Enquiry" quickly disposes of the notion that public punishments could have any positive effect upon the condemned. They are "generally" too short to achieve any significant transformation of a person's character. Moreover, the public display of criminals, it notes, is intrinsically tied to infamy. But, however horrible the imposition of infamy—and Rush thought that human beings fear it more than death—it does not improve character. Instead, the practice has the opposite effect, destroying the "sense of shame" which is "one of the strongest out-posts of virtue." In addition, infamy shatters reputations and, in a society where opportunity is tied, at least in part, to personal associations, this deprives criminals of one of their most important possessions. Finally, once subjected to public punishment, criminals passed beyond the reach of either social or corporal sanctions. "Pain has begotten insensibility to the whip; and infamy to shame" (80).

Not only do these punishments fail to reintegrate the condemned back into the community, but, Rush argued, they also endanger society itself. Criminals left "infamous," "shameless," and "insensible" to pain would "probably" possess a "spirit of revenge against the whole community" under whose laws they had suffered. So "stimulated" by vengeance, criminals would "add to the number and enormity" of their "outrages upon society" (80). And increasing the length of such punishments, as in penal labor, would only worsen these effects.

The analysis of the impact of public punishments upon criminals, however, served merely as a prelude to Rush's real concerns—the impact of these rituals upon the spectators and the spectators' unreliability as an audience. "All men, when they suffer, discover either fortitude, insensibility, or distress"; each of these reactions, he argued, undermine the deterent effects of the punishment. In fact, "so far from preventing crimes by the terror they excite," public punishments are "directly calculated to produce them" (81). This system of punishment corrupts human sensibilities; consequently, it would destroy the ties binding individuals to each other and to the community—the very ties Rush hoped to inculcate through education.

The prisoner's display of fortitude undercut penal terror by "inciting" the spectators' respect. Regardless of the justice of the sentence, fortitude, when witnessed, "never fails to weaken or to obliterate" the "destestation of the crimes with which it is connected in criminals" because it "seizes so forcible" the "esteem" of the spectators. In addition, Rush observes, the crowd's mere presence reinforces the prisoner's will. "There is something, in the presence of a number of spectators, which is calculated to excite and strengthen fortitude in a sufferer" (81). Even capital punishment fails in its purpose. It is as much the fear of dying alone as dying itself that excites terror in the criminal; public execution overcomes this fear by creating an atmosphere of communal celebration. Inevitably, the transformation of villain into hero would affect the crowd itself. By confusing the distinction between temporary bravery and heroic character, the display of fortitude on the part of the condemned might lead some members of the audience to emulate precisely the criminality the ritual was supposed to repress. Even the most well-orchestrated public punishment, Rush argued, could not eliminate this danger.

Still "more fatal" to society, in Rush's view, is the criminals' affection of insensibility. The efficacy of public punishments, he noted in the same essay, depends on terror and humiliation. If the subject of punishment appears unmoved or insensible to its burdens, the audience also ceases to fear the punishment. Criminals thus have it in their power to convert what was designed as an exhibition of the law's strength into an exposure of its weakness. Should the criminal's insensibility extend beyond the physical to the moral aspects of the punishment, the effects would be even more dangerous: it might "excite a desire" in those "made miserable" by debt or guilt to commit crimes so that they could "end their distresses in the same enviable apathy to evil" displayed by the criminal. Even worse evils would ensue if the criminal were to wrest control of the punishment from the authorities and transforms the punishment into a farce. If punishment is met with "chearfulness," the solemnity of the penal scene could shatter, especially if the condemned were to choose to "retaliate upon the inhuman curiosity of spectators by profane or indecent insults or conversation" (82). Such debased interaction would lead to moral chaos rather than disciplined virtue.

If the criminals' fortitude seduces the audience and their insensibility debases the ritual reaffirmation of law, their distress, Rush argued, effectively diminishes the human capacity for sympathy. Due to an "immutable law" of human nature, distress, "when seen," invariably "produces sympathy and a disposition to relieve it." This occurs even if the suffering caused by the authorities is just. But if the spectators respond sympathetically to the criminals' plight, they cannot reduce their suffering. The result is frustration of a basic human impulse. Sympathy, rendered "abortive," returns "empty to the bosom in which it was awakened" (82). Paradoxically, public punishment denies what it simultaneously demands. By teaching citizens to ignore distress, the rituals of the state and commands of the law work to "eradicate" active sympathy from society.

Because sympathy, the psychological basis of love, is the critical quality in Rush's moral vision, its loss would be calamitous. As the "viceregent of the divine benevolence in our world," Rush believed the "principle" of sympathy was "intended to bind up all the wounds which sin and death have made among mankind." Without the human capacity for sympathy, charity would disappear: "Misery of every kind will then be contemplated without emotion or sympathy—the widow and the orphan—the naked—the sick, and the prison, will have no avenue to our services or our charity." Equally important, sensibility, the "centinel of the moral faculty," enables individuals to distinguish virtue from vice or good from evil (83). Rush feared that elimination of this monitor would affect more than the individual. The destruction of sympathy would reduce humanity to a Hobbesian state of nature.

Finally, Rush considered the political harm that could ensue from public punishments. Pity for the distressed criminal, he was convinced, alienates the spectators from the state: "while we pity, we secretly condemn the law which inflicts the punishment." Eventually, this process would lead to a "want of respect" for the laws "in general," and thus to "a more feeble union of the great ties of government" (83). The emotion public punishments elicit in fact counteract the messages they convey in theory. Instead of representing a collective reaffirmation of communal norms, they actually help dissolve the ties binding state to citizen. If the law appears to engage in acts of cruelty, its legitimacy would dissolve.

But public punishments, Rush contended, remain self-defeating even if spectators do not identify sympathetically with the condemned. The "characters or conduct of criminals," he noted, can elicit "indignation or contempt" instead of pity. In this case the human mind is subject to corruption from within. Consequently, he aimed to prevent the development of those "passions" which habituate individuals to look upon the pain of others with indifference. If this prevention fails, these passions could affect charity in a manner similar to the frustration of sympathy, thereby precluding the fulfillment of the "obligations to universal benevolence." (84).

Still worse, indignation or contempt might destroy the basis of everyday sociability. Since convicted criminals are, after all, fellow human beings, "familiarity with such objects of horror" on the part of witnesses to punishment would inevitably lessen the cohesion of society. "If a spectator should give himself time to reflect upon such a sight of human depravity, he would naturally recoil from the embrace of friendship, and the endearments of domestic life" (84). The association of ideas, in this case the linking of "depravity" with humanity, would eliminate the trust necessary for sociability. The very human qualities and attachments Rush perceived as essential to a republican society would disappear.

But Rush's warning as to the dangers of public punishment extends even further. Besides those "generous" minds who possess "sensibility," Rush alleged, there exists another group of spectators: those either "hardened with vice" or "too young, or too ignorant to connect the ideas of crimes and punishments together." This group, he asserted, looks upon the criminal not with pity, indignation, or contempt, but with indifference. The criminal's deeds are unimportant; the punishment itself becomes the object of their curiosity. Punishments appear to be "mere arbitrary acts of cruelty" imposed by the state on the hapless criminal whose "passive behaviour . . . indicates innocence more than vice." Under these circumstances, Rush claimed, the punishment, in effect, legitimizes cruelty itself and thereby engenders a disposition to "exercise the same arbitrary cruelty over the feelings and lives" of others (84). What had been designed as a symbolic lesson in the necessity and justness of obedience to the law becomes an example, under the auspices of legal authority, of a seemingly arbitrary infliction of misery.

Having defined public punishment as the problematic site of uncontrolled communication and public corruption, Rush's argument then leads the reader almost ineluctably to the conclusion that eliminating direct contact between the community and the convicts is the only rational solution to the problem of public punishments. "If public punishments are injurious to criminals and to society, it follows, that crimes should be punished in private, or not at all. There is no alternative" (89). Beyond avoiding the problem of misinterpretation and restoring discipline to the site of their administration, private punishments would make possible the eventual reincorporation of convicts into society. Although he firmly believed in the possibility of reformation and in the obligations of Christian love and forgiveness, Rush always aimed to convince his reader that reformation and love depend on disciplined submission to the authority of knowledge.

The central feature of Rush's system of correction was to be the prison itself, which would represent order to the inmates. Its interior, he proposed, should be divided into "apartments," with space set aside for religious worship; solitary cells reserved for "refractory convicts"; and a garden where "the culprits may occasionally work, and walk. This spot will have a beneficial effect not only upon health, but morals, for it will lead to a familiarity with those pure and natural objects which are calculated to renew the connection of fallen man with his creator." Even the name of the institution should be designed to "convey an idea of its benevolent and salutary design" (87). All meanings would be carefully controlled.

In reformed punishment, knowledge and discipline would rule. "The punishments should consist of bodily pain, labour, watchfulness, solitude, and silence. They should all be joined with cleanliness and a simple diet." Oversight of this regimen would be entrusted only to men of knowledge. "To ascertain the nature, degrees, and duration of the bodily pain, will require some knowledge of the principles of sensation and of the sympathies which occur in the nervous system." Prison officials would be charged with determining which combination of punishments any inmate needed. "In the application of them," however, "the utmost possible advantages should be taken of the laws of the association of ideas, of habit, and of imitation" (89).

Rush placed such stress on reforming punishment by joining knowledge to the exercise of power because he viewed its purpose, and not merely its proper practice, in medical terms. "The great art of surgery has been said to consist in saving, not in destroying, or amputating the diseased parts of the human body. Let governments learn to imitate, in this respect, the skill and humanity of the healing art." Even nature does not eliminate "offal maters." Instead, they "are daily converted into the means of increasing the profits of industry, and the pleasures of human life." It is only the human soul, which, "when misled by passion," is "abandoned by the ignorance or cruelty of man, to unprofitable corruption, or extirpation" (93–94). The task Rush set for his public was to transfer punishment from the realm of ignorance to the realm of knowledge, where it could operate as moral surgery—and, of course, to entrust its administration to surgeons.

In "An Enquiry into the consistency of the punishment of Murder by Death, with Reason and Revelation," Rush elaborated his belief that support for public punishments derive from mistaken impressions. Here, in an impassioned attack, he argued that capital punishments are not only contrary to reason and wise social policy but also incorrectly justified on the basis of a misreading of the Bible. With the expansion of truth and corrected interpretations, support for this barbarous, unchristian practice would wither away. Knowledge would triumph.

Although the theory of punishment exemplifies the inter-relationships among knowledge, discipline, and authority in Rush's vision, it was only one segment in a continuum of his efforts to reshape character. Rush also sought to reform and discipline every-day life through culture. As a reading of "An address to the ministers of the Gospel of every denomination in the United States upon subjects interesting to morals" indicates, he attacked a wide variety of lower-class customs in pursuit of greater discipline. In this essay particularly, he called upon ministers to increase their efforts to direct the lives of those outside the school or the prison, and to preach against fairs, liquors, cock-fights, militia parades, horse-racing, clubs, and other elements of the everyday life of labor. As his attacks on lawsuits and the "licentiousness" of the press attest, however, he did not limit his vision of reform to the lower classes. The whole culture and all cultural practices needed both to be both subjected to knowledge and authority and rigorously ordered.

V

The actual product of all of these inventions, Rush's post-revolutionary citizen, emerges most clearly in the historical and biographical essays, where, in his discussions of Germans, Pennsyl-vanians, Indians, and selected individuals, he presents a morphol-ogy of social characters and an interpretation of social development. Reflecting the theory that society has proceeded through a fixed set of historical stages, each distinguished by its own particular char-acter types, these essays point to a reformed society based upon respect for property and law, and upon cultivation of labor and disciplined virtue. They set forth this vision through both a critique of social behavior and (sometimes implicitly) a prescription for the future.

Rush's thinking about historical development began with the

distinction between "civilization" and "savagery." As "An Account of the Vices Peculiar to the Indians of North America" demonstrates, his "civilized" scorn for the "savage" was typical of the period. Rush believed that the vices of Indians far outweighed their virtues and argues that they were disposed to uncleanliness, nastiness, drunkenness, gluttony, treachery, cruelty, idleness, theft, and gaming. Moreover, Indians reversed the proper relations of the sexes; women worked in the fields and were not protected properly. Even those traits which might appear to be their "virtues," Rush deprecated as "rather the qualities of necessity, than the offspring of feeling, or principle" (151–153). "Virtue," Rush wrote elsewhere, "should, in all cases, be the offspring of principle" (129). "Savage" qualities resulted from nature, not from thought; the only virtues worth having were those which resulted from reflection.

Indian culture symbolized for Rush a natural condition from which humanity had to escape in order to progress. In this process, the development of property lifted individuals out of savagery and into civilization. "Property, and a regard for law, are born together in all societies. The passion for liberty in an Indian, is as different from the passion for it in a civilized republican, as the impurity of lust, is, from the delicacy of love." Love of liberty needed to be regulated and connected with a love of law; property enabled societies to avoid both tyranny and anarchy. But Indian societies lacked the discipline of property; hence they could not balance the desire for liberty and the desire for law. "There is always an excess of law or liberty in a community where poor men are idle, or where vices of any kind are suffered with impunity" (154). Property was an essential moment in the creation and development of civilization.

Different relationships to property and law mark the different stages of "civilized" social development. Rush stated this view in "An Account of the Progress of Population, Agriculture, Manners, and Government, in Pennsylvania," an essay that, despite the title's broad scope, primarily concerns patterns of settlement and the characters of settlers and demonstrates his preoccupation with showing civilization as a triumph over savagery. "From a review of the three different species of settlers, it appears, that there are certain regular stages which mark the progress from the savage to civilized life. The first settler is nearly related to an Indian in his manners—In the second, the Indian manners are more diluted: It is in the third species of settlers only, that we behold civilization completed—It is to the third species of settlers only, that it is proper to apply the term of farmers" (129). In the progression from a lower to a higher state, each "species" possesses a greater love (and a greater amount) of property and government.

Rush hoped to see this pattern of settlement repeated in an expanding America. Contrasting Europe with America, he admits that the "passion for migration" which underlay settlement would "appear strange to an European," presenting "a picture of human nature that runs counter to the usual habits and principles of action in man" (129-130). But in America such movement fulfilled important social ends by draining away excess labor and increasing opportunities for all. Moreover, constant expansion, like the prison, would prevent settlers at different "stages" from coming in conflict with each other. Rush's first stage of settlers were not trapped within society where their "indian manners" and anti-social character could cause social disorder and upheaval.

Like Jefferson, Rush maintained that the farmer was the backbone of republican society, and he romanticized their political and moral virtues. "These are the men to whom Pennsylvania owes her ancient fame and consequence. If they possess less refinement than their southern neighbours, who cultivate their land with slaves, they possess more republican virtue" (128). This bucolic vision is depicted in some detail: in his essay on the Germans of Pennsylvania, discipline, hard work, piety, pacifism, and respect for authority and learning are treated as natural qualities of the farmer. These were the virtues upon which he hoped to build a new society.

But Rush would not limit his good society to agriculture. Rejecting the classical republican tradition's equation of commerce with corruption, he embraced a more "liberal" faith in the civilizing aspects of trade. More than merely "the avenue of the wealth of the state," commerce provided the "best security against the hereditary monopolies of land, and therefore, the surest protection against aristocracy." Its results have been "next to those of religion in humanizing mankind," and the best "means of uniting the different nations of the world together by the ties of mutual wants and obligations" (11). Imagining an agrarian republic thus civilized and enlightened, Rush, in "Information to Europeans who are Disposed to Migrate to the United States of America," encouraged emigration to America by Europeans skilled in commerce, manufacturing, and the professions, as well as in agriculture. Indeed, envisioning a constantly expanding economy, he welcomed all those willing to labor and to submit to discipline. The biographical essays present concrete models of the new citizen's characteristics: Ann Woods with her patient submission to the "Divine Will"; Benjamin Lay and Anthony Benezet, with their deep piety and commitment to humanitarian reform; Edward Drinker, whose life and maturity parallel the growth of America; William Cullen, with his commitment to the knowledge of medicine; and David Rittenhouse who points to the intellectual independence of America. Collectively, they symbolize the virtues of the properly disciplined republican.

VI

Unlike Madison, whose political philosophy was predicated upon the irreducible conflict between social interests, Rush aimed to make social and political conflict illegitimate. In repudiating the radically democratic side of the Revolution, he also repudiated the idea that the struggles of the Revolution were rooted in real, as opposed to misunderstood, social differences. Both descriptively and prescriptively, he reduced the existence of social struggles to questions of education and knowledge.

This point emerges most clearly in his writings on the problem of punishment and social discipline, which in many ways functions as a metonym for the larger context and strategy of the *Essays*. Misinterpretations plagued public punishments, as they did the entire revolutionary process. The result was that the desires and sympathies of the citizens became tied to inappropriate, anarchic examples and behaviors. Instead of allowing these conventional or customary rituals, and customary understandings, to shape republican society, he proposed to uproot them and plant more disciplined institutions in their place. These institutions would reform the republic's subjects under the supervision of disciplined and knowledgeable authority. In the process, the supervision of punishment would be taken from the public spectator and delegated to the "man of truth." The institutionalization of private punishment would inaugurate a new form of authority.

Rush's approach to the question of punishment focuses on the problem of ignorance and error, not of social division. Each problematic effect of public punishment derives from the failure—on the part of the audience—to comprehend the meaning of the ritual correctly. It was his position that this process of misinterpretation is inherent within public punishments; public punishments were errors of policy that led to errors of understanding. But, in taking this position, he denied the importance of class (and other basic social differences as well) for understanding public reaction to punishment. Rush avoids the possibility that audiences draw different lessons from the rituals of public punishment because they experience different social relationships to law and authority. Subsuming conflict under the rubric of error, Rush denied the legitimacy of conflicting interpretations by treating them as an example of a lack of wisdom.

The same reduction of social differences to levels of knowledge occurs in Rush's depiction of the three types of settlers and in his discussion of Indians. Rush codes social differencs (which he acknowledges existed constantly and simultaneously) within a narrative of historical progress. He differentiates the types of settlers not by intrinsic social conflicts (for example, between landlords and tenants, or speculators and squatters) but by social maturity. Eventually, all rural individuals would be "farmers"—disciplined, pious, sober participants in politics and society. Although Rush acknowledged these social divisions, as in his discussion of "misinterpretations" of public punishments, he reduced them to questions of education or social maturity.

At the same time, it should be noted that his description of settlement ignores the role of violence in displacing native peoples. Although Rush refers to the final type of settler as a "conqueror," he does so in a way that eliminated the term's military connotations. "The weapons with which he achieves his conquests, are the implements of husbandry: and the virtues which direct them, are industry and œconomy. Idleness—extravagance—and ignorance fly before him" (131). For Rush, the triumphant expansion of America was a story of farming, not of the brutal dislocation of conquered natives. The violence and social conflicts which marked the history of the Europeanization of America have no place in his story.

Rush was not content merely to deny the importance of social differences, however. His actual program aimed to eliminate those social spaces in which alternatives to his values might thrive. In his suggestions to ministers for moral reform, for example, he attacked the places where plebian culture flourished and the practices (such as militia elections) he thought undermined the authority of the elite. His ideas of both universal education and the prison were designed to move crucial social functions from the realms of everyday life and popular participation to the realm of expert domination. Rush aimed at no less than the re-engineering of culture and society.

The emphasis on expert interpretation emerges even in the biographical sketches that conclude the *Essays*. Here he refuses to let his characters stand on their own. Even the virtues he describes must be made reflective through the teaching of the interpreter. He continually intrudes into the description in order to instruct his readers, to make certain that they understand the true meaning of his stories. The aim of education through example drives the historical and biographical essays and makes certain that the influence of the intellectual is never absent.

The aim, once again, is to reinforce the importance of interpretation and the interpreter. And it is the importance of intellectuals and experts which stands as the centerpiece of Rush's social program. Rush endeavored to remove the discussion of social problems, as far as possible, from political debate in order to entrust it to those who, like himself, sought authority based upon their claims to knowledge of science and truth.

How then might we approach these essays? Rush's ideas need to be situated in two separate contexts. The first lies in the late eighteenth century. His stress upon such virtues as sobriety, piety and hardwork was quite conventional. The *Essays* offers an articulate presentation of that combination of religious enthusiasm and Enlightenment thought that prompted many Americans to undertake a revolution and to dream of remaking their world. At the same time, it also demonstrates the fears the revolution stimulated among many members of the elite—fears that provoked the widespread reconceptualization of politics and political institutions that led to the Constitution and the tradition of Madisonian liberalism.

The second context points more to our own time. Along with

the notable, and highly noted, tradition of political representation institutionalized by the Constitution came a quieter tradition of authority rooted in the claims of knowledge. The *Essays* helps mark the beginnings of this tradition, a tradition of institutional discipline that lies at the foundation of our political system. It was in schools and prisons, in representations and social intervention, that the citizen-subject of the American republic was created. Rush's moral visions may have been locked in the eighteenth-century present, but his social strategies indicate a future which is our present.

The text of ESSAYS *used here is that of the second edition.* Published *by Thomas and William Bradford of Philadelphia in 1806, this edition consists of all the essays in the first edition, plus "An Inquiry into the causes of Premature Deaths." In the present edited version, obviously typographical errors have been silently corrected. All notes to the text are Rush's and have been numbered sequentially within each essay. Editorial interpolations appear in the text within brackets; although Rush himself uses brackets, the context should indicate whether they have been supplied by the editor or by the author.*

ESSAYS

LITERARY, MORAL,

AND PHILOSOPHICAL

PREFACE

Most of the following Essays were published in the Museum, and Columbian Magazine, in this City, soon after the end of the revolutionary war in the United States. A few of them made their first appearance in pamphlets. They are now published in a single volume, at the request of several friends, and with a view of promoting the ends at first contemplated by them. Two of the Essays, viz: that upon the use of Tobacco, and the account of remarkable circumstances in the constitution and life of Ann Woods, are now submitted for the first time to the eye of the public. The author has omitted in this collection two pamphlets which he published in the year 1772, upon the slavery of the Negroes, because he conceived the object of them had been in part accomplished, and because the Citizens of the United States have since that time been furnished from Great-Britain and other countries, with numerous tracts upon that subject, more calculated to complete the effect intended by the author, than his early publications.

Benjamin Rush.

Philadelphia, Jan. 9, 1798.

TABLE OF CONTENTS

A PLAN FOR ESTABLISHING PUBLIC SCHOOLS IN PENNSYLVANIA, AND FOR CONDUCTING EDUCATION AGREEABLY TO A REPUBLICAN FORM OF GOVERNMENT. ADDRESSED TO THE LEGISLATURE AND CITIZENS OF PENNSYLVANIA, IN THE YEAR 1786.

BEFORE I proceed to the subject of this essay, I shall point out, in a few words, the influence and advantages of learning upon mankind.

I. It is friendly to religion, inasmuch as it assists in removing prejudice, superstition, and enthusiasm, in promoting just notions of the Deity, and in enlarging our knowledge of his works.

II. It is favourable to liberty. Freedom can exist only in the society of knowledge. Without learning, men are incapable of knowing their rights, and where learning is confined to a few people, liberty can be neither equal nor universal.

III. It promotes just ideas of laws and government. "When the clouds of ignorance are dispelled (says the Marquis of Beccaria) by the radiance of knowledge, power trembles, but the authority of laws remains immoveable."

IV. It is friendly to manners. Learning in all countries, promotes civilization, and the pleasures of society and conversation.

V. It promotes agriculture, the great basis of national wealth and happiness. Agriculture is as much a science as hydraulics, or optics, and has been equally indebted to the experiments and researches of learned men. The highly cultivated state, and the immense profits of the farms in England, are derived wholly from the patronage which agriculture has received in that country, from learned men and learned societies.

VI. Manufactures of all kinds owe their perfection chiefly to learning—hence the nations of Europe advance in manufactures, knowledge, and commerce, only in proportion as they cultivate the arts and sciences.

For the purpose of diffusing knowledge through every part of the state, I beg leave to propose the following simple plan.

I. Let there be one university in the state, and let this be established in the capital. Let law, physic, divinity, the law of nature and nations, œconomy, &c. be taught in it by public lectures in the winter season, after the manner of the European universities, and let the professors receive such salaries from the state as will enable them to deliver their lectures at a moderate price.

II. Let there be four colleges. One in Philadelphia; one at Carlisle; a third, for the benefit of our German fellow citizens, at Lancaster; and a fourth, some years hence at Pittsburg. In these colleges, let young men be instructed in mathematics and in the higher branches of science, in the same manner that they are now taught in our American colleges. After they have received a testimonial from one of these colleges, let them, if they can afford it, complete their studies by spending a season or two in attending the lectures in the university. I prefer four colleges in the state to one or two, for there is a certain size of colleges as there is of towns and armies, that is most favourable to morals and good government. Oxford and Cambridge in England are the seats of dissipation, while the more numerous, and less crouded universities and colleges in Scotland, are remarkable for the order, diligence, and decent behaviour of their students.

III. Let there be free schools established in every township, or in districts consisting of one hundred families. In these schools let children be taught to read and write the English and German languages, and the use of figures. Such of them as have parents that can afford to send them from home, and are disposed to extend their education, may remove their children from the free school to one of the colleges.

By this plan the whole state will be tied together by one system of education. The university will in time furnish masters for the colleges, and the colleges will furnish masters for the free schools, while the free schools, in their turns, will supply the colleges and the university with scholars, students and pupils. The same systems of grammar, oratory and philosophy, will be taught in every part of the state, and the literary features of Pennsylvania will thus designate one great, and equally enlightened family.

But, how shall we bear the expense of these literary institutions? I answer—these institutions will *lessen* our taxes. They will enlighten us in the great business of finance—they will teach us to encrease the ability of the state to support the government, by encreasing the profits of agriculture, and by promoting manufactures. They will teach us all the modern improvements and advantages of inland navigation. They will defend us from hasty and expensive experiment in government, by unfolding to us the experience and folly of past ages, and thus, instead of adding to our taxes and debts, they will furnish us with the true secret of lessening and discharging both of them.

But, shall the estates of orphans, batchelors and persons who have no children, be taxed to pay for the support of schools from which they can derive no benefit? I answer in the affirmative, to the first part of the objection, and I deny the truth of the latter part of it. Every member of the community is interested in the propagation of virtue and knowledge in the state. But I will go further, and add, it will be true œconomy in individuals to support public schools. The batchelor will in time save his tax for this purpose, by being able to sleep with fewer bolts and locks to his doors—the estates of orphans will in time be benefited, by being protected from the ravages of unprincipled and idle boys, and the children of wealthy parents will be less tempted, by bad company, to extravagance. Fewer pillories and whipping posts, and smaller goals, with their usual expenses and taxes, will be necessary when our youth are properly educated, than at present; I believe it could be proved, that the expenses of confining, trying and executing criminals, amount every year, in most of the counties, to more money than would be sufficient to maintain all the schools that would be necessary in each county. The confessions of these criminals generally show us, that their vices and punishments are the fatal consequences of the want of a proper education in early life.

I submit these detached hints to the consideration of the legislature and of the citizens of Pennsylvania. The plan for the free schools is taken chiefly from the plans which have long been used with success in Scotland, and in the eastern states[1] of America, where the influence of learning, in promoting religion, morals, manners, and good government, has never been exceeded in any country.

---

[1] There are 600 of these schools in the small state of Connecticut, which at this time have in them 25,000 scholars.

The manner in which these schools should be supported and governed—the modes of determining the characters and qualifications of schoolmasters, and the arrangement of families in each district, so that children of the same religious sect and nation, may be educated as much as possible together, will form a proper part of a law for the establishment of schools, and therefore does not come within the limits of this plan.

OF THE MODE OF EDUCATION PROPER IN A REPUBLIC.

THE business of education has acquired a new complexion by the independence of our country. The form of government we have assumed, has created a new class of duties to every American. It becomes us, therefore, to examine our former habits upon this subject, and in laying the foundations for nurseries of wise and good men, to adapt our modes of teaching to the peculiar form of our government.

The first remark that I shall make upon this subject is, that an education in our own, is to be preferred to an education in a foreign country. The principle of patriotism stands in need of the reinforcement of prejudice, and it is well known that our strongest prejudices in favour of our country are formed in the first one and twenty years of our lives. The policy of the Lacedemonians is well worthy of our imitation. When Antipater demanded fifty of their children as hostages for the fulfillment of a distant engagement, those wise republicans refused to comply with his demand, but readily offered him double the number of their adult citizens, whose habits and prejudices could not be shaken by residing in a foreign country. Passing by, in this place, the advantages to the community from the early attachment of youth to the laws and constitution of their country, I shall only remark, that young men who have trodden the paths of science together, or have joined in the same sports, whether of swimming, skating, fishing, or hunting, generally feel, thro' life, such ties to each other, as add greatly to the obligations of mutual benevolence.

I conceive the education of our youth in this country to be peculiarly necessary in Pennsylvania, while our citizens are composed of the natives of so many different kingdoms in Europe. Our schools of learning, by producing one general, and uniform system of education, will render the mass of the people more homogenous, and thereby fit them more easily for uniform and peaceable government.

I proceed in the next place, to enquire, what mode of education we shall adopt so as to secure to the state all the advantages that are to be derived from the proper instruction of youth; and here I beg leave to remark, that the only foundation for a useful education in a republic is to be laid in Religion. Without this there can be no virtue, and without virtue there can be no liberty, and liberty is the object and life of all republican governments.

Such is my veneration for every religion that reveals the attributes of the Deity, or a future state of rewards and punishments, that I had rather see the opinions of Confucius or Mahomed inculcated upon our youth, than see them grow up wholly devoid of a system of religious principles. But the religion I mean to recommend in this place, is that of the New Testament.

It is foreign to my purpose to hint at the arguments which establish the truth of the Christian revelation. My only business is to declare, that all its doctrines and precepts are calculated to promote the happiness of society, and the safety and well being of civil government. A Christian cannot fail of being a republican. The history of the creation of man, and of the relation of our species to each other by birth, which is recorded in the Old Testament, is the best refutation that can be given to the divine right of kings, and the strongest argument that can be used in favor of the original and natural equality of all mankind. A Christian, I say again, cannot fail of being a republican, for every precept of the Gospel inculcates those degrees of humility, self-denial, and brotherly kindness, which are directly opposed to the pride of monarchy and the pageantry of a court. A Christian cannot fail of being useful to the republic, for his religion teacheth him, that no man "liveth to himself." And lastly, a Christian cannot fail of being wholly inoffensive, for his religion teacheth him, in all things to do to others what he would wish, in like circumstances, they should do to him.

I am aware that I dissent from one of those paradoxical opinions with which modern times abound; and that it is improper to fill the minds of youth with religious prejudices of any kind, and that they should be left to choose their own principles, after they have arrived at an age in which they are capable of judging for themselves. Could we preserve the mind in childhood and youth a perfect blank, this plan of education would have more to recommend it; but this we know to be impossible. The human mind runs as naturally into principles as it does after facts. It submits with difficulty to those restraints or partial discoveries which are imposed upon it in the infancy of reason. Hence the impatience of children to be informed upon all subjects that relate to the invisible world. But I beg leave to ask, why should we pursue a different plan of education with respect to religion, from that which we pursue in teaching the arts and sciences? Do we leave our youth to acquire systems of geography, philosophy, or politics, till they have arrived at an age in which they are capable of judging for themselves? We do not. I claim no more then for religion, than for the other sciences, and I add further, that if our youth are disposed after they are of age to think for themselves, a knowledge of one system, will be the best means of conducting them in a free enquiry into other systems of religion, just as an acquaintance with one system of philosophy is the best introduction to the study of all the other systems in the world.

Next to the duty which young men owe to their Creator, I wish to see a regard to their country, inculcated upon them. When the Duke of Sully became prime minister to Henry the IVth of France, the first thing he did, he tells us, "Was to subdue and forget his own heart." The same duty is incumbent upon every citizen of a republic. Our country includes family, friends and property, and should be preferred to them all. Let our pupil be taught that he does not belong to himself, but that he is public property. Let him be taught to love his family, but let him be taught, at the same time, that he must forsake, and even forget them, when the welfare of his country requires it. He must watch for the state, as if its liberties depended upon his vigilance alone, but he must do this in such a manner as not to defraud his creditors, or neglect his family. He must love private life, but he must decline no station, however public or responsible it may be, when called to it by the suffrages of his fellow citizens. He must love popularity, but he must despise it when set in competition with the dictates of his judgement, or the real interest of his country. He must love character, and have a due sense of injuries, but he must be taught to appeal only to the laws of the state, to defend the one, and punish the other. He must love family honour, but he must be taught that neither the rank nor antiquity of his ancestors, can command respect, without personal merit. He must avoid neutrality in all questions that divide the state, but he must shun the rage, the acrimony of party spirit. He must be taught to love his fellow creatures in every part of the world, but he must cherish with a more intense and peculiar affection, the citizens of

Pennsylvania and of the United States. I do not wish to see our youth educated with a single prejudice against any nation or country; but we impose a task upon human nature, repugnant alike to reason, revelation and the ordinary dimensions of the human heart, when we require him to embrace, with equal affection, the whole family of mankind. He must be taught to amass wealth, but it must be only to increase his power of contributing to the wants and demands of the state. He must be indulged occasionally in amusements, but he must be taught that study and business should be his principal pursuits in life. Above all he must love life, and endeavour to acquire as many of its conveniences as possible by industry and œconomy, but he must be taught that this life "is not his own," when the safety of his country requires it. These are practicable lessons, and the history of the commonwealths of Greece and Rome show, that human nature, without the aids of Christianity, has attained these degrees of perfection.

While we inculcate these republican duties upon our pupil, we must not neglect, at the same time, to inspire him with republican principles. He must be taught that there can be no durable liberty but in a republic, and that government, like all other sciences, is of a progressive nature. The chains which have bound this science in Europe are happily unloosed in America. Here it is open to investigation and improvement. While philosophy has protected us by its discoveries from a thousand natural evils, government has unhappily followed with an unequal pace. It would be to dishonour human genius, only to name the many defects which still exist in the best systems of legislation. We daily see matter of a perishable nature rendered durable by certain chemical operations. In like manner, I conceive, that it is possible to combine power in such a way as not only to encrease the happiness, but to promote the duration of republican forms of government far beyond the terms limited for them by history, or the common opinions of mankind.

To assist in rendering religious, moral and political instruction more effectual upon the minds of our youth, it will be necessary to subject their bodies to physical discipline. To obviate the inconveniences of their studious and sedentary mode of life, they should live upon a temperate diet, consisting chiefly of broths, milk and vegetables. The black broth of Sparta, and the barley broth of Scotland, have been alike celebrated for their beneficial effects upon the minds of young people. They should avoid tasting Spirituous liquors. They should also be accustomed occasionally to work with their hands, in the intervals of Study, and in the busy seasons of the year in the country. Moderate sleep, silence, occasional solitude and cleanliness, should be inculcated upon them, and the utmost advantage should be taken of a proper direction of those great principles in human conduct,—sensibility, habit, imitations and association.

The influence of these physical causes will be powerful upon the intellects, as well as upon the principles and morals of young people.

To those who have studied human nature, it will not appear paradoxical to recommend, in this essay, a particular attention to vocal music. Its mechanical effects in civilizing the mind, and thereby preparing it for the influence of religion and government, have been so often felt and recorded, that it will be unnecessary to mention facts in favour of its usefulness, in order to excite a proper attention to it.

I cannot help bearing a testimony, in this place, against the custom, which prevails in some parts of America, (but which is daily falling into disuse in Europe) of crouding boys together under one roof for the purpose of education. The practice is the gloomy remains of monkish ignorance, and is as unfavorable to the improvements of the mind in useful learning, as monasteries are to the spirit of religion. I grant this mode of secluding boys from the intercourse of private families, has a tendency to make them scholars, but our business is to make them men, citizens and christians. The vices of young people are generally learned from each other. The vices of adults seldom infect them. By separating them from each other, therefore, in their hours of relaxation from study, we secure their morals from a principal source of corruption, while we improve their manners, by subjecting them to those restraints which the difference of age and sex, naturally produce in private families.

From the observations that have been made it is plain, that I consider it is possible to convert men into republican machines, This must be done, if we expect them to perform their parts properly, in the great machine of the government of the state. That republic is sophisticated with monarchy or aristocracy that does not revolve upon the wills of the people, and these must be fitted to each other by means of education before they can be made to produce regularity and unison in government.

Having pointed out those general principles, which should be inculcated alike in all the schools of the state, I proceed now to make a few remarks upon the method of conducting, what is commonly called, a liberal or learned education in a republic.

I shall begin this part of my subject, by bearing a testimony against the common practice of attempting to teach boys the learned languages, and the arts and sciences too early in life. The first twelve years of life are barely sufficient to instruct a boy in reading, writing and arithmetic. With these, he may be taught those modern languages which are necessary for him to speak. The state of the memory, in early life, is favorable to the acquisition of languages, especially when they are conveyed to the mind, through the ear. It is, moreover, in early life only, that the organs of speech yield in such a manner as to favour the just pronounciation of foreign languages.

Too much pains cannot be taken to teach our youth to read and write our American language with propriety and elegance. The study of the Greek language constituted a material part of the literature of the Athenians, hence the sublimity, purity and immortality of so many of their writings. The advantages of a perfect knowledge of our language to young men intended for the professions of law, physic, or divinity are too obvious to be mentioned, but in a state which boasts of the first commercial city in America, I wish to see it cultivated by young men, who are intended for the compting house, for many such, I hope, will be educated in our colleges. The time is past when an academical education was thought to be unnecessary to qualify a young man for merchandize. I conceive no profession is capable of receiving more embellishments from it. The French and German languages should likewise be carefully taught in all our colleges. They abound with useful books upon all subjects. So important and necessary are those languages, that a degree should never be conferred upon a young man who cannot speak or translate them.

Connected with the study of languages is the study of Eloquence. It is well known how great a part it constituted of the Roman education. It is the first accomplishment in a republic, and often sets the whole machine of government in motion. Let our youth, therefore, be instructed in this art. We do not extol it too highly when we attribute as much to the power of eloquence as to the sword, in bringing about the American revolution.

With the usual arts and sciences that are taught in our American colleges, I wish to see a regular course of lectures given upon History and Chronology. The science of government, whether it related to constitutions or laws, can only be advanced by a careful selection of facts, and these are to be found chiefly in history. Above all, let our youth be instructed in the history of the ancient republics, and the progress of liberty and tyranny in the different states of Europe. I wish likewise to see the numerous facts that relate to the origin and present state of commerce, together with the nature and principles of Money, reduced to such a system, as to be intelligible and agreeable to a young man. If we consider the commerce of our metropolis only as the avenue of the wealth of the state, the study of it merits a place in a young man's education; but, I consider commerce in a much higher light when I recommend the study of it in republican seminaries. I view it as the best security against the influence of hereditary monopolies of land, and, therefore, the surest protection against aristocracy. I consider its effects as next to those of religion in humanizing mankind, and lastly, I view it as the means of uniting the different nations of the world together by the ties of mutual wants and obligations.

Chemistry by unfolding to us the effects of heat and mixture, enlarges our acquaintance with the wonders of nature and the mysteries of art; hence it has become, in most of the universities of Europe, a necessary branch of a gentleman's education. In a young country, where improvements in agriculture and manufactures are so much to be desired, the cultivation of this science, which explains the principles of both of them, should be considered as an object of the utmost importance.

Again, let our youth be instructed in all the means of promoting national prosperity and independence, whether they relate to improvements in agriculture, manufactures, or inland navigation. Let him be instructed further in the general principles of legislation, whether they relate to revenue, or to the preservation of life, liberty or property. Let him be directed frequently to attend the courts of justice, where he will have the best opportunities of acquiring habits of comparing, and arranging his ideas by observing the discovery of truth, in the examination of witnesses, and where he will hear the laws of the state explained, with all the advantages of that species of eloquence which belongs to the bar. Of so much importance do I conceive it to be, to a young man, to attend occasionally to the decisions of our courts of law, that I wish to see our colleges established, only in county towns.

But further, considering the nature of our connection with the United States, it will be necessary to make our pupil acquainted with all the prerogatives of the national government. He must be instructed in the nature and variety of treaties. He must know the difference in the powers and duties of the several species of ambassadors. He must be taught wherein the obligations of individuals and of states are the same, and wherein they differ. In short, he must acquire a general knowledge of all those laws and forms, which unite the sovereigns of the earth, or separate them from each other.

I beg pardon for having delayed so long to say anything of the separate and peculiar mode of education proper for women in a republic. I am sensible that they must concur in all our plans of education for young men, or no laws will ever render them effectual. To qualify our women for this purpose, they should not only be instructed in the usual branches of female education, but they should be taught the principles of liberty and government; and the obligations of patriotism should be inculcated upon them. The opinions and conduct of men are often regulated by the women in the most arduous enterprizes of life; and their approbation is frequently the principal reward of the hero's dangers, and the patriot's toils. Besides, the first impressions upon the minds of children are generally derived from the women. Of how much consequence, therefore, is it in a republic, that they should think justly upon the great subjects of liberty and government!

The complaints that have been made against religion, liberty and learning, have been, against each of them in a separate state. Perhaps like certain liquors, they should only be used in a state of mixture. They mutually assist in correcting the abuses, and in improving the good effects of each other. From the combined and reciprocal influence of religion, liberty and learning upon the morals, manners and knowledge of individuals, of these, upon government, and of government, upon individuals, it is impossible to measure the degrees of happiness and perfection to which mankind may be raised. For my part, I can form no ideas of the golden age, so much celebrated by the poets, more delightful, than the contemplation of that happiness which it is now in the power of the legislature of Pennsylvania to confer upon her citizens, by establishing proper modes and places of education in every part of the state.

OBSERVATIONS UPON THE STUDY OF THE LATIN AND GREEK LANGUAGES, AS A BRANCH OF LIBERAL EDUCATION, WITH HINTS OF A PLAN OF LIBERAL EDUCATION, WITHOUT THEM, ACCOMMODATED TO THE PRESENT STATE OF SOCIETY, MANNERS, AND GOVERNMENT IN THE UNITED STATES.

IT requires the recollection of escapes from a lion and a bear, to encounter the strong and universal prejudice, in favor of the Latin and Greek languages, as a necessary branch of liberal education. If, in combating this formidable enemy of human reason, I should be less successful than the Hebrew stripling was in contending with the giant of the Philistines, I hope it will be ascribed wholly to the want of skill to direct arguments, which, in other hands, would lay this tyrant in the dust.

I shall attempt to discuss this question, by first delivering a few general propositions. I shall afterwards apply these propositions, and answer such arguments as are usually urged in favor of the Latin and Greek languages as necessary parts of an academic education.

I. The great design of a liberal education is, to prepare youth for usefulness here, and for happiness hereafter.

II. The proper time for acquiring the necessary branches of knowledge for these important purposes, is in the first eighteen years of life.

III. From four to five years are usually spent in acquiring a competent knowledge of the Latin and Greek languages.

IV. The knowledge of things always preceeds the knowledge of words. Children discover the truth of this observation every day. They know all the objects around them, long before they are able to call them by their proper names, or even to articulate sounds of any kind. It is supposed that children acquire more ideas of things in the first three years of their lives, than they acquire in any thirty years afterwards.

V. The acquisition of words lessens the ability of the mind to acquire ideas. That understanding must have uncommon strength, which does not contract an oblique direction by being employed four or five years in learning the Latin and Greek languages.

VI. The difficulty of acquiring those dead languages, and the little pleasure which accompanies the knowledge of them in early life, occasion the principal obstacles to teaching, in masters, and learning, in scholars.

The famous Busby is said to have died of "bad Latin;" that is, the ungrammatical versions of his scholars broke his heart. How few boys relish Latin and Greek lessons! The pleasure they sometimes discover in learning them, is derived either from the tales they read, or from a competition, which awakens a love of honour, and which might be displayed upon a hundred more useful subjects; or it may arise from a desire of gaining the good will of their masters or parents. Where these incentives are wanting, how bitter does the study of languages render that innocent period of life, which seems exclusively intended for happiness! "I wish I had never been born," said a boy of eleven years old, to his mother: "why, my son?" said his mother. "Because I am born into a world of trouble." "What trouble," said his mother smiling, "have you known, my son?"— "Trouble enough, mamma," said he, "two Latin lessons to get, every day." This boy was not deficient in genius nor in application to books. He often amused himself in reading natural and ancient history, was inquisitive after knowledge of every kind, and was never heard to ask a foolish or impertinent question.

VII. Many sprightly boys of excellent capacities for useful knowledge, have been so disgusted with the dead languages, as to retreat from the drudgery of schools, to low company, whereby they have become bad members of society, and entailed misery upon all who have been connected with them.

VIII. The Latin and Greek languages are the first tests of genius in schools. Where boys discover a want of capacity for them, they are generally taken from school, or remain there the butts of their companions. Dr. Swift early discovered a want of taste for the dead languages. It woud be unjust to mention this fact, without ascribing it to the voice of reason and nature speaking in this great man. He had no relish for the husks of literature. Truth and knowledge were alone commensurate to the dignity and extent of his mind.

IX. The study of some of the Latin and Greek classics is unfavourable to morals and religion. Indelicate amours, and shocking

vices both of gods and men, fill many parts of them. Hence an early
and dangerous acquaintance with vice; and hence, from an association of ideas, a diminished respect for the unity and perfections of
the true God. Those classics which are free from this censure,
contain little else but the histories of murders, perpetrated by kings,
and related in such a manner as to excite pleasure and admiration.
Hence the universal preference of the military character to all
others.—To the same cause we may ascribe the early passion for a
cockade in school boys; and the frequent adoption of the principles
and vices of armies, by young men who are destined for other
professions.

X. The study of the Latin and Greek languages is improper in
the present state of society and government in [the] United States.
While Greek and Latin are the only avenues to science, education
will always be confined to a few people. It is only by rendering
knowledge universal, that a republican form of government can be
preserved in our country.

I shall hereafter mention other reasons why the study of these
languages is improper in a peculiar manner in the United States.

XI. The cultivation of the Latin and Greek languages is a great
obstacle to the cultivation and perfection of the English language.

XII. It is likewise one of the greatest obstructions that has ever
been thrown in the way of propagating useful knowledge.

On each of these two last propositions I shall treat more fully in
another place.

I proceed now to consider the principle arguments that have
been urged in favour of the Latin and Greek languages, as necessary
parts of a liberal education.

1. A knowledge of the Latin and Greek grammar, it has been
said, is necessary for our becoming acquainted with English grammar. There was a time when the authority of a great name imposed
this opinion upon me, and even led me publicly to adopt it, but I
am now satisfied that it is wholly destitute of truth. I have known
many bachelors and masters of arts, who were incorrect English
scholars, and many persons of both sexes, ignorant of the dead
languages, who both wrote and spoke English, agreeably to the
strictest rules of modern grammar. Indeed I cannot help ascribing
the late improvements in the English language chiefly to the neglect
of the Latin and Greek languages. The Greek is supposed to be the

most perfect language both in its construction and harmony, that has ever been spoken by mortals. Now this language was not learned through the medium of any other. Hence it was acquired and spoken with equal propriety by all ranks of people, and not less by an apple woman, than by the celebrated orators of Greece. In that highly favoured nursery of human genius, the avenues to knowledge were not obstructed by two or three dead, or even foreign languages; nor was the precious season of youth, when memory is most faithful, and curiosity most active, mis-spent in learning words. Hence the fame of ancient Greece in arts and sciences, and hence the sublimity of the orations of Demosthenes, and of the poems of Homer. There was nothing in the composition of the blood, or in the structure of the nerves of the ancient Greeks, which gave them a pre-eminence over the rest of mankind. It arose entirely from their being too wise to waste the important years of education in learning to call substances, by two or three different names, instead of studying their qualities and uses. The construc-tion of the English, differs materially from that of the Latin and Greek languages; and the attempt to accommodate it to the Greek and Roman grammars has checked its improvement in many instances. I hope to prove hereafter, that a knowledge of grammar, like a knowledge of pronunciation, should be learned only by the ear in early life. The practice of teaching boys English grammar, through the medium of a dead language, is as absurd, as it would be for a parent to force his child to chew pebbles or mahogany, in order to prepare its gums or teeth to masticate bread and meat.

2. We are told that the Roman and Greek authors are the only perfect models of taste and eloquence, and that it is necessary to study them, in order to acquire their taste and spirit. Strange language indeed! what! did nature exhaust herself in Greece and Rome? Are the ancients the only repositories of the great principles of taste and genius? I reject the supposition; and will venture to assert, in opposition to it, that we shall never equal the sublime and original authors of antiquity until we cease to study them.

Nature is always the same. Let us yield to her inspiration alone, and avail ourselves of allusions to the many discoveries which have lately been made in her works. Shakespeare owes his fame, as a sublime and original poet, to his having never read (as is generally believed) a Latin or Greek author. Hence he spoke from nature, or rather, nature spoke thro' him. But it should be remembered that art, as well as nature feeds the flame of genius. By neglecting the ancients, we may borrow imagery from the many useful and well known arts which have been the inventions of modern ages, and thereby surpass the ancients in the variety and effect of our compositions. It is to this passion for ancient writers that we are to ascribe the great want of originality, that marks too many of the poems of modern times. A judicious critic has observed, that the descriptions of Spring, which are published every year in England, apply chiefly to the climates of Greece and the neighbourhood of Rome. This is the natural effect of a servile attachment to the ancient poets. It insensibly checks invention and leads to imitation. The pleasure with which the poems of the shoemaker, the milk-maid, and the Ayreshire ploughman, have been read by all classes of people, proves that an acquaintance with the Greek or Roman poets, is not necessary to inspire just ideas, or to produce harmony in poetry. Dr. Swift, as an author, owes nothing to the ancients. He has attained to what Pope calls the "majesty" and what Lord Shaftesbury calls the "divineness" of simplicity in writing. All his compositions, exemplify his own perfect definition of style. They consist of "proper words in their proper places." I have heard of a learned gentleman in Scotland, who, when any of his friends proposed to introduce a stranger to him, asked only, as a proof of his taste for composition, whether he admired Dr. Young's Night Thoughts? Were I to receive a visitor upon similar terms, my only question should be, "does he admire the style of Dr. Swift?"

Under this head I shall only add, that the most intimate acquaintance with the Roman and Greek writers will not produce perfection of style in men who are devoid of taste and genius. Hence we sometimes find the most celebrated teachers of the Latin and Greek languages extremely deficient in English composition. I acknowledge that Milton, Addison, Hume, Middleton and Boling-broke, whose styles have been so much admired, were all Latin and Greek scholars. But in these authors, a native strength of genius, and taste preserved their writings from the affectation and obscurity which are imparted to English compositions, by an adherence to the grammars and arrangement of the Latin and Greek languages.

3. It has been said that we cannot know the use or meaning of those numerous English words which are derived from the Latin

and Greek, without a knowledge of those languages. To this I may answer, that what proves too much, proves nothing at all. The argument that has been mentioned, proves that a knowledge of the Celtic, the Saxon, the German, the French, the Italian and the Dutch, is necessary to enable us to understand the use of many English words; for far the greatest part of them are derived from those languages. But I object further to this argument, that if a knowledge of the derivation of English words from the Greek and Latin languages, should be followed by a strict regard to their original meaning, it would lead us into many mistakes. The derivation of the word "angel" would lead us to contemplate a messenger, instead of a perfect finite intelligence. The derivation of the word "rebellion" would lead us to contemplate a war commenced by a conquered people: instead of a resistance to the just authority of government. Many other instances of similar incongruity might be mentioned between the meaning of certain English words, and their Roman and Greek originals. I conclude therefore that a knowledge of the derivation of words is not necessary to teach us their proper use and meaning. Custom, which is the law and rule of speech, and *what is*, instead of what *should be* common, will always govern the use of words. Where custom is unknown, modern English dictionaries will supply its place.

Here I beg leave to repeat that the study of the Greek and Latin languages by the English nation has been one of the greatest obstructions, that ever has been thrown in the way of the propagation of useful knowledge. By rendering our language unintelligible to the greatest part of the people who hear or read it, it has made it an improper vehicle of instruction. The orations of Demosthenes, we are told, were, like earthquakes in ancient Greece. They moved whole nations. The reason of this is plain. He never used a single word in any of them, but what was alike intelligible to all classes of his hearers. The effect of Indian eloquence upon the councils and wars of the savages in America, depends wholly upon its being perfectly understood and felt by every member of their communities. It has often been remarked that in England no play will succeed without action, while sentiment alone insures the loudest claps of applause, in the theatres of France. The reason of this is obvious. The English language requires action to translate it, to half the common audience of a theatre, whereas the French language, which is uniform and stationary, is understood, and, of course, the sentiment which is conveyed by it, is felt and enjoyed by all who hear it. The writings of Voltaire are quoted by the hairdressers and milliners of Paris, because they are written in the simple language of the country, while many of the most celebrated British authors cannot be understood by common readers, without the help of a dictionary or interpreter. Richardson and Fielding are an exception to this remark. They are alike intelligible and acceptable to the learned and unlearned, inasmuch as they have conveyed all their ideas in plain, but decent English words. The popularity of the methodist preachers may be ascribed in part to their speaking in a language that is intelligible to the common people. It is true, many of them are deficient in education, but this deficiency appears more in an ignorance of the construction of the English language, than in the proper use of English words, and perhaps this may be ascribed chiefly to their extempore mode of preaching. It is happy for some of those churches where the Latin and Greek languages are considered as necessary parts for education in their clergy, that part of the public worship of God is confined to reading the scriptures, and to forms of prayer, both of which are written in English, and are intelligible to every class of hearers. Such congregations are not left to the mercy of their preachers in every part of divine service. A pious woman in London who heard her minister speak of the Deity, by the name of the great Philanthropist, asked when she came home, what heathen god Philanthropist was? There are few sermons composed by Latin and Greek scholars in which there are not many hundred words, that are equally unintelligible to a majority of their hearers. Hence I cannot help thinking that were John the Baptist to appear again in our world, and to send to some of our doctors of divinity, or to many of our young preachers to enquire after the signs of their divine mission, few of them could adopt the answer of our Saviour and say that to the poor the gospel was "preached." It will require a total ignorance of the Latin and Greek languages, or an uncommon mixture of good sense and piety in a preacher who is acquainted with them, to address an audience in such a manner as to be perfectly understood by the illiterate part of them.

I wish to press the considerations that have been mentioned under this head, home to the feelings of the friends of virtue and religion. It has been demonstrated, that the study of the ancient classics is hurtful to morals. It is equally plain that the corruption of our language by the constant substitution of words of Greek and Latin origin, to those which had become familiar and universal, from long usage, has greatly retarded the progress of knowledge of all kinds, but in a more especial manner, a great proportion of that species of it which is delivered from the pulpit. I appeal to the consciences of ministers of the gospel of all denominations, whether, instead of exposing their candidates for the ministry, to temptation from that kind of learning "which puffeth up, without edifying," it would not be better to direct them to employ the time which is usually mis-spent in acquiring it, in studying the scriptures, and in making themselves masters of the English language? It is impossible to tell what great improvements would be made by these means in moral happiness in the United States.

4. We are told that a knowledge of the Greek and Roman languages, is necessary to enable us to understand the frequent allusions that are made by English writers to the mythology of those ancient nations. To this I answer, that the less we know of this subject, the better; for what is the history of the ancient fables, but an agreeable description of frauds—rapes—and murders, which, while they please the imagination, shock the moral faculty? It is high time to cease from idolizing the idolatry of Greece and Rome. Truth alone is knowledge, and spending time in studying Greek and Roman fictions, is only labouring to be more ignorant. If there is any moral contained in these fictions, it is so much involved in obscurity, as not to be intelligible to a young man at that time of life in which he usually becomes acquainted with them. Happy will it be for the present and future generations, if an ignorance of the Latin and Greek languages, should banish from modern poetry, those disgraceful invocations of heathen gods, which indicate no less a want of genius, than a want of reverence for the true God. I shall only add in this place, that the best writers in the English language seldom borrow allusions from the mythology of the Greek or Roman nations. Richardson and Fielding have passed them by, and hence arises another reason why the works of those authors are so universally intelligible and acceptable to all classes of readers.

5. It has been said, that the Latin language has become a
necessary part of liberal knowledge, inasmuch as the European
nations have by common consent made it the vehicle of their
discoveries. This argument had some weight while science consisted
only [of] learning what was known; but since the enquiries of
philosophers have been directed to new objects of observation and
experiment, the Latin language has not been able to keep pace with
the number and rapidity of their discoveries. Where shall we find
Latin words to convey just ideas of the many terms which electricity—chemistry—navigation—and many other sciences have introduced into our modern languages? It is from experience of the
insufficiency of the Latin language for this purpose, that most of the
modern nations of Europe have been obliged to adopt their own
languages, as the vehicles of their discoveries, in science. If this
argument had been acknowledged to have weight in Europe, it
should, from local circumstances, have no weight in America. Here
we have no intercourse with any part of Europe, except her commercial seaports, and in these, all business is transacted in modern
languages. America, with respect to the nations of Europe, is like
the new planet, with respect to those, whose revolutions have long
been described in the solar system. She is placed at too great a
distance from most of them, to be within the influence of a
reciprocal exchange of the rays of knowledge. Like a certain animal,
described by the naturalists, she must impregnate herself. But while
she retains a friendly intercourse with Great Britain, all the valuable
discoveries which are published in Latin, in any part of Europe, will
be transmitted to her through the medium of English translations.
    6. It has been said that a knowledge of the Latin and Greek
languages is necessary to the learned professions of law—physic—
and divinity. To this I answer, that the most useful books in each
of these professions are now translated, or written in English, in
consequence of which, knowledge in law—physic—and divinity has
been greatly multiplied and extended. I see no use at present for a
knowledge of the Latin and Greek languages, for a lawyer, a physician, or a divine, in the United States, except it be to facilitate the
remembrance of a few technical terms which may be retained
without it. Two of the most celebrated and successful lawyers in the
United States, are strangers to the Latin language. An eminent
physician, who spent several of the years of his youth in learning

this language, has assured me, that he had not more than three times in his life found any advantage from it. Very few physicians, I believe, (professors of medecine only excepted, who are obliged to review Latin theses previously to their publication) retain their knowledge of this language, after they become established in business, and if they do, it is preserved less from necessity, than from vanity, or a desire of reviving, by reading the classics, the agreeable ideas of the early and innocent part of their lives.

I know that it is commonly believed, that a knowledge of the Greek language, is necessary to enable a divine fully to understand the New Testament. But I object to this opinion, that the most useful and necessary parts of this divine book are intelligible to the lowest capacities in its present English dress: and I believe further, that there have been as many disputes among the critics, about the meaning of words, and about editions and translations of the New Testament, as there have been among unlearned christians about the meaning of its obscure and difficult passages. If a knowledge of the Greek language be necessary to enable a divine to understand the New Testament, it follows, that a critical knowledge of all the dialects in which the different parts of it were originally composed, is equally necessary for the same purpose; and, if necessary to a divine, why not to the common people, for they are equally interested in all the truths of revelation? The difficulties and absurdities into which we are led by this proposition, are too obvious to be mentioned.

We are very apt to forget the *age* in which we live. In the fifteenth century, all the knowledge of Europe was locked up in a few Greek and Latin manuscripts. In this confined state of knowledge, an acquaintance with the Latin language was thought to be necessary to civilize the human mind—hence the teachers of it acquired the title of "professors of humanity" in the European universities. But we live in an age in which knowledge has been drawn from its dead repositories, and diffused by the art of printing, in living languages, through every part of the world. Humanity has therefore changed sides. Her gentleness is now altogether in favour of modern literature.

We forget not only the age, but the country likewise in which we live. In Europe many ancient constitutions—laws—treaties—official letters—and even private deeds, are written in Latin—hence the knowledge of it has sometimes been found useful for statesmen and lawyers—but all the constitutions, laws, treaties, public letters, and private deeds of the United States, are written in English; and of course a knowledge of the Latin language is not necessary to understand them. It is therefore as useless in America, as the Spanish great-coat is in the island of Cuba, or the Dutch foot-stove, at the cape of Good Hope.

We forget further the difference of *occupation* between the inhabitants of the present, and of the fifteenth century. Formerly public prayers and war were the only business of man: but since agriculture, manufactures and commerce, have afforded such different and profitable employments to mankind, there cannot be greater folly than to learn two languages which are no ways connected with the advancement of any of them.

"I once thought health, the greatest blessing in the world," said Mr. Rittenhouse to the author of this essay, "but I do not think so now. There is one thing of much greater value, and that is time." This opinion of our excellent American philosopher, is true every where, but in a more especial manner in the United States. Here the opportunities of acquiring knowledge and of advancing private and public interest are so numerous, and the rewards of genius and industry so certain, that not a particle of time should be mis-spent or lost. We occupy a new country. Our principle business should be to explore and apply its resources, all of which press us to enterprize and haste. Under these circumstances, to spend four or five years in learning two dead languages, is to turn our backs upon a gold mine, in order to amuse ourselves in catching butterflies.

It is agreeable to hear of the progress of human reason in the gradual declension of the usual methods of teaching the Latin and Greek languages within the last forty years in Europe. Formerly boys were obliged to commit whole volumes of Latin and Greek poetry to memory, as the only means of learning those languages. Nor was this all; they were obliged to compose Latin verses, without the least regard being paid to genius, or taste for poetry. The last act of school tyranny, was to compel boys to read the ancient classics without the help of translations. All these methods of teaching the dead languages are now laid aside. The next ray of truth that irradiates human reason upon this subject, I hope will teach us to reject the Latin and Greek languages altogether, as branches of a liberal education.

The progress of human reason should likewise be acknowledged in having banished Latin and Greek quotations from sermons, and other religious tracts, which are intended for the common people. Such quotations are to be found only in books of science, addressed to the members of the learned professions, or to persons who are supposed to be acquainted with the Latin and Greek languages.

There are certain follies, like the objects of sight, which cannot be seen when the eye is placed too near them. We are struck with pity and horror in contemplating the folly discovered by our ancestors in their military expeditions to the holy land of Palestine. The generations which are to follow us, will probably view our partiality to the classic ground of Greece and Rome, with similar emotions. We laugh at the credulity of those nations who worshipped apes and crocodiles, without recollecting, that future ages will treat our superstitious veneration for the ancient poets and orators, with the same ridicule. Posterity, in reading the history of the American revolution, will wonder that in a country where so many exploits of wisdom and virtue were performed, the human understanding was fettered by prejudices in favour of the Latin and Greek languages. But I hope with the history of this folly, some historian will convey to future generations, that many of the most active and useful characters in accomplishing this revolution, were strangers to the formalities of a Latin and Greek education.

It is high time to distinguish between a philosopher, and a scholar, between things and words. "He was educated at the college of—" said a gentlemen to his friend, speaking of a young man who was known to them both. "You mean Sir," replied his friend, "he got his learning at the college of—; but as to education, he appears to have received none any where." This young man was an excellent Latin and Greek scholar, but knew nothing of men, or things.

Let it not be supposed from any thing that has been here advanced, that I wish the knowledge of the Latin and Greek languages to be extinct in the world. Far from it. My wish is to see it preserved, like the knowledge of law, or medicine, as a distinct profession. Let the persons, who devote themselves to the study of these languages, be called linguists, or interpreters, and let them be paid for their translations and explanations of Latin and Greek books, and other compositions in those languages. No more confidence will be placed by the public, in the members of this new profession, than is daily placed in lawyers and physicians, in matters of much greater importance; nor will more credit be given to them, than we are accustomed to give to travellers and historians. There can be no more reason why every man should be capable of translating or judging of a Latin or Greek book, than there can be why every man should be a lawyer or a physician, or why he should be obliged to visit Constantinople or Grand Cairo, in order to become acquainted with the situation of these two great cities. If this method of preserving and applying the dead languages should be adopted, young men will learn them as they do law and physic, by serving an apprenticeship, instead of going to school.

The following advantages would immediately attend the rejection of the Latin and Greek languages as branches of a liberal education.

1. It would improve, and finally perfect the English language, by checking the increase of those superfluous words which are derived from the Latin and Greek languages. What use have we for festivity—celebrity—hilarity—amenity—and a hundred other duplicate words, with which Johnson and Harris have corrupted and weakened our language, and which are unintelligible to three fourths of the common English readers? The rejection of the ancient languages, would further banish Latin and Greek words, such as, *exit, fecit, excudit, pinxit, acme, finis, bona fide, ipso facto, ad valorem,* and a hundred others, equally disgusting, from English compositions. It would moreover preserve our language from encroachments of French and Italian words, such as *eclat— amateur—douceur—en passant—corps—dilettanti—con cuore—piano* and many others, all of which impair the uniformity and dignity of the English language.

2. The rejection of the Latin and Greek languages from our schools, would produce a revolution in science, and in human affairs. That nation which shall first shake off the fetters of those ancient languages, will advance further in knowledge, and in happiness, in twenty years, than any nation in Europe has done, in a hundred.

3. It will have a tendency to destroy the prejudices of the common people against schools and colleges. The common people do not despise scholars, because they know more, but because they know less than themselves. A mere scholar can call a horse, or a cow, by two or three different names, but he frequently knows nothing of the qualities, or uses of those valuable animals.

4. It would be the means of banishing pride from our seminaries

of public education. Men are generally most proud of those things that do not contribute to the happiness of themselves, or others. Useful knowledge generally humbles the mind, but learning, like fine clothes, feeds pride, and thereby hardens the human heart.

5. It would greatly encrease the number of students in our colleges, and thereby extend the benefits of education through every part of our country. The excellency of knowledge would then be obvious to every body, because it would be constantly applicable to some of the necessary and useful purposes of life, and particularly to the security and order of wise and just government.

6. It would remove the present immense disparity which subsists between the sexes, in the degrees of their education and knowledge. Perhaps one cause of the misery of many families, as well as communities, may be sought for in the *mediocrity* of knowledge of the women. They should know *more* or *less*, in order to be happy themselves, and to communicate happiness to others. By ceasing to make Latin and Greek a necessary part of a liberal education, we open the doors for every species of improvement to the female part of society:—hence will arise new pleasures in their company,—and hence, too, we may expect a general reformation and refinement, in the generations which are to follow us; for principles and manners in all societies are formed chiefly by the women.

It may be asked here, how shall we employ those years of a boy, that are now usually spent in learning the Latin and Greek languages? I shall endeavour to answer this question by laying down a short plan of a liberal English education. In this undertaking, I shall strive to forget for a while all the systems of education I have ever seen, and suggest such a one as is founded in the original principles of action in the human mind.

1. Let the first eight years of a boy's time be employed in learning to speak, spell, read and write the English language. For this purpose, let him be committed to the care of a master, who speaks correctly at all times, and let the books he reads be written in a simple and correct style. During these years, let not an English grammar by any means be put into his hands. It is to most boys, under even twelve years of age, an unintelligible book. As well might we contend, that a boy should be taught the names and number of the humours of the eye, or the muscles of the tongue,

in order to learn to see, or to speak, as be taught the English language, by means of grammar. Sancho, in attempting to learn to read, by chewing the four and twenty words of the alphabet, did not exhibit a greater absurdity, than a boy of seven or eight years old does, in committing grammar rules to memory, in order to understand the English language. Did we wish to describe a ship, so as to have all its parts perfectly and speedily known, would we begin by describing its detached parts in a ship-yard, or a rope-walk? Or would we not fix every part in its proper place, and then explain the names and uses of these parts, by shewing their subserviency to each other? In like manner, I affirm, that the construction of our language should be learned by a careful attention to the places and uses of the different parts of speech in agreeable compositions, and not by contemplating them in a disjointed state in an English grammar. But I will add further, that grammar should be taught only by the ear. Pronounciation, which is far more extensive, and difficult, is learned only in this way. To teach concord in the arrangement of words, let the master converse with his pupils as well as hear them read, and let him distinctly mark and correct every deviation from grammatical propriety which they utter. This method of teaching grammar has been tried with success in the families of several gentlemen of my acquaintance. It is both rational, and practicable. It has, moreover, the authority of the wise Greeks to recommend it. Homer, Xenophon, Demosthenes, and Longinus, I believe, were all taught to speak, read, and write their native language, without the incumbrance of a Greek grammar. I do not mean by any thing that has been advanced, to insinuate that our pupil should not be instructed in the principles and laws of our language. I have reserved this part of knowledge to a much later period of his youth, at which time, he will acquire it almost as soon as Moliere's "Citizen turned Gentleman," learned to distinguish between prose and poetry. He will find that he is in possession of this knowledge, and that the business of his master will be only to give names to things with which he is already acquainted.

Under this head, I shall only add, that the perfection of the ear, as an avenue of knowledge is not sufficiently known. Ideas acquired through that organ, are much more durable, than those acquired by the eyes. We remember much longer what we hear, than what we see; hence, old men recollect voices, long after they forget faces. These facts are capable of great application to the business of education.

Having provided our pupil with a vehicle of knowledge, by teaching him to read and write, our next business should be to furnish him with ideas. Here it will be necessary to remark, that the human mind in early life first comprehends substances. From these it proceeds to actions, from actions to qualities, and from qualities to degrees. Let us therefore in education, follow this order of nature, and begin by instructing our pupil in the knowledge of substances, or things. For this purpose, let us initiate him into the knowledge of the globe on which he exists, by teaching him

2. Natural history. This study is simple and truly delightful. Animals of all kinds are often the subjects of conversation and disputes among boys in their walks and diversions. But this is not all; this study is the foundation of all useful and practical knowledge in agriculture, manufactures and commerce, as well as in philosophy, chemistry, and medecine. By making natural history the first study of a boy, we imitate the conduct of the first teacher of man. The first lesson that Adam received from his Maker in Paradise, was upon natural history. It is probable that the dominion of our great progenitor over the brute creation, and every other living creature, was founded upon a perfect knowledge of their names and qualities, for God appears in this, as well as in other instances, to have acted by the instrumentality of human reason.— Where a museum is wanting, all that is necessary for a boy to know of animals and fishes—insects—trees and herbs, may be taught by means of prints.

3. Geography, is a simple science, and accommodated to the capacity of a boy under twelve years of age. It may be perfectly understood by means of cards—globes—and maps; for each of these modes of conveying instruction, seizes upon the senses and imagination. The frequent application which a boy is obliged to make of his knowledge in geography, in reading, and conversation, will soon fix it upon his memory, and from the *time* and *manner* in which he will acquire it, he will never forget it.

I allow four years to be employed in acquiring these two fundamental branches of knowledge. After our pupil has become tolerably well acquainted with them, he should be instructed in the

4. French and German languages. These will be equally necessary, whether commerce—physic—law or divinity is the pursuit of a young man. They should be acquired only by the ear. Great care should be taken not to permit him to learn these languages before he is *twelve* years old, otherwise he will contract so much of the French and German accent as will impair the prononciation of his native tongue.

5. Arithmetic, and some of the more simple branches of the mathematics should be acquired between the twelfth and fourteenth years of his life.

6. Between his fourteenth and eighteenth years, he should be instructed in grammar—oratory—criticism—the higher branches of mathematics—philosophy—chemistry—logic—metaphysics—chronology—history—government—the principles of agriculture, and manufactures—and in every thing else that is necessary to qualify him for public usefulness, or private happiness.

7. I know it is common to introduce what is called *Moral Philosophy* into a system of liberal education. The name of this science is derived from the Pagan schools. The study of it constituted a material part of their learning. Instead of continuing this anti-christian mode of teaching morals, I would propose a course of lectures to be given upon the evidences, doctrines, and *precepts* of the Christian religion. The last part of this course might be made to include the whole circle of moral duties, and from the connection it would have with the evidences and doctrines of Christianity it would produce an impression upon the understanding which no time or circumstances would ever wear away. It is by neglecting to teach young men the Christian religion as a science, or by the separation of its morals from its principles, the colleges have become in so many instances, the nurseries of infidelity.

* * *

Extract of a letter from the reverend Mr. James Muir, principal of the academy of Alexandria in Virginia, to the Author, dated July 29, 1791.

"I have read with satisfaction, in the Museum, your observations on studying the learned languages. There is little taste for them in this place. In our academy, where there are near ninety students, not above nineteen are poring over Latin and Greek. One of these nineteen was lately addressed by a student of Arithmetic in the following language—Pray, Sir, can you resolve me, by your Latin, this question, If one bushel of corn cost four shillings, what cost fifty bushels?—A demand of this kind from a youth, is to me a proof of the taste of Americans in the present day, who prefer the *useful* to the *ornamental.*"

ANSWER *to the foregoing letter, containing further observations upon the study of the Latin and Greek languages.*

DEAR SIR, It gave me great pleasure to find, by your polite letter of July 29th, that my opinions, upon the subject of the Latin and Greek languages, have met with your approbation; and that the young gentlemen who compose your academy had discovered so much good sense in preferring *useful* to *useless*, or, at best, ornamental literature.

I have read all the replies that have been published to my opinions: and am more confirmed in the truth of them, than ever, by the weakness and fallacy of the objections that have been made to them. The style of some of those replies has established one of my propositions in the most forcible manner. It has demonstrated that a knowledge of the dead languages does not confer taste or elegance in the English language, any more than it does good breeding, or good temper. I except from this remark the candid and ingenious letters published in the Federal Gazette, said to be written by Dr. Stuber, of this city.

To persuade men, that white is *black*, or black, *white*, it is necessary sometimes to make them believe that they are *grey*. The mind requires a resting point, in passing from error to truth, upon many subjects. I shall avail myself of this weakness in human nature, and take the liberty of suggesting a method of teaching the Latin and Greek languages, which I conceive, will be accommodated to the present state of the prejudices of our countrymen in their favour.

The late Dr. Franklin used to say, that the learning of a dead or foreign language might be divided into *ten* parts. That it required *five* only to learn to read it—*seven* to speak it—and the whole *ten* to write it. Now, when we consider how seldom we are called upon to *speak* or *write* the Latin or Greek languages, suppose we teach our boys only to *read* them. This will cut off one half the difficulty of learning them, and enable a boy to acquire as much of *both*, in two years, as will be necessary for him. He will, moreover, by this plan, be able to read more of the classics than are read at present in our schools. The classics are now read only for the sake of acquiring a knowledge of the construction of the languages in which they are written; but by the plan I have proposed, they would be read for the sake of the matter they contained, and there would be time enough to read each book from its beginning to its end. At present, what boy ever reads all the Aenead of Virgil, or the Iliad of Homer? In short, few boys ever carry with them from school, any thing but a smattering of the classics. They peep into a dozen of them; but are taught to attend to every thing they contain, more than to the *subjects* which are treated of by them.

In the way I have proposed, a boy would be able to translate all the Latin and Greek books he would meet with, and from the perfect knowledge he would acquire of them at school, he would probably retain that knowledge as long as he lived.

To carry this mode of teaching the Latin and Greek languages into effect, it is absolutely necessary that a boy should first be instructed in *history* and *geography*. Let him read an account of the rise, progress, and fall of the Greek and Roman nations; and exam-ine, upon maps, the countries they inhabited and conquered, and their languages will soon become interesting to him. The neglect of this natural and easy mode of instruction, is an inversion of all order. The absurdity of it was once happily exposed by a boy of eight years old, who, with a Latin Grammar in his hand, gravely asked his father, "who made the Latin language, and what was it made for?" Had this boy been previously instructed in the Roman history, he would not have asked such a question. Considering his age, it was as natural, as it was foolish.

There is no play common among children, that strikes me with an idea of half the folly that I am struck with, every time I look into a Latin school, and see thirty or forty little boys pinioned down to benches, and declining nouns, conjugating verbs, or writing Latin versions. I consider the highest attainment in this kind of learning, as nothing more than successful dostards, but far less use-ful than those which are exhibited in the useful athletic exercises of school boys.

By adopting the plan I have proposed, a boy will not open a Latin or Greek book, till he is fourteen or fifteen years old; so that the dead languages, instead of being the first, will be the last things he will learn at school. At this age, he will learn them with half the trouble, and understand them much better than he would have done at nine or ten years of age. For though languages are acquired with most ease by the *ear* under puberty, yet they are acquired most easily by the *eye*, after that period of life. But there is another advantage in making the Latin and Greek languages the last things that are taught at school. The bent of a young man's inclinations is generally known at fourteen or fifteen, and seldom sooner. Now if he incline to commerce—to a military—or a naval life—or to a mechanical employment, in all of which it is agreed, Latin and Greek are unnecessary, it will be improper to detain him any longer at school, by which means much money will be saved by the parents, and much time saved by the boy, both of which are wasted by the present indiscriminate and preposterous mode of teaching the dead languages.

The idea of the necessity of a knowledge of those languages, as an introduction to the knowledge of the English language, begins to lose ground. It is certainly a very absurd one. We have several English schools in our city, in which boys and girls of twelve and fourteen years old have been taught to speak and write our native language with great grammatical propriety. Some of these children would disgrace our bachelors and masters of arts, who have spent four or five years in the study of the Latin and Greek languages in our American colleges. It is true, these Latin and Greek scholars, after a while, acquire a knowledge of our language: but it is in the same slow way, in which some men acquire a knowledge of the forms of good breeding. Three months instruction will often impart more of both, than a whole life spent in acquiring them simply by imitation.

Where there is one Latin scholar, who is obliged, in the course of his life, to *speak* or *write* a Latin sentence, there are hundreds who are not under that necessity. Why then should we spend years in teaching that which is so rarely required in future life? For some years to come, the reading of the language, may be necessary; but a young man of fourteen or fifteen, may be taught to do this perfectly in one year, without committing a single grammar rule to memory, or without *spoiling his hand by* writing a single version.

Much more, in my opinion, might be said in favour of teaching our young men to *speak* the Indian languages of our country, than to *speak* or write Latin. By their means, they might qualify themselves to become ambassadors to our Indian nations, or introduce among them a knowledge of the blessings of civilization and religion.

We have lately seen a large portion of power wrested from the hands of kings and priests, and exercised by its lawful owners. Is it not high time to wrest the power over the education of our youth, out of the hands of ignorant or prejudiced schoolmasters, and place it in the hands of men of more knowledge and experience in the affairs of the world? We talk much of our being an *enlightened* people, but I know not with what reason, while we tolerate a system of education in our schools, which is as disgraceful to the human understanding as the most corrupt tenets or practices of the pagan religion, or of the Turkish government.

With great respect for your character, as well as for your present honourable and useful employment, I am, dear sir,

Your friend and most obedient servant.

BENJAMIN RUSH.

Philadelphia, August 24, 1791.

Thoughts upon the Amusements and Punishments which are Proper for Schools. Addressed to George, Clymer, Esq.

DEAR SIR,

The last time I had the pleasure of being in your company, you did me the honour to request my opinion upon the AMUSEMENTS and PUNISHMENTS which are proper for schools. The subjects are of a very opposite nature, but I shall endeavour to comply with your wishes, by sending you a few thoughts upon each of them. I am sure you will not reject my opinions because they are contrary to received practices, for I know that you are accustomed to think for yourself, and that every proposition that has for its objects the interests of humanity and your country, will be treated by you with attention and candor.

I shall begin with the subjects of AMUSEMENTS. Montesquieu informs us that the exercises of the last day of the life of Epaminondas, were the same as his amusements in his youth. Herein we have an epitome of the perfection of education. The amusements of Epaminondas were of a military nature; but as the profession of arms is the business of only a small part of mankind, and happily much less necessary in the United States than in ancient Greece, I would propose that the amusements of our youth, at school, should consist of such exercises as will be most subservient to their future employments in life. These are; 1. agriculture; 2. mechanical occupations; and 3. the business of the learned professions.

I. There is a variety in the employments of agriculture which may readily be suited to the genius, taste, and strength of young people. An experiment has been made of the efficacy of these employments, as amusements, in the Methodist College at Abington, in Maryland; and, I have been informed, with the happiest effects. A large lot is divided between the scholars, and premiums are adjudged to those of them who produce the most vegetables from their grounds, or who keep them in the best order.

II. As the employments of agriculture cannot afford amusement at all seasons of the year, or in cities, I would propose, that children should be allured to seek amusements in such of the mechanical arts as are suited to their strength and capacities. Where is the boy who does not delight in the use of a hammer—a chisel—or a saw? and who has not enjoyed a high degree of pleasure in his youth, in constructing a miniature house? How amusing are the machines which are employed in the manufactory of cloathing of all kinds! and how full of various entertainment are the mixtures which take place in the chemical arts! each of these might be contrived upon such a scale, as not only to amuse young people, but to afford a profit to their parents or masters. The Moravians, at Bethlehem in our state, have proved that this proposition is not a chimerical one. All the amusements of their children are derived from their performing the subordinate parts of several of the mechanical arts; and a considerable portion of the wealth of that worthy and happy society is the product of the labour of their little hands.—

If, in these amusements, an appeal should be made to that spirit of competition which is so common among young people, it would be the means of producing more pleasure to the children, and more profit to all who are connected with them. The wealth of those manufacturing towns in England, which employ the children of poor people, is a proof of what might be expected from connecting amusement and labour together, in all our schools. The product from the labour obtained in this way, from all the schools in the United States, would amount to a sum which would almost exceed calculation.

III. To train the youth who are intended for the learned professions or for merchandize, to the duties of their future employments, by means of useful amusements, which are *related* to those employments, will be impracticable; but their amusements may be derived from cultivating a spot of ground; for where is the lawyer, the physician, the divine, or the merchant, who has not indulged or felt a passion, in some part of his life, for rural improvements?— Indeed I conceive the seeds of knowledge in agriculture will be the most productive, when they are planted in the minds of this class of scholars.

I have only to add under this head, that the common amusements of children have no connection with their future occupations. Many of them injure their cloaths, some of them waste their strength, and impair their health, and all of them prove more or less, the means of producing noise, or of exciting angry passions, both of which are calculated to beget vulgar manners. The Methodists have wisely banished every species of play from their college. Even the healthy and pleasurable exercise of swimming, is not permitted to their scholars, except in the presence of one of their masters.

Do not think me too strict if I here exclude *gunning* from among the amusements of young men. My objections to it are as follow.

1. It hardens the heart, by inflicting unnecessary pain and death upon animals.

2. It is unnecessary in civilized society, where animal food may be obtained from domestic animals, with greater facility.

3. It consumes a great deal of time, and thus creates habits of idleness.

4. It frequently leads young men into low, and bad company.

5. By imposing long abstinance from food, it leads to intemperance in eating, which naturally leads to intemperance in drinking.

6. It exposes to fevers, and accidents. The newspapers are occasionally filled with melancholy accounts of the latter, and every physician must have met with frequent and dangerous instances of the former, in the course of his practice.

I know the early use of a gun is recommended in our country, to teach our young men the use of firearms, and thereby to prepare them for war and battle. But why should we inspire our youth, by such exercises, with hostile ideas towards their fellow creatures?—Let us rather instill into their minds sentiments of universal benevolence to men of all nations and colours. Wars originate in error and vice. Let us eradicate these, by proper modes of education, and wars will cease to be necessary in our country. The divine author and lover of peace "will then suffer no man to do us wrong; yea, he will reprove kings for our sake, saying, touch not my annointed and do my people no harm." Should the nations with whom war is a trade, approach our coasts, they will retire from us, as Satan did from our Saviour, when he came to assault him; and for the same reason, because they will "find nothing in us" congenial to their malignant dispositions; for the flames of war can be spread from one nation to another, only by the conducting mediums of vice and error.

I have hinted at the injury which is done to the health of young people by some of their amusements; but there is a practice common in all our schools, which does more harm to their bodies than all the amusements that can be named, and that is, obliging them to sit too long in *one place*, or crowding too many of them together *in one room*. By means of the former, the growth and shape of the body have been impaired; and by means of the latter, the seeds of fevers have often been engendered in schools. In the course of my business, I have been called to many hundred children who have been seized with indispositions in school, which evidently arose from the action of morbid effluvia, produced by the confined breath and perspiration of too great a number of children in one room. To obviate these evils, children should be permitted, after they have said their lessons, to amuse themselves in the open air, in some of the useful and agreeable exercises which have been mentioned. Their minds will be strengthened, as well as their bodies relieved by them. To oblige a sprightly boy to sit *seven* hours in a day, with his little arms pinioned to his sides, and his neck unnaturally bent towards his book; and for *no crime!*—what cruelty and folly are manifested, by such an absurd mode of instructing or governing young people!

I come next to say a few words upon the subject of PUNISHMENTS which are proper in schools.

In barbarous ages every thing partook of the complexion of the times. Civil, ecclesiastical, military, and domestic punishments were all of a cruel nature. With the progress of reason and christianity, punishments of all kinds have become less severe. Solitude and labour are now substituted in many countries, with success, in the room of the whipping-post and the gallows.—The innocent infirmities of human nature are no longer proscribed, and punished by the church. Discipline, consisting in the vigilance of officers, has lessened the supposed necessity of military executions; and husbands—fathers—and masters now blush at the history of the times, when wives, children, and servants, were governed only by force. But unfortunately this spirit of humanity and civilization has not reached our schools. The rod is yet the principal instrument of governing them, and a school-master remains the only despot now known in free countries. Perhaps it is because the little subjects of their arbitrary and capricious power have not been in a condition to complain. I shall endeavour therefore to plead their cause, and to prove that corporal punishments (except to children under four or five years of age) are never necessary, and always hurtful, in schools.—The following arguments I hope will be sufficient to establish this proposition.

1. Children are seldom sent to school before they are capable of feeling the force of rational or moral obligation. They may therefore be deterred from committing offences, by motives less disgraceful than the fear of corporal punishments.

2. By correcting children for ignorance and negligence in school, their ideas of *improper* and *immoral* actions are confounded, and hence the moral faculty becomes weakened in after life. It would not be more cruel or absurd to inflict the punishment of the whipping-post upon a man, for not dressing fashionably or neatly, than it is to ferule a boy for blotting his copy book, or mis-spelling a word.

3. If the natural affection of a parent is sometimes insufficient, to restrain the violent effects of a sudden gust of anger upon a child, how dangerous must the power of correcting children be when lodged in the hands of a school-master, in whose anger there is no mixture of parental affection! Perhaps those parents act most wisely, who never trust themselves to inflict corporal punishments upon their children, after they are four or five years old, but endeavour to punish, and reclaim them, by confinement, or by abridging them of some of their usual gratifications, in dress, food or amusements.

4. Injuries are sometimes done to the bodies, and sometimes to the intellects of children, by corporal punishments. I recollect, when a boy, to have lost a school-mate, who was said to have died in consequence of a severe whipping he received in school. At that time I did not believe it possible, but from what I now know of the disproportion between the violent emotions of the mind, and the strength of the body in children, I am disposed to believe, that not only sickness, but that even *death* may be induced, by the convulsions of a youthful mind, worked up to a high sense of shame and resentment.

The effects of thumping the head, boxing the ears, and pulling the hair, in impairing the intellects, by means of injuries done to the brain, are too obvious to be mentioned.

5. Where there is *shame*, says Dr. Johnson, there may be *virtue*. But corporal punishments, inflicted at school, have a tendency to destroy the sense of shame, and thereby to destroy all moral sensibility. The boy that has been often publicly whipped at school, is under great obligations to his maker, and his parents, if he afterwards escape the whipping-post or the gallows.

6. Corporal punishments, inflicted at school, tend to beget a spirt of violence in boys towards each other, which often follows them through life; but they most certainly beget a spirit of hatred, or revenge, towards their masters, which too often becomes a ferment of the same baneful passions towards other people. The celebrated Dr. afterwards Baron Haller declared, that he never saw, without horror, during the remaining part of his life, a schoolmaster, who had treated him with unmerited severity, when he was only ten years old. A similar anecdote is related of the famous M. de Condamine. I think I have known several instances of this vindictive, or indignant spirit, to continue towards a cruel and tyrannical school-master, in persons who were advanced in life, and who were otherwise of gentle and forgiving dispositions.

7. Corporal punishments, inflicted at schools, beget a hatred to instruction in young people. I have sometimes suspected that the Devil, who knows how great an enemy knowledge is to his kingdom, has had the address to make the world believe that *ferruling, pulling* and *boxing ears, cudgelling, horsing, &c.* and, in boarding-schools, a *little starving*, are all absolutely necessary for the government of young people, on purpose that he might make both schools, and school-masters odious, and thereby keep our world in ignorance; for ignorance is the best means the Devil ever contrived, to keep up the number of his subjects in our world.

8. Corporal punishments are not only hurtful, but altogether unnecessary, in schools. Some of the most celebrated and successful school-masters, that I have known, never made use of them.

9. The fear of corporal punishments, by debilitating the body, produces a corresponding debility in the mind, which contracts its capacity of acquiring knowledge. This capacity is enlarged by the tone which the mind acquires from the action of hope, love, and confidence upon it; and all these passions might easily be cherished, by a prudent and enlightened school-master.

10. As there should always be a certain ratio between the strength of a remedy, and the excitability of the body in diseases, so there should be a similar ratio between the force employed in the government of a school, and the capacities and tempers of children. A kind rebuke, like fresh air in a fainting fit, is calculated to act upon a young mind with more effect, than stimulants of the greatest power; but corporal punishments level all capacities and tempers, as quack-medicines do, all constitutions and diseases. They dishonour and degrade our species; for they suppose a total absence of all moral and intellectual feeling from the mind. Have we not often seen dull children suddenly improve, by changing their schools? The reason is obvious. The successful teacher only accommodated his manner and discipline to the capacities of his scholars.

11. I conceive corporal punishments, inflicted in an arbitrary manner, to be contrary to the spirit of liberty, and that they should not be tolerated in a free government. Why should not children be protected from violence and injuries, as well as white and black servants?—Had I influence enough in our legislature to obtain only a single law, it should be to make the punishment for striking a school boy, the same as for assaulting and beating an adult member of society.

To all these arguments I know some well disposed people will reply, that the *rod* has received a divine commission from the sacred Scriptures, as the instrument of correcting children. To this I answer that the *rod*, in the Old Testament, by a very common figure in Rhetoric, stands for punishments of *any* kind, just as the *sword*, in the New Testament, stands for the faithful and general administration of justice, in such a way as is most calculated to reform criminals, and to prevent crimes.

The following method of governing a school, I apprehend, would be attended with much better effects, than that which I have endeavoured to shew to be contrary to reason, humanity, religion, liberty, and the experience of the wisest and best teachers in the world.

Let a school-master endeavour, in the first place, to acquire the confidence of his scholars, by a prudent deportment. Let him learn to command his passions and temper, at all times, in his school,—Let him treat the name of the Supreme Being with reverence, as often as it occurs in books, or in conversation with his scholars.—Let him exact a respectful behaviour towards himself, in his school;

but in the intervals of school hours, let him treat his scholars with gentleness and familiarity. If he should even join in their amusements, he would not lose, by his condescension, any part of his authority over them. But to secure their affection and respect more perfectly, let him, once or twice a year, lay out a small sum of money in penknives, and books, and distribute them among his scholars, as rewards for proficiency in learning, and for good behaviour. If these prudent and popular measures should fail of preventing offences at school, then let the following modes of punishment be adopted.

1. *Private* admonition. By this mode of rebuking, we imitate the conduct of the divine Being towards his offending creatures, for his *first* punishment is always inflicted *privately*, by means of the *still* voice of conscience.

2. Confinement after school-hours are ended; but with the knowledge of the parents of the children.

3. Holding a small sign of disgrace, of any kind, in the middle of the floor, in the presence of a whole school.

If these punishments fail of reclaiming a bad boy, he should be dismissed from school, to prevent his corrupting his schoolmates. It is the business of parents, and not of school-masters, to use the last means for eradicating idleness and vice from their children.

The world was created in love. It is sustained by love. Nations and families that are happy, are made so only by love. Let us extend this divine principle, to those little communities which we call schools. Children are capable of loving in a high degree. They may therefore be governed by love.

The occupation of a school-master is truly dignified. He is, next to mothers, the most important member of civil society. Why then is there so little rank connected with that occupation? Why do we treat it with so much neglect or contempt? It is because the voice of reason, in the human heart, associates with it the idea of despotism and violence. Let school-masters cease to be tyrants, and they will soon enjoy the respect and rank, which are naturally connected with their profession.

We are grossly mistaken in looking up wholly to our governments, and even to ministers of the gospel, to promote public and private order in society. Mothers and school-masters plant the seeds of nearly all the good and evil which exist in our world. Its reformation must therefore be begun in nurseries and in schools. If the habits we acquire there, were to have no influence upon our future happiness, yet the influence they have upon our governments, is a sufficient reason why we ought to introduce new modes, as well as new objects of education into our country.

You have lately been employed in an attempt to perpetuate our existence as a free people, by establishing the means of national credit and defence;[1] but these are feeble bulwarks against slavery, compared with habits of labour and virtue, disseminated among our young people. Let us establish schools for this purpose, in every township in the United States, and conform them to reason, humanity, and the present state of society in America. Then, Sir, will the generations who are to follow us, realize the precious ideas of the dignity and excellence of republican forms of government, which I well recollect you cherished with so much ardor, in the beginning of the American revolution, and which you have manifested ever since, both by your public and private conduct.

We suffer so much from traditional error of various kinds, in education, morals, and government, that I have been led to wish, that it were possible for us to have schools established, in the United States, for teaching *the art of forgetting*. I think three-fourths of all our school-masters, divines, and legislators would profit very much, by spending two or three years in such useful institutions.

An apology may seem necessary, not only for the length of this letter, but for some of the opinions contained in it. I know how apt mankind are to brand every proposition for innovation, as visionary and Utopian. But good men should not be discouraged, by such epithets, from their attempts to combat vice and error. There never was an improvement, in any art or science, nor even a proposal for meliorating the condition of man, in any age or country, that has not been considered in the light of what has been called, since Sir Thomas More's time, an *Utopian scheme*. The application of the magnet to navigation, and of steam to mechanical purposes, have both been branded as Utopian projects. The great idea in the mind of Columbus, of exploring a new world, was long viewed, in most of the courts of Europe, as the dream of a visionary sailor. But why do we go to ancient times, for proofs of important innovations in human affairs having been treated as Utopian schemes. You and

---

[1] Mr. Clymer was one of the Representatives of Pennsylvania, in the first Congress of the United States which met in New York, in the year 1789.

I recollect the time, when the abolition of negro slavery in our
state, as also when the independence of the United States, and the
present wise and happy confederacy of our republics, were all considered by many of our sober prudent men, as subjects of an
Utopian nature.

If those benefactors of mankind, who have levelled mountains
in the great road of human life, by the discoveries or labours which
have been mentioned, have been stigmatized with obloquy, as
visionary projectors, why should an individual be afraid of similar
treatment, who has only attempted to give to that road, from its
beginning, a straight direction.

If but a dozen men like yourself, approve of my opinions, it will
overbalance the most illiberal opposition they may meet with, from
all the learned vulgar of the United States.

For the benefit of those persons who consider opinions as
improved, like certain liquors, by time; and who are opposed to
innovations, only because they did not occur to their ancestors,
I shall conclude my letter with an anecdote of a minister in London,
who, after employing a long sermon, in controverting what he
supposed to be an heretical opinion, concluded it with the following
words, "I tell you, I tell you my brethren,—I tell you again,—that an
old error is better than a new truth."

With great regard I am,
Dear Sir,
Your's sincerely,

BENJAMIN RUSH.

Philadelphia, August 20th, 1790.

P.S. Since writing the above letter, an ingenious German friend
of mine has informed me, that a curious work has lately appeared
in Germany, entitled, "A treatise on human misery," written by a
Mr. Salzman, an enlightened school-master, in which a striking
view is given of the misery inflicted upon part of the human race,
by the present absurd, and cruel modes of conducting education in
public schools. The author concludes this part of his work, my
friend informs me, with a dream, in which he beholds with ineffable
joy, the avenging angel descending from heaven, and afterwards
consuming in an immense bonfire, certain absurd school-books,
and *all the ferrules* in the world.

THOUGHTS UPON FEMALE EDUCATION,
ACCOMMODATED TO THE PRESENT STATE OF
SOCIETY, MANNERS, AND GOVERNMENT, IN THE
UNITED STATES OF AMERICA. ADDRESSED TO
THE VISITORS OF THE YOUNG LADIES'
ACADEMY IN PHILADELPHIA, 28TH JULY, 1787, AT
THE CLOSE OF THE QUARTERLY EXAMINATION,
AND AFTERWARDS PUBLISHED AT THE REQUEST
OF THE VISITORS.

GENTLEMEN,

I have yielded with diffidence to the solicitations of the Principal of the Academy, in undertaking to express my regard for the prosperity of this seminary of learning, by submitting to your candor, a few Thoughts upon Female Education.

The first remark that I shall make upon this subject, is, that female education should be accommodated to the state of society, manners, and government of the country, in which it is conducted.

This remark leads me at once to add, that the education of young ladies, in this country, should be conducted upon principles very different from what it is in Great Britain, and in some respects, different from what it was when we were part of a monarchical empire.

There are several circumstances in the situation, employments, and duties of women in America, which require a peculiar mode of education.

I. The early marriages of our women, by contracting the time allowed for education, renders it necessary to contract its plan, and to confine it chiefly to the more useful branches of literature.

II. The state of property in America, renders it necessary for the greatest part of our citizens to employ themselves, in different occupations, for the advancement of their fortunes. This cannot be done without the assistance of the female members of the community. They must be the stewards, and guardians of their husbands' property. That education, therefore, will be most proper for our women, which teaches them to discharge the duties of those offices with the most success and reputation.

III. From the numerous avocations from their families, to which professional life exposes gentlemen in America, a principal share of the instruction of children naturally devolves upon the women. It becomes us therefore to prepare them by a suitable education, for the discharge of this most important duty of mothers.

IV. The equal share that every citizen has in the liberty, and the possible share he may have in the government of our country, make it necessary that our ladies should be qualified to a certain degree by a peculiar and suitable education, to concur in instructing their sons in the principles of liberty and government.

V. In Great Britain the business of servants is a regular occupation; but in America this humble station is the usual retreat of unexpected indigence; hence the servants in this country possess less knowledge and subordination than are required from them; and hence, our ladies are obliged to attend more to the private affairs of their families, than ladies generally do, of the same rank in Great Britain. "They are good servants," said an American lady of distinguished merit,[1] in a letter to a favorite daughter,[2] "who will do well with good looking after." This circumstance should have great influence upon the nature and extent of female education in America.

The branches of literature most essential for a young lady in this country, appear to be,

I. A knowledge of the English language. She should not only read, but speak and spell it correctly. And to enable her to do this, she should be taught the English grammar, and be frequently examined in applying its rules in common conversation.

II. Pleasure and interest conspire to make the writing of a fair an legible hand, a necessary branch of a lady's education. For this purpose she should be taught not only to shape every letter properly, but to pay the strictest regard to points and capitals.[3]

---

[1] Mrs. Graeme.

[2] Mrs. Elizabeth Ferguson.

[3] The present mode of writing among persons of taste is to use a capital letter only for the first word of a sentence, and for names of persons, places and months, and for the first word of every line in poetry. The words should be so shaped that a straight line may be drawn between two lines, without touching the extremities of the words in either of them.

I once heard of a man who professed to discover the temper and disposition of persons by looking at their hand writing. Without enquiring into the probability of this story; I shall only remark, that there is one thing in which all mankind agree upon this subject, and that is, in considering writing that is blotted, crooked, or illegible, as a mark of vulgar education. I know of few things more rude or illiberal, than to obtrude a letter upon a person of rank or business, which cannot be easily read. Peculiar care should be taken to avoid every kind of ambiguity and affectation in writing *names*. I have now a letter in my possession upon business, from a gentleman of a liberal profession in a neighbouring state, which I am unable to answer, because I cannot discover the name which is subscribed to it.[4] For obvious reasons I would recommend the writing of the first or christian name at full length, where it does not consist of more than two syllables. Abbreviations of all kind in letter writing, which always denote either haste or carelessness, should likewise be avoided. I have only to add under this head that the Italian and inverted hands which are read with difficulty, are by no means accommodated to the active state of business in America, or to the simplicity of the citizens of a republic.

III. Some knowledge of figures and book-keeping is absolutely necessary to qualify a young lady for the duties which await her in this country. There are certain occupations in which she may assist her husband with this knowledge; and should she survive him, and agreeably to the custom of our country be the executrix of his will, she cannot fail of deriving immense advantages from it.

IV. An acquaintance with geography and some instruction in chronology will enable a young lady to read history, biography, and travels, with advantage; and thereby qualify her not only for a general intercourse with the world, but to be an agreeable companion for a sensible man. To these branches of knowledge may be added, in some instances, a general acquaintance with the first principles of astronomy, natural philosophy and chemistry, particularly, with such parts of them as are calculated to prevent superstition, by

---

[4] Dr. Franklin received many letters while he was in France during the American war, from persons who wished to migrate to America, and who appeared to possess knowledge and talents that would have been useful to his country, but their names were subscribed to their letters in so artificial and affected a manner, that he was unable to decypher them, and of course, did not answer them.

explaining the causes, or obviating the effects of natural evil, and such, as are capable of being applied to domestic, and culinary purposes.

V. Vocal music should never be neglected, in the education of a young lady, in this country. Besides preparing her to join in that part of public worship which consists in psalmody, it will enable her to soothe the cares of domestic life. The distress and vexation of a husband—the noise of a nursery, and, even, the sorrows that will sometimes intrude into her own bosom, may all be relieved by a song, where sound and sentiment unite to act upon the mind. I hope it will not bring thought foreign to this part of our subject to introduce a fact here which has been suggested to me by my profession, and that is, that the exercise of the organs of the breast, by singing, contributes very much to defend them from those diseases to which our climate; and other causes, have of late exposed them.—Our German fellow citizens are seldom afflicted with consumptions, nor have I ever known but one instance of spitting blood among them. This, I believe, is in part occasioned by the strength which their lungs acquire, by exercising them frequently in vocal music, for this constitutes an essential branch of their education. The music-master of our academy[5] has furnished me with an observation still more in favour of this opinion. He informed me that he had known several instances of persons who were strongly disposed to the consumption, who were restored to health, by the moderate exercise of their lungs in singing.

VI. DANCING is by no means an improper branch of education for an American lady. It promotes health, and renders the figure and motions of the body easy and agreeable. I anticipate the time when the resources of conversation shall be so far multiplied, that the amusement of dancing shall be wholly confined to children. But in our present state of society and knowledge, I conceive it to be an agreeable substitute for the ignoble pleasures of drinking, and gaming, in our assemblies of grown people.

VII. The attention of our young ladies should be directed, as soon as they are prepared for it, to the reading of history—travels—poetry—and moral essays. These studies are accommodated, in a peculiar manner, to the present state of society in America, and

---

[5] Mr. Adgate.

when a relish is excited for them, in early life, they subdue that passion for reading novels, which so generally prevails among the fair
sex. I cannot dismiss this species of writing and reading without
observing, that the subjects of novels are by no means accommodated to our present manners. They hold up *life*, it is true, but
it is not as yet *life* in America. Our passions have not as yet "overstepped the modesty of nature," nor are they "torn to tatters," to use
the expressions of the poet, by extravagant love, jealousy, ambition,
or revenge. As yet the intrigues of a British novel, are as foreign to
our manners, as the refinements of Asiatic vice. Let it not be said,
that the tales of distress, which fill modern novels, have a tendency
to soften the female heart into acts of humanity. The fact is the
reverse of this. The abortive sympathy which is excited by the recital
of imaginary distress, blunts the heart to that which is real; and,
hence, we sometimes see instances of young ladies, who weep away
a whole forenoon over the criminal sorrows of a fictitious Charlotte
or Werter, turning with disdain at three o'clock from the sight of a
beggar, who solicits in feeble accents or signs, a small portion only
of the crumbs which fall from their fathers' tables.

VIII. It will be necessary to connect all these branches of education with regular instruction in the christian religion. For this
purpose the principles of the different sects of christians should be
taught and explained, and our pupils should early be furnished with
some of the most simple arguments in favour of the truth of christianity.[6] A portion of the bible (of late improperly banished from
our schools) should be read by them every day, and such questions
should be asked, after reading it as are calculated to imprint upon
their minds the interesting stories contained in it.

Rousseau has asserted that the great secret of education consists
in "wasting the time of children profitably." There is some truth in
this observation. I believe that we often impair their health, and
weaken their capacities, by imposing studies upon them, which are
not proportioned to their years. But this objection does not apply
to religious instruction. There are certain simple propositions in the
christian religion, which are suited in a peculiar manner, to the
infant state of reason and moral sensibility. A clergyman of long

---

[6] Baron Haller's letters to his daughter on the truths of the christian religion, and
Dr. Beatie's "evidences of the christian religion briefly and plainly stated" are excellent little tracts, and well adapted for his purpose.

experience in the instruction of youth[7] informed me, that he always found children acquired religious knowledge more easily than knowledge upon other subjects; and that young girls acquired this kind of knowledge more readily than boys. The female breast is the natural soil of christianity; and while our women are taught to believe its doctrines, and obey its precepts, the wit of Voltaire, and the stile of Bolingbroke, will never be able to destroy its influence upon our citizens.

I cannot help remarking in this place, that christianity exerts the most friendly influence upon science, as well as upon the morals and manners of mankind. Whether this be occasioned by the unity of truth, and the mutual assistance which truths upon different subjects afford each other, or whether the faculties of the mind be sharpened and corrected by embracing the truths of revelation, and thereby prepared to investigate and perceive truths upon other subjects, I will not determine, but I believe that the greatest discoveries in science have been made by christian philosophers, and that there is the most knowledge in those countries where there is the most christianity.[8] If this remark be well founded, then those philosophers who reject christianity, and those christians, whether parents or school-masters, who neglect the religious instruction of their children and pupils, *reject* and *neglect* the most effectual means of promoting knowledge in our country.

IX. If the measures that have been recommended for inspiring our pupils with a sense of religious and moral obligation be adopted, the government of them will be easy and agreeable. I shall only remark under this head, that *strictness* of discipline will always render *severity* unnecessary, and that there will be the most instruction in that school, where there is the most order.

---

[7] The Rev. Mr. Nicholas Collin, minister of the Swedish church in Wicocoe.

[8] This is true in a peculiar manner in the science of medecine. A young Scotch physician of enterprizing talents, who conceived a high idea of the state of medecine in the eastern countries, spent two years in enquiries after medical knowledge in Constantinople, and Grand Cairo. On his return to Britain, he confessed to an American physician whom he met at Naples, that after all his researches and travels, he "had discovered nothing except a single fact relative to the plague, that he thought worth remembering or communicating." The science of medecine in China, according to the accounts of De Halde is in as imperfect a state as among the Indians of North America.

I have said nothing in favour of instrumental music as a branch of female education, because I conceive it is by no means accommodated to the present state of society and manners in America. The price of musical instruments, and the extravagant fees demanded by the teachers of instrumental music, form but a small part of my objections to it.

To perform well, upon a musical instrument, requires much time and long practice. From two to four hours in a day, for three or four years appropriated to music, are an immense deduction from that short period of time which is allowed by the peculiar circumstances of our country for the acquisition of the useful branches of literature that have been mentioned. How many useful ideas might be picked up in these hours from history, philosophy, poetry, and the numerous moral essays with which our language abounds, and how much more would the knowledge acquired upon these subjects add to the consequence of a lady, with her husband and with society, than the best performed pieces of music upon a harpsicord or a guittar! Of the many ladies whom we have known, who have spent the most important years of their lives, in learning to play upon instruments of music, how few of them do we see amuse themselves or their friends with them, after they become mistresses of families! Their harpsicords serve only as side-boards for their parlours, and prove by their silence, that necessity and circumstances, will always prevail over fashion, and false maxims of education.

Let it not be supposed from these observations that I am insensible of the charms of instrumental music, or that I wish to exclude it from the education of a lady where a musical ear irresistibly disposes to it, and affluence at the same time affords a prospect of such an exemption from the usual cares and duties of the mistress of a family, as will enable her to practise it. These circumstances form an exception to the general conduct that should arise upon this subject, from the present state of society and manners in America.

It is agreeable to observe how differently modern writers, and the inspired author of the Proverbs, describe a fine woman. The former confine their praises chiefly to personal charms, and ornamental accomplishments, while the latter celebrates only the virtues of a valuable mistress of a family, and a useful member of society. The one is perfectly acquainted with all the fashionable languages of Europe; the other, "opens her mouth with wisdom" and is perfectly acquainted with all the uses of the needle, the distaff, and the loom. The business of the one, is pleasure; the pleasure of the other, is business. The one is admired abroad; the other is honoured and beloved at home. "Her children arise up and call her blessed, her husband also, and he praiseth her." There is no fame in the world equal to this; nor is there a note in music half so delightful, as the respectful language with which a grateful son or daughter perpetuates the memory of a sensible and affectionate mother.

It should not surprize us that British customs, with respect to female education, have been transplanted into our American schools and families. We see marks of the same incongruity, of time and place, in many other things. We behold our houses accommodated to the climate of Great Britain, by eastern and western directions. We behold our ladies panting in a heat of ninety degrees, under a hat and cushion, which were calculated for the temperature of a British summer. We behold our citizens condemned and punished by a criminal law, which was copied from a country, where maturity in corruption renders public executions a part of the amusements of the nation. It is high time to awake from this servility—to study our own character—to examine the age of our country—and to adopt manners in every thing, that shall be accommodated to our state of society, and to the forms of our government. In particular it is incumbent upon us to make ornamental accomplishments yield to principles and knowledge, in the education of our women.

A philosopher once said "let me make all the ballads of a country and I care not who makes its laws." He might with more propriety have said, let the ladies of a country be educated properly, and they will not only make and administer its laws, but form its manners and character. It would require a lively imagination to describe, or even to comprehend, the happiness of a country, where knowledge and virtue, were generally diffused among the female sex. Our young men would then be restrained from vice by the terror of being banished from their company. The loud laugh, and the malignant smile, at the expence of innocence, or of personal infirmities—the feats of successful mimicry—and the low priced wit, which is borrowed from a misapplication of scripture phrases, would no more be considered as recommendations to the society of the ladies. A double entendre in their presence, would then exclude a gentleman forever from the company of both sexes, and probably oblige him to seek an asylum from contempt, in a foreign country. The influence of female education would be still more extensive and useful in domestic life. The obligations of gentlemen to qualify themselves by knowledge and industry to discharge the duties of benevolence, would be encreased by marriage; and the patriot—the hero—and the legislator, would find the sweetest regard of their toils, in the approbation and applause of their wives. Children would discover the marks of maternal prudence and wisdom in every station of life; for it has been remarked that there have been few great or good men who have not been blessed with wise and prudent mothers. Cyrus was taught to revere the gods, by his mother Mandane—Samuel was devoted to his prophetic office before he was born, by his mother Hannah—Constantine was rescued from paganism by his mother Constantia—and Edward the sixth inherited those great and excellent qualities which made him the delight of the age in which he lived, from his mother, lady Jane Seymour. Many other instances might be mentioned, if necessary, from ancient and modern history, to establish the truth of this proposition.

I am not enthusiastical upon the subject of education. In the ordinary course of human affairs, we shall probably too soon follow the footsteps of the nations of Europe in manners and vices. The first marks we shall perceive of our declension, will appear among our women. Their idleness, ignorance, and profligacy will be the harbingers of our ruin. Then will the character and performance of a buffoon on the theatre, be the subject of more conversation and praise, than the patriot or the minister of the gospel;—then will our language and pronunciation be enfeebled and corrupted by a flood of French and Italian words;—then will the history of romantic amours, be preferred to the pure and immortal writings of Addison, Hawkesworth and Johnson;—then will our churches be neglected, and the name of the supreme being never be called upon, but in profane exclamations;—then will our Sundays be appropriated, only to feasts and concerts?—and then will begin all that train of domestic and political calamities—But, I forbear. The prospect is so painful, that I cannot help, silently, imploring the great arbiter of human, affairs, to interpose his almighty goodness, and to deliver us from these evils, that, at least one spot of the earth may be reserved as a monument of the effects of good education, in order to shew in some degree, what our species was, before the fall, and what it shall be, after its restoration.

Thus, gentlemen, have I briefly finished what I proposed. If I am wrong in those opinions in which I have taken the liberty of departing from general and fashionable habits of thinking, I am sure you will discover, and pardon my mistakes. But if I am right, I am equally sure you will adopt my opinions; for to enlightened minds truth is alike acceptable, whether it comes from the lips of age, or the hand of antiquity, or whether it be obtruded by a person, who has no other claim to attention, than a desire of adding to the stock of human happiness.

I cannot dismiss the subject of female education without remarking, that the city of Philadelphia first saw a number of gentlemen associated for the purpose of directing the education of young ladies. By means of this plan, the power of teachers is regulated and restrained, and the objects of education are extended. By the separation of the sexes in the unformed state of their manners, female delicacy is cherished and preserved. Here the young ladies may enjoy all the literary advantages of a boarding-school, and at the same time live under the protection of their parents.[9] Here emulation may be excited without jealousy,—ambition without envy,—and competition without strife. The attempt to establish this new mode of education for young ladies, was an experiment, and the success of it hath answered our expectations. Too much praise cannot be given to our principal[10] and his assistants, for the abilities and fidelity with which they have carried the plan into execution. The proficiency which the young ladies have discovered in reading—writing—spelling—arithmetic—grammar—geography—music—and their different catechisms, since the last examination, is a less equivocal mark of the merit of our teachers, than any thing I am able to express in their favour.

---

[9] Unnatural confinement makes a young woman embrace with avidity every pleasure when she is set free. To relish domestic life, one must be acquainted with it; for it is in the house of her parents a young woman acquires the relish." Lord Kaims's thoughts upon education, and the culture of the heart.

[10] Andrew Brown.

But the reputation of the academy must be suspended, till the public are convinced, by the future conduct and character of our pupils, of the advantages of the institution. To you, therefore, YOUNG LADIES, an important problem is commited for solution; and that is, whether our present plan of education be a wise one, and whether it be calculated to prepare you for the duties of social and domestic life. I know that the elevation of the female mind, by means of moral, physical and religious truth, is considered by some men as unfriendly to the domestic character of a woman. But this is the prejudice of little minds, and springs from the same spirit which opposes the general diffusion of knowledge among the citizens of our republics. If men believe that ignorance is favourable to the government of the female sex, they are certainly deceived; for a weak and ignorant woman will always be governed with the greatest difficulty. I have sometimes been led to ascribe the invention of ridiculous and expensive fashion in female dress, entirely to the gentlemen,[11] in order to divert the ladies from improving their minds, and thereby to secure a more arbitrary and unlimited authority over them. It will be in your power, LADIES, to correct the mistakes and practice of our sex upon these subjects, by demonstrating, that the female temper can only be governed by reason, and that the cultivation of reason in women, is alike friendly to the order of nature, and to private as well as public happiness.

---

[11] The very expensive prints of female dresses which are published annually in France, are invented and executed wholly by GENTLEMEN.

A DEFENCE OF THE USE OF THE BIBLE AS A SCHOOL BOOK. ADDRESSED TO THE REV. JEREMY BELKNAP, OF BOSTON.

DEAR SIR,

It is now several months, since I promised to give you my reasons for prefering the bible as a school book, to all other compositions. I shall not trouble you with an apology for my delaying so long to comply with my promise, but shall proceed immediately to the subject of my letter.

Before I state my arguments in favour of teaching children to read by means of the bible, I shall assume the five following propositions.

I. That christianity is the only true and perfect religion, and that in proportion as mankind adopt its principles, and obey its precepts, they will be wise, and happy.

II. That a better knowledge of this religion is to be acquired by reading the bible, than in any other way.

III. That the bible contains more knowledge necessary to man in his present state, than any other book in the world.

IV. That knowledge is most durable, and religious instruction most useful, when imparted in early life.

V. That the bible, when not read in schools, is seldom read in any subsequent period of life.

My arguments in favor of the use of the bible as a school book are founded,

I. In the constitution of the human mind.

1. The memory is the first faculty which opens in the minds of children. Of how much consequence, then, must it be, to impress it with the great truths of christianity, before it is pre-occupied with less interesting subjects! As all the liquors, which are poured into a cup, generally taste of that which first filled it, so all the knowledge, which is added to that which is treasured up in the memory from the bible, generally receives an agreeable and useful tincture from it.

2. There is a peculiar aptitude in the minds of children for religious knowledge. I have constantly found them in the first six or seven years of their lives, more inquisitive upon religious sub-

jects, than upon any others: and an ingenious instructor of youth has informed me, that he has found young children more capable of receiving just ideas upon the most difficult tenets of religion, than upon the most simple branches of human knowledge. It would be strange if it were otherwise; for God creates all his means to suit all his ends. There must of course be a fitness between the human mind, and the truths which are essential to its happiness.

3. The influence of *prejudice* is derived from the impressions, which are made upon the mind in early life; prejudices are of two kinds, true and false. In a world where *false* prejudices do so much mischief, it would discover great weakness not to oppose them, by such as are *true*.

I grant that many men have rejected the prejudices derived from the bible: but I believe no man ever did so, without having been made *wiser* or *better*, by the early operation of these prejudices upon his mind. Every just principle that is to be found in the writings of Voltaire, is borrowed from the bible: and the morality of the Deists, which has been so much admired and praised, is, I believe, in most cases, the effect of habits, produced by early instruction in the principles of christianity.

4. We are subject, by a general law in our natures, to what is called *habit*. Now if the study of the scriptures be necessary to our happiness at any time of our lives, the sooner we begin to read them, the more we shall be attached to them; for it is peculiar to all the acts of habit, to become easy, strong and agreeable by repetition.

5. It is a law in our natures, that we remember *longest* the knowledge we acquire by the greatest number of our senses. Now a knowledge of the contents of the bible, is acquired in school by the aid of the *eyes* and the *ears*; for children after getting their lessons, always say them to their masters in an audible voice; of course there is a presumption, that this knowledge will be retained much longer than if it had been acquired in any other way.

6. The interesting events and characters, recorded and described in the Old and New Testaments, are accommodated above all others to seize upon all the faculties of the minds of children. The understanding, the memory, the imagination, the passions, and the moral powers, are all occasionally addressed by the various inci-

dents which are contained in those divine books, insomuch that
not to be delighted with them, is to be devoid of every principle of
pleasure that exists in a sound mind.

7. There is a native love of *truth* in the human mind. Lord
Shaftesbury says, that "truth is so congenial to our minds, that we
love even the *shadow* of it:" and Horace, in his rules for composing
an epick poem, establishes the same law in our natures, by advising
the "fictions in poetry to resemble truth." Now the bible contains
more truths than any other book in the world: so true is the
testimony that it bears of God in his works of creation, providence,
and redemption, that it is called *truth* itself, by way of pre-eminence
above things that are only simply true. How forcibly are we struck
with the evidences of truth, in the history of the Jews, above what
we discover in the history of other nations? Where do we find a
hero, or an historian record his own faults or vices except in the Old
Testament? Indeed, my friend, from some accounts which I have
read of the American revolution, I begin to grow sceptical to all
history except to that which is contained in the bible. Now if this
book be known to contain nothing but what is materially true, the
mind will naturally acquire a love for it from this circumstance: and
from this affection for the truths of the bible, it will acquire a
discernment of truth in other books, and a preference of it in all
the transactions of life.

8. There is a wonderful property in the *memory*, which enables
it in old age, to *recover* the knowledge it had acquired in early life,
after it had been apparently forgotten for forty or fifty years. Of how
much consequence, then, must it be, to fill the mind with that
species of knowledge, in childhood and youth, which, when *recalled*
in the decline of life, will support the soul under the infirmities of
age, and smooth the avenues of approaching death? The bible is the
only book which is capable of affording this support to old age; and
it is for this reason that we find it resorted to with so much diligence
and pleasure by such old people as have read it in early life. I can
recollect many instances of this kind in persons who discovered no
attachment to the bible, in the meridian of their lives, who have
notwithstanding, spent the evening of them, in reading no other
book. The late Sir John Pringle, Physician to the Queen of Great
Britain, after passing a long life in camps and at court, closed it by

studying the scriptures. So anxious was he to increase his knowledge in them, that he wrote to Dr. Michaelis, a learned professor of divinity in Germany, for an explanation of a difficult text of scripture, a short time before his death.

9. My second argument in favour of the use of the bible in schools, is founded upon an implied command of God, and upon the practice of several of the wisest nations of the world.—In the 6th chapter of Deuteronomy, we find the following words, which are directly to my purpose, "And thou shalt love the Lord thy God, with all thy heart and with all thy soul, and with all thy might. And these words which I command thee this day shall be in thine heart. And thou *shalt teach them diligently unto thy children*, and shalt talk of them when thou sittest in thine house, and when thou walkest by the way, and when thou liest down, and when thou risest up."

It appears, moreover, from the history of the Jews, that they flourished as a nation, in proportion as they honoured and read the books of Moses, which contained, a written revelation of the will of God, to the children of men. The law was not only neglected, but lost during the general profligacy of manners which accompanied the long and wicked reign of Manassah. But the discovery of it, in the rubbish of the temple, by Josiah, and its subsequent general use, were followed by a return of national virtue and prosperity. We read further, of the wonderful effects which the reading of the law by Ezra, after his return from his captivity in Babylon, had upon the Jews. They hung upon his lips with tears, and showed the sincerity of their repentance, by their general reformation.

The learning of the Jews, for many years consisted in nothing but a knowledge of the scriptures. These were the text books of all the instruction that was given in the schools of their prophets. It was by means of this general knowledge of their law, that those Jews that wandered from Judea into our countries, carried with them and propagated certain ideas of the true God among all the civilized nations upon the face of the earth. And it was from the attachment they retained to the old Testament, that they procured a translation of it into the Greek language, after they lost the Hebrew tongue, by their long absence from their native country. The utility of this translation, commonly called the septuagint, in facilitating the progress of the gospel, is well known to all who are acquainted with the history of the first age of the christian church.

But the benefits of an early and general acquaintance with the bible, were not confined only to the Jewish nations. They have appeared in many countries in Europe, since the reformation. The industry, and habits of order, which distinguish many of the German nations, are derived from their early instruction in the principles of christianity, by means of the bible. The moral and enlightened character of the inhabitants of Scotland, and of the New England States, appears to be derived from the same cause. If we descend from nations to sects, we shall find them wise and prosperous in proportion as they become early acquainted with the scriptures. The bible is still used as a school book among the quakers. The morality of this sect of christians is universally acknowledged. Nor is this all,—their prudence in the management of their private affairs, is as much a mark of their society, as their sober manners.

I wish to be excused for repeating here, that if the bible did not convey a single direction for the attainment of future happiness, it should be read in our schools in preference to all other books, from its containing the greatest portion of that kind of knowledge which is calculated to produce private and publick temporal happiness.

We err not only in human affairs, but in religion likewise, *only* because "we do not know the scriptures." The opposite systems of the numerous sects of christians arise chiefly from their being more instructed in catechisms, creeds, and confessions of faith, than in the scriptures. Immense truths, I believe, are concealed in them. The time, I have no doubt, will come, when posterity will view and pity our ignorance of these truths, as much as we do the ignorance of the disciples of our Saviour, who knew nothing of the meaning of those plain passages in the old testament which were daily fulfilling before their eyes. Whenever that time shall arrive, those truths which have escaped our notice, or, if discovered, have been thought to be opposed to each other, or to be inconsistent with themselves, will then like the stones of Solomon's temple, be found so exactly to accord with each other, that they shall be cemented without noise or force, into one simple and sublime system of religion.

But further, we err, not only in religion but in philosophy likewise, because we "do not know or *believe* the scriptures." The sciences have been compared to a circle of which religion composes a part. To understand any one of them perfectly it is necessary to have some knowledge of them all. Bacon, Boyle, and Newton included the scriptures in the inquiries to which their universal geniuses disposed them, and their philosophy was aided by their knowledge in them. A striking agreement has been lately discovered between the history of certain events recorded in the bible and some of the operations and productions of nature, particularly those which are related in Whitehurst's observations on the deluge—in Smith's account of the origin of the variety of colour in the human species, and in Bruce's travels. It remains yet to be shown how many other events, related in the bible, accord with some late important discoveries in the principles of medecine. The events, and the principles alluded to, mutually establish the truth of each other. From the discoveries of the christian philosophers, whose names have been last mentioned, I have been led to question whether most harm has been done to revelation, by those divines who have unduly multiplied the objects of faith, or by those deists who have unduly multiplied the objects of reason, in explaining the scriptures.

I shall now proceed to answer some of the objections which have been made to the use of the bible as a school book.

I. We are told, that the familiar use of the bible in our schools, has a tendency to lessen a due reverence for it. This objection, by proving too much, proves nothing at all. If familiarity lessens respect for divine things, then all those precepts of our religion, which enjoin the daily or weekly worship of the Deity, are improper. The bible was not intended to represent a Jewish ark; and it is an anti-christian idea, to suppose that it can be profaned, by being carried into a school house, or by being handled by children. But where will the bible be read by young people with more reverence than in a school? Not in most private families; for I believe there are few parents, who preserve so much order in their houses, as is kept up in our common English schools.

II. We are told, that there are many passages in the old testament, that are improper to be read by children, and that the greatest part of it is no way interesting to mankind under the present dispensation of the gospel. There are I grant, several chapters, and many verses in the old testament, which in their present unfortunate translation, should be passed over by children. But I deny that any of the books of the old testament are not interesting to mankind, under the gospel dispensation. Most of the characters, events, and ceremonies, mentioned in them, are personal, providential, or instituted types of the Messiah: All of which have been, or remain yet to be, fulfilled by him. It is from an ignorance or neglect of these types, that we have so many deists in christendom; for so irrefragably do they prove the truth of christianity, that I am sure a young man who had been regularly instructed in their meaning, could never doubt afterwards of the truth of any of its principles. If any obscurity appears in these principles, it is only (to use the words of the poet) because *they are dark, with excessive bright.*

I know there is an objection among many people to teach children doctrines of any kind, because they are liable to be controverted. But where will this objection lead us?—The being of a God, and the obligations of morality, have both been controverted; and yet who has objected to our teaching these doctrines to our children?

The curiosity and capacities of young people for the mysteries of religion, awaken much sooner than is generally supposed. Of this we have two remarkable proofs in the old testament. The first is mentioned in the twelfth chapter of Exodus. "And it shall come when your *children* shall say unto you, '*What mean you by this service?*' that ye shall say, 'It is the sacrafice of the Lord's passover, who passed over the houses of the children of Israel in Egypt, when he smote the Egyptians, and delivered our houses. And the children of Israel went away, and did as the Lord had commanded Moses and Aaron.'" A second proof of the desire of children to be instructed in the mysteries of religion, is to be found in the sixth chapter of Deuteronomy. "And when thy son *asketh* thee in the time to come saying, 'What mean the testimonies—and the statutes—and the judgments which the Lord our God hath commanded you?' Then thou shalt say unto thy son, 'We were Pharoah's bondmen in Egypt, and the Lord our God brought us out of Egypt with a mighty hand.'" These enquiries from the mouths of children are perfectly natural; for where is the parent who has not had similar questions proposed to him by his children upon their being first conducted to a place of worship, or upon their beholding, for the first time, either of the sacraments of our religion?

Let us not be wiser than our Maker. If moral precepts alone could have reformed mankind, the mission of the Son of God into our world, would have been unnecessary. He came to promulgate a system of *doctrines*, as well as a system of morals. The perfect morality of the gospel rests upon a *doctrine*, which, though often controverted, has never been refuted, I mean the vicarious life and death of the Son of God. This sublime and ineffable doctrine delivers us from the absurd hypotheses of modern philosophers, concerning the foundation of moral obligation, and fixes it upon the eternal and self moving principle of LOVE. It concentrates a whole system of ethics in a single text of scripture. *"A new command-ment I give unto you, that ye love one another, even as I have loved you."* By withholding the knowledge of this doctrine from children, we deprive ourselves of the best means of awakening moral sensibility in their minds. We do more, we furnish an argument, for withholding from them a knowledge of the morality of the gospel likewise; for this, in many instances, is as supernatural, and therefore as liable to be controverted, as any of the doctrines or miracles which are mentioned in the new testament. The miraculous conception of the saviour of the world by a virgin, is not more opposed to the ordinary course of natural events, nor is the doctrine of the atonement more above human reason, than those moral precepts, which command us to love our enemies, or to die for our friends.

III. It has been said, that the division of the bible into chapters and verses, renders it more difficult to be read, by children than many other books.

By a little care in a master, this difficulty may be obviated, and even an advantage derived from it. It may serve to transfer the attention of the scholar to the *sense* of a subject; and no person will ever read well, who is guided by any thing else, in his stops, empha-sis, or accents. The division of the bible into chapters and verses, is not a greater obstacle to its being read with ease, than the bad punctuation of most other books. I deliver this stricture upon other books, from the authority of Mr. Rice, the celebrated author of the art of speaking, whom I heard declare in a large company in Lon-don, that he had never seen a book properly pointed in the English Language. He exemplified, notwithstanding, by reading to the same company a passage from Milton, his perfect knowledge of the art of reading.

Some people, I know, have proposed to introduce extracts from the bible, into our schools, instead of the bible itself. Many excellent works of this kind, are in print, but if we admit any one of them, we shall have the same inundation of them that we have had of grammars, spelling books, and lessons for children, many of which are published for the benefit of the authors only, and all of them have tended greatly to increase the expence of education. Besides, these extracts or abridgements of the bible, often contain the tenets of particular sects or persons, and therefore, may be improper for schools composed of the children of different sects of christians. The bible is a cheap book, and is to be had in every bookstore. It is, moreover, esteemed and preferred by all sects; because each finds its peculiar doctrines in it. It should therefore be used in preference to any abridgements of it, or histories extracted from it.

I have heard it proposed that a portion of the bible should be read every day by the master, as a means of instructing children in it: But this is a poor substitute for obliging children to read it as a school book; for by this means we insensibly *engrave*, as it were, its contents upon their minds: and it has been remarked that children, instructed in this way in the scriptures, seldom forget any part of them. They have the same advantage over those persons, who have only heard the scriptures read by a master, that a man who has worked with the tools of a mechanical employment for several years, has over the man who has only stood a few hours in a work shop and seen the same business carried on by other people.

In this defence of the use of the bible as a school book, I beg you would not think that I suppose the Bible to contain the only revelation which God has made to man. I believe in an internal revelation, or a moral principle, which God has implanted in the heart of every man, as the precursor of his final dominion over the whole human race. How much this internal revelation accords with the external, remains yet to be explored by philosophers. I am disposed to believe, that most of the doctrines of christianity revealed in the bible might be discovered by a close examination of all the principles of action in man: But who is equal to such an enquiry? It certainly does not suit the natural indolence, or laborious employments of a great majority of mankind. The internal revelation of the gospel may be compared to the straight line which is made through a wilderness by the assistance of a compass, to a distant country, which few are able to discover, while the bible resembles a public road to the same country, which is wide, plain, and easily found. "And a highway shall be there, and it shall be called the way of holiness. The way faring men, though fools, shall not err therein."

Neither let me in this place exclude the Revelation which God has made of himself to man in the works of creation. I am far from wishing to lessen the influence of this species of Revelation upon mankind. But the knowledge of God obtained from this source, is obscure and feeble in its operation, compared with that which is derived from the bible. The visible creation speaks of the Deity in hyeroglyphics, while the bible describes all his attributes and perfections in such plain, and familiar language that "he who runs may read."

How kindly has our maker dealt with his creatures, in providing three different cords to draw them to himself! But how weakly do some men act, who suspend their faith, and hopes upon only one of them! By laying hold of them all, they would approach more speedily and certainly to the centre of all happiness.

To the arguments I have mentioned in favour of the use of the bible as a school book, I shall add a few reflections.

The present fashionable practice of rejecting the bible from our schools, I suspect has originated with the deists. They discover great ingenuity in this new mode of attacking christianity. If they proceed in it, they will do more in half a century, in extirpating our religion, than Bolingbroke or Voltaire could have effected in a thousand years. I am not writing to this class of people. I despair of changing the opinions of any of them. I wish only to alter the opinions and conduct of those lukewarm, or superstitious christians, who have been misled by the deists upon this subject. On the ground of the good old custom, of using the bible as a school book, it becomes us to entrench our religion. It is the last bulwark the deists have left it; for they have rendered instruction in the principles of christianity by the pulpit and the press, so unfashionable, that little good for many years seems to have been done by either of them.

The effects of the disuse of the bible, as a school book have appeared of late in the neglect and even contempt with which scripture names are treated by many people. It is because parents have not been early taught to know or respect the characters and exploits of the old and new testament worthies, that their names are

exchanged for those of the modern kings of Europe, or of the principal characters in novels and romances. I conceive there may be
some advantage in bearing scripture names. It may lead the persons
who bear them, to study that part of the scriptures, in which their
names are mentioned, with uncommon attention, and perhaps it
may excite a desire in them to possess the talents or virtues of their
ancient namesakes. This remark first occurred to me, upon hearing
a pious woman whose name was Mary, say, that the first passages
of the bible, which made a serious impression on her mind, were
those interesting chapters and verses in which the name of Mary is
mentioned in the New Testament.

It is a singular fact, that while the names of kings and emperors
of Rome, are now given chiefly to *horses* and *dogs*, scripture names
have hitherto been confined only to the human species. Let the
enemies and contemners of those names take care, lest the names
of more modern kings be given hereafter only to the same animals,
and lest the names of the modern heroines of romances be given to
animals of an inferior species.

It is with great pleasure, that I have observed the bible to be the
only book read in the Sunday schools in England. We have adopted
the same practice in the Sunday schools, lately established in this
city. This will give our religion (humanly speaking) the chance of
a longer life in our country. We hear much of the persons educated
in free schools in England, turning out well in the various walks of
life. I have enquired into the cause of it, and have satisfied myself,
that it is wholly to be ascribed to the general use of the bible in
those schools, for it seems the children of poor people are of too
little consequence to be guarded from the supposed evils of reading
the scriptures in early life, or in an unconsecrated school house.

However great the benefits of reading the scriptures in schools
have been, I cannot help remarking, that these benefits might be
much greater, did schoolmasters take more pains to explain them to
their scholars. Did they demonstrate the divine original of the bible
from the purity, consistency, and benevolence of its doctrines and
precepts—did they explain the meaning of the levitical institutions,
and show their application to the numerous and successive gospel
dispensations—did they inform their pupils that the gross and
abominable vices of the Jews were recorded *only* as proofs of depravity of human nature, and of the insufficiency of the law, to produce

moral virtue and thereby to establish the necessity and perfection of the gospel system—and above all, did they often enforce the discourses of our Saviour, as the best rule of life, and the surest guide to happiness, how great would be the influence of our schools upon the order and prosperity of our country! Such a mode of instructing children in the christian religion, would convey knowledge into their *understandings*, and would therefore be preferable to teaching them creeds, and catechisms, which too often convey, not knowledge, but *words* only, into their *memories*. I think I am not too sanguine in believing, that education, conducted in this manner, would, in the course of two generations, eradicate infidelity from among us, and render civil government scarcely necessary in our country.

In contemplating the political institutions of the United States, I lament, that we waste so much time and money in punishing crimes, and take so little pains to prevent them. We profess to be republicans, and yet we neglect the only means of establishing and perpetuating our republican forms of government, that is, the universal education of our youth in the principles of christianity, by means of the bible; for this divine book, above all others, favours that equality among mankind, that respect for just laws, and all those sober and frugal virtues, which constitute the soul of republicanism.

I have now only to apologize for having addressed this letter to you, after having been assured by you, that your opinion, respecting the use of the bible as a school book, coincided with mine. My excuse for what I have done is, that I knew you were qualified by your knowledge, and disposed by your zeal in the cause of truth, to correct all the errors you would discover in my letter. Perhaps a further apology may be necessary for my having presumed to write upon a subject so much above my ordinary studies. My excuse for it is, that I thought a single mite from a member of a profession, which has been frequently charged with scepticism in religion, might attract the notice of persons who had often overlooked the more ample contributions upon this subject, of gentlemen of other professions. With great respect, I am, dear sir, your sincere friend.

BENJAMIN RUSH.

Philadelphia, March 10, 1791.

AN ADDRESS TO THE MINISTERS OF THE GOSPEL OF EVERY DENOMINATION IN THE UNITED STATES, UPON SUBJECTS INTERESTING TO MORALS.

FROM the nature of your pursuits, and from your influence in society, I am encouraged to address you upon subjects of the utmost importance to the present and future happiness of your fellow-citizens, as well as to the prosperity of the United States.

Under the great diversity of opinions, you entertain in religion, you are all united in inculcating the necessity of morals. In this business you are neither catholics nor protestants—churchmen nor dissenters. One spirit actuates you all. From the success, or failure, of your exertions in the cause of virtue, we anticipate the freedom or slavery of our country. Even the new government of the United States, from which so many advantages are expected, will neither restore order, nor establish justice among us, unless it be accompanied and supported by morality, among all classes of people. Impressed with a sense of the truth of these observations, I shall briefly point out a few of those practices, which prevail in America, which exert a pernicious influence upon morals, and thereby prepare our country for misery and slavery.

I shall begin by pointing out, in the first place, the mischevious effects of spirituous liquors upon the morals of our citizens.

1. They render the temper peevish and passionate. They beget quarrels, and lead to profane and indecent language. They are the parents of idleness and extravagance, and the certain forerunners of poverty, and frequently of jails, wheelbarrows, and the gallows. They are likewise injurious to health and life, and kill more than the pestilence, or the sword. Our legislatures, by permitting the use of them, for the sake of the paltry duty collected from them, act as absurdly as a prince would do, who should permit the cultivation of a poisonous nut, which every year carried off ten thousand of his subjects, because it yielded a revenue of thirty thousand pounds a year. These ten thousand men would produce annually by their labour, or by paying a trifling impost upon any one of the necessaries of life, twenty times that sum. In order to put an end

to the desolating effects of spirituous liquors, it will be proper for our ministers to preach against, not the abuse of them only, but their use altogether. They are never necessary but in sickness: and then they are better applied to the outside, than to the inside of the body.

II. Militia laws have an unfriendly influence upon morals, more especially where they authorise the election of the officers by the privates. The meetings of citizens for militia exercises are generally attended with intemperance in drinking, quarrelling, profane swearing, and acts of violence to the property of the persons who live near the place where those meetings are held. It is a mistake to suppose that the defence of liberty requires a well organized militia in the time of peace.

The United States proved in the beginning of the late war, and France has proved since, that armies of disciplined irresistable troops may be formed in a short time out of the peasants of a country. War has lately become a simple art. All that is practical in it, may be acquired in a few weeks. The most gallant exploits were performed during the late war, by men who had been but a few days in the practice of handling fire arms.

III. Fairs are a Pandora's box opened twice a year, in many of the states. They are wholly unnecessary, since shops are so common in all the civilized parts of the country. They tempt to extravagance—gaming—drunkenness—and uncleanness. They are proper only in despotic states, where—the more a people are corrupted, the more readily they submit to arbitrary government.

IV. Law-suits should be discouraged as much as possible. They are highly disreputable between persons who profess christianity. The attendance upon courts exposes to idleness—drinking—and gaming; and the usual delays of justice seldom fail of entailing hereditary discord among neighbours. It is with inexpressible pleasure that I have lately seen an account of a recommendation from the presbyterian synod of New York and Philadelphia, to all the churches under their care, to settle their disputes after the manner of the primitive christians and friends, by arbitration. Blessed event in the history of mankind! may their practice spread among all sects of christians, and may it prove a prelude of that happy time foretold in the scriptures, when war and murder shall be no more.

V. The licentiousness of the press is a fruitful source of the corruption of morals. Men are deterred from injuring each other, chiefly by the fear of detection or punishment. Now both of these are removed by the usual secrecy of a licentious press. Hence revenge, scandal, and falsehood are cherished and propagated in a community. By means of this engine of malice, we sometimes see not only reputation but even life, itself, taken away. The patriotic Mr. Cummins, and the amiable Dr. Hawkesworth, it is said, both died of a broken heart, in consequence of being attacked by persons, who concealed themselves behind a licentious press in London. Personal disputes and attacks in a newspaper, may be compared to duels, or to the Indian mode of fighting, according as they are carried on with, or without the names of their authors. They shew in both cases, a degree of the same spirit, which leads to open murder or private assassination. But further: the cause of liberty is greatly injured by personal publications, which are not true, or which have no connection with the public; for who will believe a truth that is told of a bad man, who has been accustomed to read falsehoods published every day, of a good man? Printers who vend scurrility, would do well in considering, that the publisher of scandal, is as bad as the author of it, in the same manner that the receiver of stolen goods, is as bad as the thief.

VI. Horse-racing and cock-fighting are unfriendly amusements to morals, and of course to the liberties of our country. They occasion idleness, fraud, gaming, and profane swearing, and harden the heart against the feelings of humanity. These vulgar sports should be forbidden by law in all christian and republican countries.

VII. Clubs of all kinds, where the only business of the company, is feeding (for that is [the] true name of a gratification that is simply animal) are hurtful to morals. The society in taverns where clubs are usually held, is seldom subject to much order. It exposes men to idleness, prodigality, and debt. It is in private families, only that society is innocent, or improving. Here manners are usually kept within the bounds of decency by the company of females, who generally compose a part of all private families; and manners, it is well known, have an influence upon morals.

VIII. Amusements of every kind, on Sundays, beget habits of idleness and a love of pleasure, which extend their influence to every day of the week. In those manufacturing towns in England, where the Sundays are spent in idleness or frolicking, little or no work is ever done on the ensuing day; hence it is called St. Monday. If there were no hereafter—individuals and societies would be great gainers, by attending public worship every Sunday. Rest from labour in the house of God, winds up the machine of both soul and body, better than any thing else, and thereby invigorates it for the labours and duties of the ensuing week. Should I ever travel into a christian country, and wish to know whether the laws of that country were wise and just, and whether they were duly obeyed, the only question I would ask, should be "do the people spend Sunday at church, or in pleasurable entertainments at home and abroad?" The Sunday schools in England have been found extremely useful in reforming the children of poor people. Who can witness the practices of swimming, sliding and skating, which prevail so universally on Sundays, in most of the cities of the United States, and not wish for similar institutions to rescue our poor children from destruction? I shall conclude my remarks upon this subject, by declaring, that I do not wish to see any new laws made to enforce the keeping of the Sabbath. I call upon ministers of the gospel only, to increase and extend, by their influence, the pure and useful spirit of their religion. In riding through our country, we may always tell, by the appearance of the people we meet with on the road, or see at taverns, whether they enjoy the benefit of public worship, and of a vigilant and faithful ministry. Where a settlement enjoys these inestimable blessings, we generally find taverns deserted on a Sunday, and a stillness pervading the whole neighbourhood, as if nature herself had ceased from her labours, to share with man in paying her weekly homage to God for his creating goodness.

Thus I have briefly pointed out the principal sources of vice in our country. They are all of a public nature, and affect, in a direct manner, the general interests of society. I shall now suggest a few sources of vice, which are of a domestic nature, and which indirectly affect the happiness of our country.

I. The frequent or long absence of the master and mistress from home, by dissolving the bounds of domestic government, proves a fruitful source of vice among children and servants. To prevent in some degree, the inconveniencies which arise from the necessary absence of the heads of the family, from home, it would be a good practice to invest the eldest son or daughter, when of a suitable age, with the government of the family and to make them responsible for their conduct, upon the return of their parents. Government in a family is like an electric rod to a house. Where it is wanting a family is exposed to the attacks of every folly and vice, that come within the sphere of its attraction.

II. Frequent and large entertainments weaken domestic government, by removing children and servants too long from the eye of the authority. They moreover, expose children and servants to the temptation of eating and drinking to excess.

III. Boys and girls should never be admitted as servants—into a genteel family. They are seldom instructed properly, by their masters or mistresses. Their leisure hours are moreover spent in bad company: and all the vices which they pick up, are spread among the children of the family, who are generally more prone to associate with them, than with any other. Where poverty or death makes it necessary to bind out children, they should be bound to those persons only, who will work with them. By these means, they will be trained to industry, and kept from idleness and vice.

IV. Servants, both male and female should always be hired by the year, otherwise no proper government can be established over them. The impertinence and irregular conduct of servants, arise from their holding their places by too short a tenure. It would be a good law to fine every person, who hired a servant, without a written good character, signed by his last master, and countersigned by a magistrate. This practice would soon drive bad servants out of the civilized parts of our country and thereby prevent much evil both in families and society. How many young men and women have carried through life the sorrowful marks in their consciences or characters, of their being early initiated into the mysteries of vice, by unprincipled servants of both sexes! Servants that are married, should be preferred to such as are single. Matrimony in all ranks of people lessens the temptation to vice, and furnishes fresh motives to just conduct.

V. Apprentices should always board and lodge, if possible, with their masters and mistresses, when they are separated from their parents. Young people seldom fall into bad company in the day time. It is in the evening, when they cease to be subject to government, that they are in the most danger of corruption: and this danger can be obviated only by subjecting all their hours to the direction of their masters or mistresses.

I shall conclude this address, by suggesting to ministers of the gospel, a plan of a new species of federal government for the advancement of morals in the United States. Let each sect appoint a representative in a general convention of christians, whose business shall be, to unite in promoting the general objects of christianity. Let no matters of faith or opinion ever be introduced into this convention, but let them be considered as badges of the sovereignty of each particular sect. To prevent all disputes, let the objects of the deliberations of this general convention be ascertained with the same accuracy, that the powers of the national government are defined in the new constitution of the United States. By this previous compact, no encroachments will ever be made by the general government, upon the principles—discipline— or habits of any one sect—for in the present state of human nature, the division of christians into sects, is as necessary to the existence and preservation of christianity, as the division of mankind into nations, and of nations into separate families are necessary to promote general and private happiness. By means of such an institution, christian charity will be promoted, and the discipline of each church will be strengthened—for I would propose, that a dismission for immorality, from any one church, should exclude a man from every church in the ecclesiastical union. But the advantages of this christian convention will not end here. It will possess an influence over the laws of the United States. This influence will differ from that of most of the ecclesiastical associations that have existed in the world. It will be the influence of reason over the passions of men. Its objects will be morals, not principles, and the design of it will be, not to make men zealous members of any one church, but to make them—good neighbours—good husbands—good fathers— good masters—good servants—and of course good rulers and good citizens. The plan is certainly a practicable one. America has taught the nations of Europe by her example to be free, and it is to be hoped she will soon teach them to govern themselves. Let her advance one step further—and teach mankind, that it is possible for christians of different denominations to love each other, and to unite in the advancement of their common interests. By the gradual operation of such natural means, the kingdoms of this world are probably to become the kingdoms of the prince of righteousness and peace.

Philadelphia, June 21, 1788.

AN ENQUIRY INTO THE CONSISTENCY OF OATHS WITH REASON AND CHRISTIANITY.

IN discussing this question, I shall first mention the objections to oaths, which are founded in reason; and, secondly, the objections to them which are derived from the precepts and spirit of the christian religion.

I. Oaths produce an idea in the minds of men, that there are *two* kinds or degrees of truth; the one intended for common, and the other for solemn occasions. Now, this idea is directly calculated to beget a want of reverence for the *inferior* kind of truth; hence men are led to trifle with it in the common affairs of human life. I grant that some men will tell the truth, when urged to it by the solemn formalities of an oath, who would not otherwise do it: But this proves the great mischief of oaths in society; for as men are called upon to speak the truth 999 *times* in common life, to *once* they are called upon to *swear* to it, we have exactly 999 falsehoods to *one* truth told by them. How extensive, then, must be the mischief of this great disproportion between truth and falsehood, in all the affairs of human life! It is wrong to do any thing that shall create an idea of two kinds of truth. There is a scale of falsehoods; but truth has no degrees or subdivisions. Like its divine author, it is an eternal unchangeable UNIT.

II. The practice of swearing according to human laws, appears to be the cause of all profane swearing, which is so universal among all ranks of people in common conversation; for if there are two modes of speaking the truth, it is natural for men to prefer that mode which the laws of our country have entitled to the first degree of credibility: hence men swear, when they wish to be believed, in common conversation.

III. Oaths have been multiplied upon so many trifling occasions, that they have ceased, in a great degree, to operate with any force upon the most solemn occasions: hence the universal prevalence of *perjury* in courts, armies and custom-houses, all over the world. This fact is so notorious in Jamaica, that a law has lately been passed in that island, which requires a bond of £. 200, instead of an oath, from every captain that enters his vessel in the custom-house, as a security for his veracity in the manifest of his cargo, and for the amount of his duties to the government.

Reason and scripture (when perfectly understood) are never *contrary* to each other; and revelation from God can never give a sanction to that which is so evidently absurd, and unfriendly to the interests of human society. Let us proceed then to examine the bible, and here we shall find, that oaths are as contrary to the precepts and spirit of christianity as they are to sound reason.

Before I mention either the precepts or the spirit of the gospel, which militate against oaths, I shall mention a few of the cases of swearing which I find upon record in the New Testament. I shall first mention the precedents in favour of this practice, and then the precepts and precedents against it.

The *first* precedent I shall produce, is taken from the example of the devil, who addresses our Saviour in an oath, in Mark v. 7. "What have I to do with thee, Jesus, thou son of the most high God? I adjure thee by God that thou torment me not."

A *second* precedent is taken from the example of the high priest, who addresses our Saviour in an oath in Matthew, xxvi. 63. "I adjure thee," says he, just before he consents to his death, "by the *living God*, that thou tell us whether thou be the Christ the son of God." It has been said that there was no impropriety in this mode of expression, otherwise our Saviour would have rebuked it: but let it be remembered, that he stood before the tribunal of a high priest, as a *prisoner*, and not as a *teacher*; and hence we find he submits in *silence* to all the prophane insults that were offered him. In this silent submission to insult, he moreover fulfilled an ancient prophesy "he is brought as a lamb to the slaughter and as a sheep before his shearers is dumb, so he openeth not his mouth" Isaiah liii. 7.

Peter furnishes a *third* instance of swearing. "And again he *denied*" (says Matthew chap. xxvi. 72.) "with an *oath*, I know not the man." It would seem from this account, that a bare *affirmation* was so characteristic of a disciple of Jesus Christ, that Peter could not use a more direct method to convince the maid, who charged him with being a follower of Jesus of Nazareth, that he was *not a christian*, than by having recourse to the Jewish and pagan practice of taking an oath.

Herod furnishes a *fourth* instance of swearing, in Matthew xiv. 7, when he promised to give the daughter of Herodias whatever she should ask of him: she asked for John the baptist's head in a

charger: the king repented of his hasty promise; "nevertheless, for
the oath's sake, and them which sat with him at meat, he commanded it to be given her." Here it is evident he would have violated
a common promise. But if common promises are not held sacred,
and binding, there is an end of a great portion of truth in society,
and of all the order and happiness which arise from it. To secure
constant and universal truth, men should swear *always* or *not at all*.
A *fifth* precedent for swearing we find in the xix of Acts and 13th
verse. "Then certain of the vagabond Jews, exorcists, took upon
them to call over them which had evil spirits, the name of the Lord
Jesus, saying, *we adjure thee*, by Jesus whom Paul preacheth. And the
man in whom the evil spirit was, leaped on them, and overcame
them; so that they fled out of the house naked and wounded."

The *last* precedent for swearing that I shall mention, is the one
related in Acts xxiii. 21st. It contains an account of forty men who
had bound themselves, by *an oath*, not to eat or drink, until they
had killed St. Paul. It would seem that these banditti knew each
other perfectly, and thay they would not act together under the
form of a common obligation. The occasion indeed, seems to
require an oath. It was an association to commit murder. I am disposed to suspect that oaths were introduced originally to compel
men to do all things that were contrary to justice, or to their
consciences.

In mentioning the precepts and precedents that are to be found
in the new testament against swearing, the following striking
passage, taken from Matthew v. 34, 35, 36, 37, should alone determine the question. "Swear not at all, neither by heaven, for it is
God's throne; nor by the earth, for it is his footstool; nor by
Jerusalem, for it is the city of the great king. Neither shalt thou
swear by thy head, because thou canst not make one hair white or
black. But let your communication be yea, yea; nay, nay; for what-
soever is more than these, cometh of evil."

The words of the apostle James, are equally pointed against
swearing, chap. v. 12, "But above all things my brethren, swear not,
neither by heaven, neither by the earth, neither by any other oath;
but let your yea, be yea, and your nay, nay; lest ye fall into condemnation."

I know, these passages are said to be levelled only against profane
swearing in common conversation, but this will appear improbable

when we reflect, that our Saviour's words were addressed exclusively to his disciples, and that the epistle of St. James, from whence the prohibition of swearing is taken, is directed to a number of pious converts to christianity, none of whom, any more than the disciples of our Lord, could be suspected of profane swearing in common conversation. Both passages equally condemn oaths of every kind, and demonstrate their contrariety to the gospel dispensation.

There is a peculiar meaning in the reason which is given for the prohibition of swearing in the precept, of our Saviour, viz. that any thing more than a bare affirmation, *cometh of evil*. Yes, it came originally from the universal prevalance of falsehood in society; but the christian religion, by opening new sources of moral and religious obligation, and by discovering more fully the beauty and rewards of truth and deformity, and future punishment of falsehood, has rendered the obligation of oaths wholly unnecessary. They comported with the feeble discoveries of the Jewish, and the numerous corruptions of the pagan religions; but they are unnecessary under that full and clear manifestation of the divine will which is contained in the gospel. Caesar's wife should not be suspected.—With how much more propriety should this be said of the veracity of a christian, than of the chastity of the wife of a heathen emperor. Every time a christian swears, he exposes the purity and truth of his religion to suspicion. "As for you, Petrarch, your word is sufficient," said the cardinal Colonna, in an enquiry into the cause of a riot that had happened in his family, while that celebrated poet was a member of it; and in which he exacted an oath from every other member of his family, not excepting his own brother, the bishop of Luna. The same address should be made to every christian, when he is called upon to declare the truth. "You believe in a future state of rewards and punishment—you profess to be the follower of that Being who has inculcated a regard for truth, under the awful consideration of his omniscience, and who has emphatically styled himself the TRUTH." *Your word, therefore, is sufficient.*

A nobleman is permitted, by the laws of England, to declare the truth upon his *honour*. The profession of christianity is declared in scripture to be an high calling, and christians are said to be *priests* and *kings*. Strange! that persons of such high rank, should be treated with less respect than English noblemen; and still more strange! that persons possessing these august titles, should betray their illustrious birth and dignity, by conforming to a practice which tends so much to invalidate the truth and excellency of their religion.

It is very remarkable, that in all the accounts we have of the intercourse of our Saviour with his disciples, and of their subsequent intercourse with each other, there is no mention made of a single oath being taken by either of them.

Perhaps there never was an event in which the highest degrees of evidence were more necessary, than they were to establish the truth of the resurrection of our Saviour, as on the truth of this miracle depended the credibility of the christian religion. But in the establishment of the truth of this great event, no oath is taken, or required. The witnesses of it simply relate what they saw, and are believed by all the disciples except one, who still remembered too well the prohibition of his master, "swear not at all," to ask for an oath to remove his unbelief.

It is worthy of notice likewise, that no preposterous oath of office is required of the disciples when they assume the apostolic character, and are sent forth to preach the gospel to all nations. How unlike the spirit of the gospel are those human constitutions and laws, which require oaths of fidelity, every year! and which appear to be founded in the absurd idea that men are at all times the guardians of their own virtue.

There can be no doubt of christians having uniformly refused to take an oath in the first ages of the church: nor did they conform to this pagan custom, till after christianity was corrupted by a mixture with many other parts of the pagan and Jewish religions.

There are two arguments in favour of oaths which are derived from the new testament, and which remain to be refuted.—Ist. St. Paul uses several expressions in his epistles which amount to oaths, and even declares "an oath to be the end of strife." It was the character of St. Paul, that he became all things to all men. He circumcised as well as baptized Jews, and he proves the truth of revelation by a quotation from a heathen poet. Oaths were a part of the Jewish and pagan institutions—and, like several other ceremonies, for some time, continued to retain a strong hold of the prejudices of the new converts to christianity. But the above words of the Apostle, which have been urged in favor of swearing, are by no means intended to apply to common life. They have a retrospect to the promise made to Abraham of the coming of the Messiah, and were designed to shew the certainty of that event in a language which was accommodated to the idea of the Jewish nation.

2d. It has been said, that the great Jehovah frequently swears, both in the old and new testament, and that the angel who is to sound the last trumpet will "swear that time shall be no more." Every expression of this kind should be considered as an accommodation to Jewish and pagan customs, in order to render the truths of revelation more intelligible and acceptable. The Supreme Being, for the same reasons, often assumes to himself the violent passions, and even the features and senses of men; and yet who can suppose it proper to ascribe either of them to a Being, one of whose perfections consists in his existing as a pure unchangeable spirit.

If oaths are contrary to reason, and have a pernicious influence upon morals and the order of society; and above all, if they are contrary to the precepts and spirt of the gospel; it becomes legislators and ministers of the gospel to consider how far they are responsible for all the falsehood, profane swearing and perjury that exist in society. It is in the power of legislators to abolish oaths, by expunging them from our laws; and it is in the power of ministers of the gospel, by their influence and example, to render truth so simple and obligatory, that human governments shall be ashamed to ask any other mode of declaring it, from *Christians*, than by a bare affirmation.

The friends of virtue and freedom have beheld, with great pleasure, a new constitution established in the United States, whose objects are *peace, union* and *justice*. It will be in the power of the first congress that shall act under this constitution, to set the world an example of enlightened policy, by framing laws that shall command obedience without the absurd and improper obligation of oaths. By this means they will add the restoration and establishment of TRUTH, to the great and valuable objects of the constitution that have been mentioned.

Jan. 20, 1789.

AN ENQUIRY INTO THE EFFECTS OF PUBLIC PUNISHMENTS UPON CRIMINALS, AND UPON SOCIETY. READ IN THE SOCIETY FOR PROMOTING POLITICAL ENQUIRIES, CONVENED AT THE HOUSE OF BENJAMIN FRANKLIN, ESQ. IN PHILADELPHIA, MARCH 9TH, 1787.

"Accustomed to look up to those nations from whom we have derived our origin, for our laws, our opinions, and our manners; we have retained, with undistinguishing reverence, their errors, with their improvements; have blended, with our public institutions, the policy of dissimilar countries; and have grafted, on an infant commonwealth, the manners of ancient and corrupted monarchies." PREFACE TO THE LAWS OF THE SOCIETY FOR POLITICAL ENQUIRIES.

THE design of punishment is said to be, 1st, to reform the person who suffers it; 2dly, to prevent the perpetration of crimes, by exciting terror in the minds of spectators; and, 3dly, to remove those persons from society, who have manifested, by their tempers and crimes, that they are unfit to live in it.

From the first institution of governments, in every age and country (with but a few exceptions) legislators have thought that punishments should be *public*, in order to answer the two first of these intentions. It will require some fortitude to combat opinions that have been sanctified by such long and general prejudice, and supported by universal practice. But truth in government, as well as in philosophy, is of progressive growth. As in philosophy, we often arrive at truth by rejecting the evidence of our senses; so in government, we often arrive at it, after divorcing our first thoughts. Reason, though deposed and oppressed, is the only just sovereign of the human mind. Discoveries, it is true, have been made by accident; but they have derived their credit and usefulness only from their according with the decisions of reason.

In medicine, above every other branch of philosophy, we perceive many instances of the want of relation between the apparent cause and effect. Who, by reasoning *a priori*, would suppose, that the hot regimen was not preferable to the cold, in the treatment of the small-pox? But experience teaches us, that this is not the case. Cause and effect appear to be related in philosophy, like the objects of chemistry. Similar bodies often repel each other, while bodies that are dissimilar in figure, weight and quality, often unite together with impetuosity. With our present imperfect degrees of knowledge of the properties of bodies, we can discover these chemical relations only by experiment. The same may be said of the connection between *cause* and *effect*, in many parts of government. This connection often accords with reason, while it is repugnant to our senses—and when this is not the case, from our inability to perceive it, it forces our consent from the testimony of experience and observation.

It has been remarked, that the profession of arms owes its present rank, as a science, to its having been rescued, since the revival of letters, from the hands of mere soldiers, and cultivated by men acquainted with other branches of literature. The reason of this is plain. Truth is an unit. It is the same thing in war—philosophy—medicine—morals—religion and government; and in proportion as we arrive at it in one science, we shall discover it in others.

After this apology, for dissenting from the established opinions and practice, upon the subject of public punishments, I shall take the liberty of declaring, that the great ends proposed, are not to be obtained by them; and that, on the contrary, all *public* punishments tend to bad make men worse, and to increase crimes, by their influence upon society.

I. The reformation of a criminal can never be effected by a public punishment, for the following reasons.

1st. As it is always connected with infamy, it destroys in him the sense of shame, which is one of the strongest out-posts of virtue.

2dly. It is generally of such short duration, as to produce none of those changes in body or mind, which are absolutely necessary to reform obstinate habits of vice.

3dly. Experience proves, that public punishments have increased propensities to crimes. A man who has lost his character at a whipping-post, has nothing valuable left to lose in society. Pain has begotten insensibility to the whip; and infamy to shame. Added to his old habits of vice, he probably feels a spirit of revenge against the whole community, whose laws have inflicted his punishment upon him; and hence he is stimulated to add to the number and enormity of his outrages upon society. The long duration of the punishment, when public, by increasing its infamy, serves only to increase the evils that have been mentioned. The criminals, who were sentenced to work in the presence of the City of London, upon the Thames, during the late war, were prepared by it, for the perpetration of every crime, as soon as they were set at liberty from their confinement. I proceed,

II. To shew, that public punishments, so far from preventing crimes by the terror they excite in the minds of spectators, are directly calculated to produce them.

All men, when they suffer, discover either fortitude, insensibility, or distress. Let us inquire into the effects of each of these upon the minds of spectators.

1st. Fortitude is a virtue, that seizes so forcible upon our esteem, that wherever we see it, it never fails to weaken, or to obliterate, our detestation of the crimes with which it is connected in criminals. "I call upon you," said major Andre, at the place of execution to his attendants "to bear witness, gentlemen, that I die like a brave man." The effect of this speech upon the American army is well known. The spy was lost in the hero: and indignation, every where, gave way to admiration and praise. But this is not all: the admiration, which fortitude, under suffering, excites, has in some instances excited envy. In Denmark uncommon pains are taken to prepare criminals for death, by the conversation and instructions of the clergy. After this, they are conducted to the place of execution with uncommon pomp and solemnity. The criminals, under these circumstances, suffer death with meekness—piety—and sometimes with dignity. [The] effects of this, I have been well informed have been, in several instances, to induce deluded people to feign or confess crimes, which they had never committed, on purpose to secure to themselves a conspicuous death, and a certain entrance into happiness. There is something in the presence of a number of spectators, which is calculated to excite and strengthen fortitude in a sufferer. "It is not so difficult a thing," said Lewis XIV. to his courtiers, who stood round his death-bed, "to die, as I expected." "No wonder," says Voltaire, who relates this anecdote, "for all men die with fortitude, who die in company." The bravery of soldiers is derived in a great degree, from the operation of this principle in the human mind.

2dly. If criminals discover insensibility under their punishments, the effect of it must be still more fatal upon society. It removes, instead of exciting terror. In some instances, I conceive it may excite a desire in the minds of persons whom debt or secret guilt has made miserable, to seek an end of their distresses in the same enviable apathy to evil. Should this insensibility be connected with chearfulness, which is sometimes the case, it must produce still more unfriendly effects upon society. But terrible must be the consequence of this insensibility and chearfulness, if they should lead criminals to retaliate upon the inhuman curiosity of spectators, by profane or indecent insults or conversation.

3rdly. The effects of distress in criminals, though less obvious are not less injurious to society, than fortitude or insensibility. By an immutable law of our nature, distress of all kinds, when *seen*, produces sympathy, and a disposition to relieve it. This sympathy, in generous minds, is not lessened by the distress being the offspring of crimes: on the contrary, even the crimes themselves are often palliated by the reflection that they were unfortunate consequences of extreme poverty—of seducing company—or of the want of a virtuous education, from the loss or negligence of parents in early life. Now, as the distress which the criminals suffer, is the effect of a law of the state, which cannot be resisted, the sympathy of the spectator is rendered abortive, and returns empty to the bosom in which it was awakened. Let us briefly examine the consequences of this abortive sympathy in society. It will not be necessary here to dwell upon all the advantages of this principle in human nature. It will be sufficient to observe, that it is the vicegerent of the divine benevolence in our world. It is intended to bind up all the wounds which sin and death have made among mankind. It has founded hospitals—erected charity-schools—and connected the extremes of happiness and misery together in every part of the globe. Above all, sensibility is the centinel of the moral faculty. It decides upon the quality of the actions before they reach that divine principle of the soul. It is of itself, to use the words of an elegant female poet,[1] "A hasty moral—a sudden sense of right."

If such are the advantages of sensibility, now what must be the consequences to society, of extirpating or weakening it in the human breast? But public punishments are calculated to produce

---

[1] Miss Moore.

this effect. To prove this, I must borrow an analogy from the animal œconomy.—The sensibility of the human body is said to be *active* and *passive*. The first is connected with motion and sensation; the second only with sensation. The first is increased, the second is diminished, by the repetition of impressions. The same phaenomena take place in the human mind. Sensibility here is both *active* and *passive*. Passive sensibility is lessened, while that which is active is increased by habit. The passive sensibility of a physician, to the distress of his patients, is always, diminished, but his active sensibility is always increased by time; hence we find young physicians *feel* most—but old physicians, with less feeling, *discover* most sympathy with their patients.

If such be the constitution of our minds, then the effects, of distress upon them will be, not only to destroy passive, but to eradicate active sensibility from them. The principle of sympathy, after being often opposed by the law of the state, which forbids it to relieve the distress it commiserates, will cease to act altogether; and, from this defect of action, and the habit arising from it, will soon lose its place in the human breast. Misery of every kind will then be contemplated without emotion or sympathy.—The widow and the orphan—the naked—the sick, and the prisoner, will have no avenue to our services or our charity—and what is worse than all, when the centinel of our moral faculty is removed, there is nothing to guard the mind from the inroads of every positive vice.

I pass over the influence of this sympathy in its first operation upon the government of the state. While we pity, we secretly condemn the law which inflicts the punishment: hence, arises a want of respect for [laws] in general, and a more feeble union of the great ties of government.

I have only to add, upon this part of my subject, that the pernicious effects of sympathy, where it does not terminate in action, are happily provided against by the Jewish law. Hence we read of a prohibition against it where persons suffer for certain crimes. To spectators, the voice of heaven, under such circumstances, is, "thine eye shall not pity him."

4thly. But it is possible the characters or conduct of criminals may be such, as to excite indignation or contempt instead of pity, in the minds of spectators. Let us there enquire, briefly, into the effects of these passions upon the human mind. Every body acknowledges our obligations to universal benevolence; but these cannot be fulfilled, unless we love the whole human race, however diversified they may be by weakness or crimes. The indignation or contempt which is felt for this unhappy part of the great family of mankind, must necessarily extinguish a large portion of this universal love. Nor is this all the men, or perhaps the women whose persons we detest, possess souls and bodies composed of the same materials as those of our friends and relations. They are bone of their bone; and were originally fashioned with the same spirits. What, then, must be the consequence of a familiarity with such objects of horror, upon our attachments and duties to our friends and connections, or to the rest of mankind? If a spectator should give himself time to reflect upon such a sight of human depravity, he would naturally recoil from the embraces of friendship, and the endearments of domestic life, and perhaps say with an unfortunate great man, after having experienced an instance of treachery in a friend, "Oh! that I were a dog, that I might not call man my brother." The Jewish law forbade more than nine and thirty lashes, lest the sufferer should afterwards become "vile" in the sight of spectators. It is the prerogative of God alone, to contemplate the vices of bad men, without withdrawing from them the support of his benevolence. Hence we find, when he appeared in the world, in the person of his Son, he did not exclude criminals from the benefits of his goodness. He dismissed a woman caught in the perpetration of a crime, which was capital by the Jewish law, with a friendly admonition: and he opened the gates of paradise to a dying thief.

5thly. But let us suppose, that criminals are viewed without sympathy—indignation—or contempt.—This will be the case, either when the spectators are themselves hardened with vice, or when they are too young, or too ignorant, to connect the ideas of crimes and punishments together. Here, then, a new source of injury arises from the public nature of punishments. Every portion of them will appear, to spectators of this description, to be mere arbitrary acts of cruelty: hence will arise a disposition to exercise the same arbitrary cruelty over the feelings and lives of their fellow creatures. To see blows, or a halter, imposed in cold blood upon a criminal, whose passive behaviour, operating with the ignorance of the spectators, indicates innocence more than vice, cannot fail of removing the natural obstacles to violence and murder in the human mind.

6thly. Public punishments make many crimes known to persons who would otherwise have passed through life in a total ignorance of them. They moreover produce such a familiarity, in the minds of spectators, with the crimes for which they are inflicted, that, in some instances, they have been known to excite a propensity for them. It has been remarked, that a certain immorality has always kept pace with public admonitions in the churches in the eastern states. In proportion as this branch of ecclesiastical discipline has declined, fewer children have been born out of wedlock.

7thly. Ignominy is universally acknowledged to be a worse punishment than death. Let it not be supposed, from this cir-cumstance, that it operates more than the fear of death in prevent-ing crimes. On the contrary, like the indiscriminate punishment of death, it not only confounds and levels all crimes, but by increasing the disproportion between crimes and punishments, it creates a hatred of all law and government; and thus disposes to the perpetra-tion of every crime. Laws can only be respected and obeyed, while they bear an exact proportion to crimes.—The law which punishes the shooting of a swan with death, in England, has produced a thousand murders. Nor is this all the mischievous influence, which the punishment of ignominy has upon society. While murder is punished with death, the man who robs on the high-way, or breaks open a house, must want the common feelings and principles which belong to human nature, if he does not add murder to theft, in order to screen himself, if he should be detected, from that punish-ment which is acknowledged to be more terrible than death.

It would seem strange, that ignominy should ever have been adopted, as a milder punishment than death, did we not know that the human mind seldom arrives at truth upon any subject, till it has first reached the extremity of error.

8thly. But may not the benefit derived to society, by employing criminals to repair public roads, or to clean streets, overbalance the evils that have been mentioned? I answer, by no means. On the con-trary, besides operating in *one*, or in *all* the ways that have been described, the practice of employing criminals in public labour, will render labour of every kind disreputable, more especially that species of it, which has for its objects the convenience or improve-ment of the state. It is a well-known fact, that white men soon decline labour in the West Indies, and in the southern states, only because the agriculture, and mechanical employments of those countries, are carried on chiefly by negro slaves. But I object further to the employment of criminals on the high-ways and streets, from the idleness it will create, by alluring spectators from their business, and thereby depriving the state of greater benefits from the industry of its citizens, than it can ever derive from the labour of criminals.

The history of public punishments, in every age and country, is full of facts, which support every principle that has been advanced. What has been the operation of the seventy thousand executions, that have taken place in Great Britain from the year 1688, to the present day, upon the morals and manners of the inhabitants of that island? Has not every prison-door that has been opened, to conduct criminals to public shame and punishment, unlocked, at the same time, the bars of moral obligation upon the minds of ten times the number of people? How often do we find pockets picked under a gallows, and highway robberies committed in sight of a gibbet? From whence arose the conspiracies, with assassinations and poisonings, which prevailed in the decline of the Roman empire? Were they not favoured by the public executions of the amphitheatre? It is therefore to the combined operation of indolence, prejudice, ignorance and the defect of culture of the human heart, alone, that we are to ascribe the continuance of public punishments, after such long and multiplied experience of their inefficacy to reform bad men, or to prevent the commission of crimes.

III. Let it not be supposed, from any thing that has been said, that I wish to abolish punishments. Far from it: I wish only to change the place and manner of inflicting them, so as to render them effectual for the reformation of criminals, and beneficial to society. Before I propose a plan for this purpose, I beg leave to deliver the following general axioms:

1st. The human mind is disposed to exaggerate every thing that is removed from it, by time or place.

2dly. It is equally disposed to enquire after, and to magnify such things as are sacred.

3dly. It always ascribes the extremes in qualities, to things that are unknown; and an excess in duration, to indefinite time.

4thly. Certain and definite evil, by being long contemplated, ceases to be dreaded or avoided. A soldier soon loses, from habit the fear of death in battle; but retains, in common with other people, the terror of death from sickness or drowning.

5thly. An attachment to kindred and society is one of the strongest feelings of the human heart. A separation from them, therefore has ever been considered as one of the severest punishments that can be inflicted upon man.

6thly. Personal liberty is so dear to all men, that the loss of it, for an indefinite time, is a punishment so severe that death has often been preferred to it.

These axioms being admitted (for they cannot be controverted) I shall proceed next to apply them, by suggesting a plan for the punishment of crimes, which, I flatter myself, will answer all the ends that have been proposed by them.

1. Let a large house be erected in a convenient part of the state. Let it be divided into a number of apartments, reserving one large room for public worship. Let cells be provided for the solitary confinement of such persons as are of a refractory temper. Let the house be supplied with the materials, and instruments for carrying on such manufactures as can be conducted with the least instruction, or previous knowledge. Let a garden adjoin this house, in which the culprits may occasionally work, and walk. This spot will have a beneficial effect not only upon health, but morals, for it will lead them to a familiarity with those pure and natural objects which are calculated to renew the connection of fallen man with his creator. Let the name of this house convey an idea of its benevolent and salutary design, but let it by no means be called a prison, or by any other name that is associated with what is infamous in the opinion of mankind. Let the direction of this institution be committed to persons of established characters for probity, discretion and humanity, who shall be amenable at all times to the legislature, or courts of the state.

2dly. Let the various kinds of punishment, that are to be inflicted on crimes, be defined and fixed by law. But let no notice be taken, in the law, of the punishment that awaits any particular crime. By these means, we shall prevent the mind from accustoming itself to the view of these punishments, so as to destroy their terror by habit. The indifference and levity with which some men suffer the punishment of hanging, is often occasioned by an insensibility which is contracted by the frequent anticipation of it, or by the appearance of the gallows suggesting the remembrance of scenes of criminal festivity, in which it was the subject of humour or ridicule. Besides, punishments should always be varied in degree, according to the temper of criminals, or the progress of their reformation.

3dly. Let the duration of punishments, for all crimes, be limitted: but let this limitation be unknown. I conceive this secret to be of the utmost importance in reforming criminals, and preventing crimes. The imagination, when agitated with uncertainty, will seldom fail of connecting the longest duration of punishment, with the smallest crime.

I cannot conceive any thing more calculated to diffuse terror through a community, and thereby to prevent crimes, than the combination of the three circumstances that have been mentioned in punishments. Children will press upon the evening fire in listening to the tales that will be spread from this abode of misery. Superstition will add to its horrors: and romance will find in it ample materials for fiction, which cannot fail of increasing the terror of its punishments.

Let it not be objected, that the terror produced by the history of these secret punishments, will operate like the abortive sympathy I have described. *Active* sympathy can be fully excited only through the avenues of the eyes and the ears. Besides, the recollection that the only design of punishment is the reformation of the criminal will suspend the action of sympathy altogether. We listen with paleness to the history of a tedious and painful operation in surgery, without a wish to arrest the hand of the operator. Our sympathy, which in this case is of the *passive* kind, is mixed with pleasure, when we are assured, that there is a certainty of the operation being the means of saving the life of the sufferer.

Nor let the expence of erecting and supporting a house of repentance, for the purposes that have been mentioned, deter us from the undertaking. It would be easy to demonstrate, that it will not cost one fourth as much as the maintenance of the numerous jails that are now necessary in every well regulated state. But why should receptacles be provided and supported at an immense expence, in every country, for the relief of persons afflicted with bodily disorders, and an objection be made to providing a place for the cure of the diseases of the mind?

The nature, degrees and duration of the punishments should all be determined beyond a certain degree, by a court properly constituted for that purpose, and whose business it should be to visit the receptacle for criminals once or twice a year.

I am aware of the prejudices of freemen, against entrusting power to a discretionary court. But let it be remembered, that no power is committed to this court, but what is possessed by the different courts of justice in all free countries; nor so much as is now wisely and necessarily possessed by the supreme and inferior courts, in the execution of the penal laws of Pennsylvania. I shall spend no time in defending the consistency of private punishments, with a safe and free government. Truth, upon this subject, cannot be divided. If public punishments are injurious to criminals and to society, it follows that crimes should be punished in private, or not punished at all. There is no alternative. The opposition to private punishments, therefore is founded altogether in prejudice, or in ignorance of the true principles of liberty.

The safety and advantages of private punishments, will appear, further, when I add, that the best governed families and schools are those, in which the faults of servants and children are rebuked privately, and where confinement and solitude are preferred for correction, to the use of the rod.

In order to render these punishments effectual they should be accommodated to the constitutions and tempers of the criminals, and the peculiar nature of their crimes. Peculiar attention should be paid, likewise, in the nature, degrees, and duration of punishments, to crimes, as they arise from passion, habit or temptation.

The punishments, should consist of bodily pain, labour, watchfulness, solitude, and silence. They should all be joined with cleanliness and a simple diet. To ascertain the nature, degrees, and duration of the bodily pain, will require some knowledge of the principles of sensation, and of the sympathies which occur in the nervous system. The labour should be so regulated and directed, as to be profitable to the state. Besides employing criminals in laborious and useful manufactures, they may be compelled to derive all their subsistance from a farm and a garden, cultivated by their own hands, adjoining the place of their confinement.

These punishments may be used separately, or more or less combined, according to the nature of the crimes, or according to the variations of the constitution and temper of the criminals. In the application of them, the utmost possible advantages should be taken of the laws of the association of ideas, of habit, and of imitation.

To render these physical remedies more effectual they should be accompanied by regular instruction in the principles and obligations of religion, by persons appointed for that purpose.

Thus far I am supported, in the application of the remedies I have mentioned, for the cure of crimes, by the facts contained in Mr. Howard's history of prisons, and by other observations. It remains yet to prescribe the *specific* punishment that is proper for each *specific* crime. Here my subject begins to oppress me. I have no more doubt of every crime having its cure in moral and physical influence, than I have of the efficacy of the Peruvian bark in curing the intermitting fever. The only difficulty is, to find out the proper remedy or remedies for particular vices. Mr. Dufriche de Valaye, in his elaborate treatise upon penal laws, has performed the office of a pioneer upon this difficult subject. He has divided crimes into classes; and has affixed punishments to each of them, in a number of ingenious tables. Some of the connections he has established, between crimes and punishments, appear to be just. But many of his punishments are contrary to the first principles of action in man; and all of them are, in my opinion, improper, as far as he orders them to be inflicted in the *eye* of the *public*. His attempt, however, is laudable, and deserves the praise of every friend to mankind.

If the invention of a machine for facilitating labour, has been repaid with the gratitude of a country, how much more will that man deserve, who shall invent the most speedy and effectual methods of restoring the vicious part of mankind to virtue and happiness, and of extirpating a portion of vice from the world? Happy condition of human affairs! when humanity, philosophy and christianity, shall unite their influence to teach men, that they are brethren; and to prevent their preying any longer upon each other! Happy citizens of the United States, whose governments permit them to adopt every discovery in the moral or intellectual world, that leads to these benevolent purposes!

Let it not be objected, that it will be impossible for men, who have expiated their offences by the mode of punishment that has been proposed, to recover their former connections with society. This objection arises from an unfortunate association of ideas. The infamy of criminals is derived, not so much from the remembrance of their crimes, as from the recollection of the ignominy of their punishments. Crimes produce a stain, which may be washed out by reformation, and which frequently wears away by time; but public punishments leave scars, which disfigure the whole character; and hence persons, who have suffered them, are ever afterwards viewed with horror or aversion. If crimes were expiated by private discipline, and succeeded by reformation, criminals would probably suffer no more in character from them, than men suffer in their reputation or usefulness from the punishments they have undergone when boys at school.

I am so perfectly satisfied of the truth of this opinion, that methinks I already hear the inhabitants of our villages and townships counting the years that shall complete the reformation of one of their citizens. I behold them running to meet him on the day of his deliverance. His friends and family bathe his cheeks with tears of joy; and the universal shout of the neighbourhood is, "This our brother was lost, and is found—was dead and is alive."

It has long been a desideratum in government, that there should exist in it no pardoning power, since the *certainty* of punishment operates so much more than its severity, or infamy, in preventing crimes. But where punishments are excessive in degree, or infamous from being public, a pardoning power is absolutely necessary. Remove their severity and public infamy, and a pardoning power ceases to be necessary in a code of criminal jurisprudence. Nay, further—it is such a defect in penal laws, as in some measure defeats every invention to prevent crimes, or to cure habits of vice.

If punishments were moderate, just, and private, they would exalt the feelings of public justice and benevolence so far above the emotions of humanity in witnesses, juries and judges, that they would forget to conceal, or to palliate crimes; and the *certainty* of punishment, by extinguishing all hope of pardon in the criminal, would lead him to connect the beginning of his repentance with the last words of his sentence of condemnation. To obtain this great and salutary end, there should exist *certain* portions of punishment, both in duration and degree, which should be placed by law beyond the power of the discretionary court before mentioned, to shorten or mitigate.

I have said nothing upon the manner of inflicting death as a punishment for crimes, because I consider it as an improper punishment for *any* crime. Even murder itself is propagated by the punishment of death for murder. Of this we have a remarkable proof in Italy. The duke of Tuscany soon after the publication of the marquis of Beccaria's excellent treatise upon this subject, abolished death as a punishment for murder. A gentleman, who resided five years at Pisa, informed me, that only five murders had been perpetrated in his dominions in twenty years. The same gentleman added, that after his residence in Tuscany, he spent three months in Rome, where death is still the punishment of murder, and where executions, according to Dr. Moore, are conducted with peculiar circumstances of public parade. During this short period, there were sixty murders committed in the precincts of that city. It is remarkable, the manners, principles, and religion, of the inhabitants of Tuscany and Rome, are exactly the same. The abolition of death alone, as a punishment for muder, produced this difference in the moral character of the two nations.

I suspect the attachment to death, as a punishment for murder, in minds otherwise enlightened, upon the subject of capital punishments, arises from a false interpretation of a passage contained in the old testament, and that is, "he that sheds the blood of man, by man shall his blood be shed." This has been supposed to imply that blood could only be expiated by blood. But I am disposed to believe, with a late commentator[2] upon this text of scripture, that it is rather a *prediction* than a *law*. The language of it is simply, that such will be the depravity and folly of man, that murder, in every age, shall beget murder. Laws, therefore, which inflict death for murder, are, in my opinion, as unchristian as those which justify or tolerate revenge; for the obligations of christianity upon individuals, to promote repentance, to forgive injuries, and to discharge the duties of universal benevolence, are equally binding upon states.

The power over human life, is the sole prerogative of him who gave it. Human laws, therefore, rise in rebellion against this prerogative, when they transfer it to human hands.

If society can be secured from violence, by confining the murderer so as to prevent a repetition of his crime, the end of extirpation will be answered. In confinement, he may be reformed: and

---

[2] The reverend Mr. William Turner, in the second vol. of Memoirs of the Literary and Philosophical Society of Manchester.

if this should prove impracticable, he may be restrained for a term of years, that will probably, be coeval with his life.

There was a time, when the punishment of captives with death or servitude, and the indiscriminate destruction of peaceable husbandmen, women, and children, were thought to be essential, to the success of war, and the safety of states. But experience has taught us, that this is not the case. And in proportion as humanity has triumphed over these maxims of false policy, wars have been less frequent and terrible, and nations have enjoyed longer intervals of internal tranquility. The virtues are all parts of a circle. Whatever is humane, is wise—whatever is wise, is just—and whatever is wise, just, and humane, will be found to be the true interest of states, whether criminals or foreign enemies are the objects of their legislation.

I have taken no notice of perpetual banishment, as a legal punishment, as I consider it the next in degree, in folly and cruelty, to the punishment of death. If the receptacle for criminals, which has been proposed, is erected in a remote part of the state, it will act with the same force upon the feelings of the human heart, as perpetual banishment. Exile, when perpetual, by destroying one of the most powerful principles of action in man, viz. the love of kindred and country, deprives us of all the advantages, which might be derived from it, in the business of reformation. While certain passions are weakened, this noble passion is strengthed by age: hence, by preserving this passion alive, we furnish a principle, which, in time may become an overmatch for those vicious habits, which separated criminals from their friends and from society.

Notwithstanding this testimony against the punishment of death and perpetual banishment, I cannot help adding, that there is more mercy to the criminal, and less injury done to society, by both of them, than by public infamy and pain, without them.

The great art of surgery has been said to consist in saving, not in destroying, or amputating the diseased parts of the human body. Let governments learn to imitate, in this respect, the skill and humanity of the healing art. Nature knows no waste in any of her operations. Even putrefaction itself is the parent of useful productions to man. Human ingenuity imitates nature in a variety of arts. Offal maters, of all kinds, are daily converted into the means of increasing the profits of industry, and the pleasures of human life.

The soul of man alone, with all its moral and intellectual powers, when misled by passion, is abandoned, by the ignorance or cruelty of man, to unprofitable corruption, or extirpation.

A worthy prelate of the church of England once said upon seeing a criminal led to execution, "There goes my wicked self." Considering the vices to which the frailty of human nature exposes whole families of every rank and class in life, it becomes us, whenever we see a fellow creature led to public infamy and pain, to add further. "There goes my unhappy father, my unhappy brother, or my unhappy son," and afterwards to ask ourselves, whether *private* punishments are not to be preferred to *public*.

For the honour of humanity it can be said, that in every age and country, there have been found persons in whom uncorrupted nature has triumphed over custom and law. Else, why do we hear of houses being abandoned near to places of public execution? Why do we see doors and windows shut on the days or hours of criminal exhibitions? Why do we hear of aid being secretly afforded to criminals, to mitigate or elude the severity of their punishments? Why is the public executioner of the law an object of such general detestation? These things are latent struggles of reason, or rather the secret voice of God himself, speaking in the human heart, against the folly and cruelty of public punishment.

I shall conclude this enquiry by observing, that the same false religion and philosophy, which once kindled the fire on the alter of persecution, now doom the criminal to public ignominy and death. In proportion as the principles of philosophy and christianity are understood, they will agree in extinguishing the one, and destroying the other. If these principles continue to extend their influence upon government, as they have done for some years past, I cannot help entertaining a hope, that the time is not very distant, when the gallows, the pillory, the stocks, the whipping-post and the wheel-barrow, (the usual engines of public punishments) will be connected with the history of the rack and the stake, as marks of the barbarity of ages and countries, and as melancholy proofs of the feeble operation of reason and religion upon the human mind.

AN ENQUIRY INTO THE CONSISTENCY OF THE PUNISHMENT OF MURDER BY DEATH, WITH REASON AND REVELATION.

I. THE Punishment of Murder by Death, is contrary to *reason*, and to the order and happiness of society.

1. It lessens the horror of taking away human life, and thereby tends to multiply murders.

2. It produces murder by its influence upon people who are tired of life, and who, from a supposition that murder is a less crime than suicide, destroy a life (and often that of a near connection) and afterwards deliver themselves up to the laws of their country, that they may escape from their misery by means of a halter.

3. The punishment of murder by death multiplies murders, from the difficulty it creates of convicting persons who are guilty of it. Humanity, revolting at the idea of the severity and certainty of a capital punishment, often steps in, and collects such evidence in favour of a murderer, as screens him from death altogether, or palliates his crime into manslaughter. Even the law itself favours the acquital of a murderer by making the circumstance of premeditation and malice, necessary to render the offence, a capital crime. Mr. Townsend tells us in his travels into Spain[1] that seventy murders were perpetrated in Malaga in the 16 months which preceeded his visit to that city, all of which escaped with impunity, and probably from the causes which have been mentioned. If the punishment of murder consisted in long confinement, and hard labour, it would be proportioned to the measure of our feelings of justice, and every member of society would be a watchman, or a magistrate, to apprehend a destroyer of human life, and to bring him to punishment.

4. The punishment of murder by death checks the operations of universal justice, by preventing the punishment of every species of murder.

5. The punishment of murder by death has been proved to be contrary to the order and happiness of society, by the experiments of some of the wisest legislators in Europe. The Empress of Russia,

---

[1] Vol. 3.

the King of Sweden, and the Duke of Tuscany, have nearly extirpated murder from their dominions, by converting its punishments into the means of benefiting society, and reforming the criminals who perpetrate it.

II. The punishment of murder by death is contrary to *divine revelation*. A religion which commands us to forgive, and even to do good to, our enemies, can never authorise the punishment of murder by death. "Vengence is mine," said the Lord; "I will repay." It is to no purpose to say here, that this vengeance is taken out of the hands of an individual, and directed against the criminal by the hand of government. It is equally an usurpation of the prerogative of heaven, whether it be inflicted by a single person, or by a whole community.

Here I expect to meet with an appeal from the letter and spirit of the gospel, to the law of Moses, which declares, "he that killeth a man shall be put to death." Forgive, indulgent heaven! the ignorance and cruelty of man, which, by the misapplication of this text of scripture, has so long and so often stained the religion of Jesus Christ with folly and revenge.

The following considerations, I hope, will prove that no argument can be deduced from this law, to justify the punishment of murder by death;—on the contrary, that several arguments against it, may be derived from a just and rational explanation of that part of the Levitical institutions.

1. There are many things in scripture above, but nothing contrary to, reason. Now, the punishment of murder by death, is contrary to reason. It cannot, therefore, be agreeable to the will of God.

2. The order and happiness of society cannot fail of being agreeable to the will of God. But the punishment of murder by death, destroys the order and happiness of society. It must therefore be contrary to the will of God.

3. Many of the laws given by Moses, were accommodated to the ignorance, wickedness, and "hardness of heart," of the Jews. Hence their divine legislator expressly says, "I gave them statutes that were not good, and judgments whereby they should not live." Of this, the law which respects divorces, and the law of retaliation, which required, "an eye for an eye, and a tooth for a tooth," are remarkable instances.

But we are told, that the punishment of murder by death, is founded not only on the law of Moses, but upon a positive precept given to Noah and his posterity, that "whoso sheddeth man's blood, by man shall his blood be shed." If the interpretation of this text given in a former essay[2] be not admitted, I shall attempt to explain it by remarking, that soon after the flood, the infancy and weakness of society rendered it impossible to punish murder by confinement. There was therefore no medium between inflicting death upon a murderer, and suffering him to escape with impunity, and thereby to perpetrate more acts of violence against his fellow creatures. It pleased God, in this condition of the world, to permit a less, in order to prevent a greater evil. He therefore commits for a while his exclusive power over human life, to his creatures for the safety and preservation of an infant society, which might otherwise have perished, and with it, the only stock of the human race. The command indirectly implies that the crime of murder was not punished by death in the mature state of society which existed before the flood. Nor is this the only instance upon record in the scriptures in which God has delegated his power over human life to his creatures. Abraham expresses no surprise at the command which God gave him to sacrifice his son. He submits to it as a precept founded in reason and natural justice, for nothing could be more obvious, than that the giver of life had a right to claim it, when and in such manner as he pleased. 'Till men are able to give life, it becomes them to tremble at the thought of taking it away. Will a man rob God?—Yes—he robs him of what is infinitely dear to him—of his darling attribute of mercy, every time he deprives a fellow creature of life.

4. If the Mosaic law, with respect to murder, be obligatory upon Christians, it follows that it is equally obligatory upon them to punish adultery, blasphemy and other capital crimes that are mentioned in the Levitical law, by death. Nor is this all: it justifies the extirpation of the Indians, and the enslaving of the Africans; for the command to the Jews to destroy the Canaanites, and to make slaves of their heathen neighbours, is as positive as the command which declares, "that he that killeth a man, shall surely be put to death."

5. Every part of the Levitical law, is full of types of the Messiah.

---

[2] Enquiry into the effects of public punishments.

May not the punishment of death, inflicted by it, be intended to represent the demerit and consequences of sin, as the cities of refuge were the offices of the Messiah? And may not the enlargement of murderers who had fled to those cities of refuge, upon the death of a high priest, represent the eternal abrogation of the law which inflicted death for murder, by the meritorious death of the Saviour of the world?

6. The imperfection and severity of these laws were probably intended farther—to illustrate the perfection and mildness of the gospel dispensation. It is in this manner that God has manifested himself in many of his acts. He created darkness first, to illustrate by comparison the beauty of light, and he permits sin, misery, and death in the moral world, that he may hereafter display more illustriously the blessings of the righteousness, happiness, and immortal life. This opinion is favoured by St. Paul, who says, "the law made nothing perfect, and that it was a shadow of good things to come."

How delightful to discover such an exact harmony between the dictates of reason, the order and happiness of society, and the precepts of the gospel! There is a perfect unity in truth. Upon all subjects—in all ages—and in all countries—truths of every kind agree with each other. I shall now take notice of some of the common arguments, which are made use of, to defend the punishment of murder by death.

1. It has been said, that the common sense of all nations, and particularly of savages, is in favour of punishing murder by death.

The common sense of all nations is in favour of the commerce and slavery of their fellow creatures. But this does not take away from the immorality. Could it be proved that the Indians punish murder by death, it would not establish the right of man over the life of a fellow creature; for revenge we know in its utmost extent is the universal and darling passion of all savage nations. The practice moreover, (if it exist) must have originated in *necessity*: for a people who have no settled place of residence, and who are averse from all labour, could restrain murder in no other way. But I am disposed to doubt whether the Indians punish murder by death among their own tribes. In all those cases where a life is taken away by an Indian of a foreign tribe, they always demand the satisfaction of life for life. But this practice is founded on a desire of preserving a balance in their numbers and power; for among nations which consist of only a few warriors, the loss of an individual often destroys this balance, and thereby exposes them to war or extermination. It is for the same purpose of keeping up an equality in numbers and power, that they often adopt captive children into their nations and families. What makes this explanation of the practice of punishing murder by death among the Indians more probable, is, that we find the same bloody and vindictive satisfaction is required of a foreign nation, whether the person lost, be killed by an accident, or premeditated violence. Many facts might be mentioned from travellers to prove that the Indians do not punish murder by death within the jurisdiction of their own tribes. I shall mention only one, which is taken from the Rev. Mr. John Megapolensis's account of the Mohawk Indians, lately published in Mr. Hazard's historical collection of state papers.—"There is no punishment, (says our author) here for murder, but every one is his own avenger. The friends of the deceased revenge themselves upon the murderer until peace is made with the next a kin. But although they are so cruel, yet there are not half so many murders committed among them as among Christians, notwithstanding their severe laws, and heavy penalties."

2. It has been said, that the horrors of a guilty conscience proclaim the justice and necessity of death, as a punishment for murder. I draw an argument of another nature from this fact. Are the horrors of conscience the punishment that God inflicts upon murder? Why, then should we shorten or destroy them by death, especially as we are taught to direct the most atrocious murderers to expect pardon in the future world? No, let us not counteract the government of God in the human breast: let the murderer live—but let it be to suffer the reproaches of a guilty conscience; let him live, to make compensation to society for the injury he has done it, by robbing it of a citizen; let him live to maintain the family of the man whom he has murdered; let him live, that the punishment of his crime may become universal; and, lastly, let him live, that murder may be extirpated from the list of human crimes!

Let us examine the conduct of the moral Ruler of the world towards the first murderer.—See Cain, returning from his field, with his hands reeking with the blood of his brother! Do the heavens gather blackness, and does a flash of lightning blast him to the earth? No. Does his father Adam, the natural legislator and judge of the world, inflict upon him the punishment of death? No. The infinitely wise God becomes his judge and executioner. He expels him from the society of which he was a member. He fixes in his conscience a never dying worm. He subjects him to the necessity of labour; and to secure a duration of his punishment, proportioned to his crime, he puts a mark of prohibition upon him, to prevent his being put to death, by weak and angry men; declaring, at the same time, that "whosoever slayeth Cain, vengeance shall be taken on him seven-fold."

But further, if a necessary connection existed between the crime of murder and death in the mind and laws of the Deity, how comes it that Moses and David escaped it? They both imbrued their hands in innocent blood, and yet the horrors of a guilty conscience were their only punishment. The subsequent conduct of those two great and good men, proves that the heart may retain a sound part after committing murder, and that even murderers, after repentance, may be the vehicles of great temporal and spiritual blessings to mankind.

3. The declaration of St. Paul before Festus, respecting the punishment of death,[3] and the speech of the dying thief on the cross,[4] are said to prove the lawfulness of punishing murder by death: but they prove only that the punishment of death was agreeable to the Roman law. Human life was extremely cheap under the Roman government. Of this we need no further proof than the head of John the Baptist forming a part of a royal entertainment. From the frequency of public executions, among those people, the *sword* was considered as an emblem of public justice. But to suppose, from the appeals which are sometimes made to it as a sign of justice, that capital punishments are approved of in the New Testament, is as absurd as it would be to suppose that horse-racing was a christian exercise, from St. Paul's frequent allusions to the Olympic games.

The declaration of the barbarians upon seeing the snake fasten upon St. Paul's hand, proves nothing but the ignorance of those uncivilized people;—"and when the barbarians saw the venomous beast hang on his hand, they said among themselves, no doubt this

---

[3] For if I be an offender, and have committed any thing worthy of death, I refuse not to die."—Acts xxv. and 11.

[4] "We indeed suffer *justly*, for we receive the due reward of our deeds."—Luke xxiii. and 41.

man is a murderer, whom, though he hath escaped the sea, yet vengeance suffereth not to live."—Acts xxvii. and 4th.

Here it will be proper to distinguish between the sense of justice so universal among all nations, and an approbation of death as a punishment for murder. The former is written by the finger of God upon every human heart, but like his own attribute of justice, it has the happiness of individuals and of society for its objects. It is always misled, when it seeks for satisfaction in punishments that are injurious to society, or that are disproportioned to crimes. The satisfaction of this universal sense of justice by the punishments of imprisonment and labour, would far exceed that which is derived from the punishment of death; for it would be of longer duration, and it would more frequently occur; for, upon a principle formerly mentioned, scarcely any species of murder would escape with impunity.[5]

The conduct and discourses of our Saviour should outweigh every argument that has been or can be offered in favour of capital punishment for any crime. When the woman caught in adultery was brought to him, he evaded inflicting the bloody sentence of the Jewish law upon her. Even the *maiming* of the body appears to be offensive in his sight; for when Peter drew his sword, and smote off the ear of the servant of the high priest, he replaced it by miracle, and at the same time declared, that "all they who take the sword, shall perish with the sword." He forgave the crime of murder, on his cross; and after his resurrection, he commanded his disciples to preach the gospel of forgiveness, *first* at Jerusalem, where he well knew his murderers still resided. These striking facts are recorded for our imitation, and seem intended to shew that the Son of God died, not only to reconcile God to man, but to reconcile men to each other. There is one passage more, in the history of our Saviour's life which would of itself overset the justice of the punish-

---

[5] A scale of punishments, by means of imprisonment and labour, might easily be contrived, so as to be accommodated to the different degrees of atrocity in murder. For example—for the first or highest degree of guilt, let the punishment be solitude and darkness, and a total *want* of employment. For the second, solitude and labour, with the benefit of light. For the third, confinement and labour. The *duration* of these punishments should likewise be governed by the atrocity of the murder, and by the signs of contrition and amendment in the criminal.

ment of death for murder, if every other part of the Bible had been silent upon the subject. When two of his disciples, actuated by the spirit of vindictive legislators, requested permission of him to call down fire from Heaven to consume the inhospitable Samaritans, he answered them "The Son of Man is not come to *destroy* men's *lives* but to save them." I wish these words composed the motto of the arms of every nation upon the face of the earth. They inculcate every duty that is calculated to preserve, restore, or prolong human life. They militate alike against war—and capital punishments—the objects of which, are the unprofitable destruction of the lives of men. How precious does a human life appear from these words, in the sight of heaven! Pause, Legislators, when you give your votes for inflicting the punishment of death for any crime. You frustrate in one instance, the design of the mission of the Son of God into the world, and thereby either deny his appearance in the flesh, or reject the truth of his gospel. You, moreover, strengthen by your conduct the arguments of the Deists against the particular doctrines of the Christian revelation. You do more, you preserve a bloody fragment of the Jewish institutions.—"The Son of Man came not to *destroy* men's lives, but to *save* them." Excellent words! I require no others to satisfy me of the truth and divine original of the Christian religion; and while I am able to place a finger, upon this text of scripture, I will not believe an angel from heaven, should he declare that the punishment of death, for *any* crime, was inculcated, or permitted by the spirit of the gospel.

The precious nature of human life in the eyes of the Saviour of mankind, appears further in the comparative value which he has placed upon it in the following words.[6] "For what is a man profited, if he shall gain the whole world, & lose his life, or what shall a man give in exchange for his *life*." I have rejected the word *soul* which is used in the common translation of this verse. The original word in the Greek, signifies *life*, and it is thus happily and justly translated in the verse which precedes it.

4. It has been said, that a man who has committed a murder, has discovered a malignity of heart, that renders him ever afterwards unfit to live in human society. This is by no means true in many,

---

[6] Matthew, x. v. 26.[Matthew xvi. 26]

and perhaps in most of the cases of murder. It is most frequently
the effect of a sudden gust of passion, and has sometimes been the
only stain of a well-spent, or inoffensive life. There are many crimes
which unfit a man much more for human society, than a single
murder; and there have been instances of murderers, who have
escaped, or bribed the laws of their country, who have afterwards
become peaceable and useful members of society. Let it not be supposed that I wish to palliate, by this remark, the enormity of murder.
Far from it. It is only because I view murder with such superlative
horror, that I wish to deprive our laws of the power of perpetuating
and encouraging it.

It has been said, that the confessions of murderers have, in many
instances, sanctioned the justice of their punishment. I do not wish
to lessen the influence of such vulgar errors as tend to prevent
crimes, but I will venture to declare, that many more murderers
escape discovery, than are detected, or punished.—Were I not afraid
of trespassing upon the patience of my readers, I might mention a
number of facts, in which circumstances of the most trifling nature
have become the means of detecting theft and forgery; from which
I could draw as strong proofs of the watchfulness of Providence
over the property of individuals, and the order of society, as have
been drawn from the detection of murder. I might mention
instances, likewise, of persons in whom conscience has produced
restitution for stolen goods, or confession of the justice of the
punishment which was inflicted for theft. Conscience and
knowledge always keep pace with each other, both with respect to
divine and human laws.

The acquiescence of murderers in the justice of their execution,
is the effect of prejudice and education. It cannot flow from a conscience acting in concert with reason or religion—for they both
speak a very different language.

The world has certainly undergone a material change for the
better within the last two hundred years. This change has been
produced chiefly, by the secret and unacknowledged influence of
Christianity upon the hearts of men. It is agreeable to trace the
effects of the Christian religion in the extirpation of slavery—in the
diminution of the number of capital punishments, and in the miti-
gation of the horrors of war. There was a time when masters possessed a power over the lives of their slaves. But Christianity has

deposed this power, and mankind begin to see every where that slavery is alike contrary to the interests of society, and the spirit of the gospel. There was a time when torture was part of the punishment of death, and when the number of capital crimes in Great Britain, amounted to one hundred and sixty-one.—Christianity has abolished the former, and reduced the latter to not more than six or seven. It has done more. It has confined, in some instances, capital punishments to the crime of murder—and in some countries it has abolished it altogether. The influence of Christianity upon the modes of war, has still been more remarkable. It is agreeable to trace its progress.

1st. In rescuing women and children from being the objects of the desolations of war, in common with men.

2dly. In preventing the destruction of captives taken in battle, in cold blood.

3dly. In protecting the peaceable husbandman from sharing in the carnage of war.

4thly. In producing an exchange of prisoners, instead of dooming them to perpetual slavery.

5thly. In avoiding the invasion or destruction, in certain cases, of private property.

6thly. In declaring all wars to be unlawful but such as are purely defensive.

This is the only tenure by which war now holds its place among Christians. It requires but little ingenuity to prove that a defensive war cannot be carried on successfully without offensive operations. Already the princes and nations of the world discover the struggles of opinion or conscience in their preparations for war. Witness the many national disputes which have been lately terminated in Europe by negociation, or mediation. Witness too, the establishment of the constitution of the United States without force or bloodshed. These events indicate an improving state of human affairs. They lead us to look forward with expectation to the time, when the weapons of war shall be changed into implements of husbandry, and when rapine and violence shall be no more. These events are the promised fruits of the gospel. If they do not come to pass, the prophets have deceived us. But if they do—war must be as contrary to the spirit of the gospel, as fraud, or murder, or any other of the vices which are reproved or extirpated by it.

P.S. Since the publication of this essay and the preceeding one, the Author has had the pleasure of seeing his principles reduced to practice in the State of Pennsylvania, in the abolition of the punishment of death for all crimes, (the highest degree of murder expected) and in private punishments being substituted to those which were public. The effects of this reformation in the penal laws of our state have been, a remarkable diminution of crimes of all kinds, and a great encrease of convictions in a given number of offenders. The expenses of the house appropriated to the punishment of criminals have been more than defrayed by the profits of their labor. Many of them have been reformed, and become useful members of society, and very few have relapsed into former habits of vice.

The Author is happy in adding, that a reformation in the penal laws of the states of New York and New Jersey has taken place, nearly similar to that which has been mentioned, in Pennsylvania.

It would be an act of injustice in this place not to acknowledge that the principles contained in the foregoing essays, would probably have never been realized, had they not been supported and enforced by the eloquence of the late William Bradford Esq. and the zeal of Caleb Lownes. To both these gentlemen, humanity and reason owe great obligations. Mr. Lownes has demonstrated by facts, the success of schemes of philanthrophy, once deemed visionary and impracticable. His plans for employing, and reforming his unfortunate fellow creatures in the Philadelphia prison, discover great knowledge of the œconomy of the body, and of the principles of action in the mind. To comprehend fully the ingenuity and benevolence of these plans, it will be necessary to visit the prison. There science and religion exhibit a triumph over vice and misery, infinitely more sublime and affecting, than all the monuments of ancient conquests. It is thus the father of the human race has decreed the ultimate extermination of all evil, viz. by manifestations of love to his fallen creatures. For the details of the discipline, order, products of labor, &c. of this prison, the reader is referred to two elegant pamphlets, the one by Mr. De Liancourt, of France, the other by Mr. Turnbull of South Carolinas.

July 4, 1797.

A PLAN OF A PEACE-OFFICE FOR THE UNITED STATES.

AMONG the defects which have been pointed out in the federal constitution by its antifederal enemies, it is much to be lamented that no person has taken notice of its total silence upon the subject of an office of the utmost importance to the welfare of the United States, that is, an *office* for promoting and preserving perpetual *peace* in our country.

It is to be hoped that no objection will be made to the establishment of such an office, while we are engaged in a war with the Indians, for as the *War-Office* of the United States was established in the *time of peace*, it is equally reasonable that a *Peace-Office* should be established in the *time of war*.

The plan of this office is as follows:

I. Let a Secretary of the Peace be appointed to preside in this office, who shall be perfectly free from all the present absurd and vulgar European prejudices upon the subject of government; let him be a genuine republican and a sincere Christian, for the principles of republicanism and Christianity are no less friendly to universal and perpetual peace, than they are to universal and equal liberty.

II. Let a power be given to this Secretary to establish and maintain free-schools in every city, village and township of the United States; and let him be made responsible for the talents, principles, and morals, of all his schoolmasters. Let the youth of our country be carefully instructed in reading, writing, arithmetic, and in the doctrines of a religion of some kind: the Christian religion should be preferred to all others; for it belongs to this religion exclusively to teach us not only to cultivate peace with men, but to forgive, nay more—to love our very enemies. It belongs to it further to teach us that the Supreme Being alone possesses a power to take away human life, and that we rebel against his laws, whenever we undertake to execute death in any way whatever upon any of his creatures.

III. Let every family in the United States be furnished at the public expense, by the Secretary of this office, with a copy of an American edition of the BIBLE. This measure has become the more necessary in our country, since the banishment of the bible, as a school-book, from most of the schools in the United States. Unless the price of this book be paid for by the public, there is reason to fear that in a few years it will be met with only in courts of justice or in magistrates' offices; and should the absurd mode of establishing truth by kissing this sacred book fall into disuse, it may probably, in the course of the next generation, be seen only as a curiosity on a shelf in a public museum.

IV. Let the following sentence be inscribed in letters of gold over the doors of every State and Court house in the United States.

THE SON OF MAN CAME INTO THE WORLD, NOT TO DESTROY MEN'S LIVES, BUT TO SAVE THEM.

V. To inspire a veneration for human life, and an horror at the shedding of human blood, let all those laws be repealed which authorise juries, judges, sheriffs, or hangmen to assume the resentments of individuals and to commit murder in cold blood in any case whatever. Until this reformation in our code of penal jurisprudence takes place, it will be in vain to attempt to introduce universal and perpetual peace in our country.

VI. To subdue that passion for war, which education, added to human depravity, have made universal, a familiarity with the instruments of death, as well as all military shows, should be carefully avoided. For which reason, militia laws should every where be repealed, and military dresses and military titles should be laid aside: reviews tend to lessen the horrors of a battle by connecting them with the charms of order; militia laws generate idleness and vice, and thereby produce the wars they are said to prevent; military dresses fascinate the minds of young men, and lead them from serious and useful professions; were there no *uniforms*, there would probably be no armies; lastly, military titles feed vanity, and keep up ideas in the mind which lessen a sense of the folly and miseries of war.

VII. In the last place, let a large room, adjoining the federal hall, be appropriated for transacting the business and preserving all the records of this *office*. Over the door of this room let there be a sign, on which the figures of a LAMB, a DOVE and an OLIVE BRANCH

should be painted, together with the following inscriptions in letters
of gold:

PEACE ON EARTH—GOOD-WILL TO MAN. AH! WHY WILL MEN FORGET THAT THEY ARE BRETHERN?

Within this apartment let there be a collection of ploughshares
and pruning-hooks made out of swords and spears; and on each of
the walls of the apartment, the following pictures as large as the life:

1. A lion eating straw with an ox, and an adder playing upon
the lips of a child.

2. An Indian boiling his venison in the same pot with a citizen
of Kentucky.

3. Lord Cornwallis and Tippoo Saib, under the shade of a
sycamore-tree in the East Indies, drinking Madeira wine together
out of the same decanter.

4. A group of French and Austrian soldiers dancing arm and
arm, under a bower erected in the neighbourhood of Mons.

5. A St. Domingo planter, a man of color, and a native of
Africa, legislating together in the same colonial assembly.[1]

To complete the entertainment of this delightful apartment, let
a group of young ladies, clad in white robes, assemble every day at
a certain hour, in a gallery to be erected for the purpose, and sing
odes, and hymns, and anthems in praise of the blessings of peace.
One of these songs should consist of the following lines.

> Peace o'er the world her olive wand extends,
> And white-rob'd innocence from heaven descends;
> All crimes shall cease, and ancient frauds shall fail,
> Returning justice lifts aloft her scale.

---

[1] At the time of writing this, there existed wars between the United States and
the American Indians, between the British nation and Tippoo Saib, between the
planters of St. Domingo and their African slaves, and between the French nation
and the emperor of Germany.

In order more deeply to affect the minds of the citizens of the United States with the blessings of peace, by *contrasting* them with the evils of war, let the following inscriptions be painted upon the sign, which is placed over the door of the War-Office.

1. An office for butchering the human species.
2. A Widow and Orphan making office.
3. A broken bone making office.
4. A Wooden leg making office.
5. An office for creating public and private vices.
6. An office for creating a public debt.
7. An office for creating speculators, stock Jobbers, and Bankrupts.
8. An office for creating famine.
9. An office for creating pestilential diseases.
10. An office for creating poverty, and the destruction of liberty, and national happiness.

In the lobby of this office let there be painted representations of all the common military instruments of death, also human skulls, broken bones, unburied and putrifying dead bodies, hospitals crouded with sick and wounded Soldiers, villages on fire, mothers in besieged towns eating the flesh of their children, ships sinking in the ocean, rivers dyed with blood, and extensive plains without a tree or fence, or any other object, but the ruins of deserted farm houses.

Above this group of woeful figures,—let the following words be inserted, in red characters to represent human blood,

"NATIONAL GLORY"

INFORMATION TO EUROPEANS WHO ARE DISPOSED TO MIGRATE TO THE UNITED STATES OF AMERICA. IN A LETTER TO A FRIEND IN GREAT BRITAIN.

AGREEABLY to your request contained in your letter of the 29th of August, 1789, I have at last sat down to communicate such facts to you, upon the subject of migration to this country, as have been the result of numerous enquiries and observation. I am aware that this subject has been handled in a masterly manner by Doctor Franklin, in his excellent little pamphlet, entitled "Advice to those who would wish to remove to America," but as that valuable little work is very general, and as many important changes have occurred in the affairs of the United States since its publication, I shall endeavour to comply with your wishes, by adding such things as have been omitted by the Doctor, and shall accommodate them to the present state of our country.

I shall begin this letter by mentioning the descriptions of people, who ought not to come to America.

I. Men of independent fortunes who can exist only in company, and who can converse only upon public amusements, should not think of settling in the United States. I have known several men of that character in this country, who have rambled from State to State, complaining of the dulness of each of them, and who have finally returned and renewed their former connexions and pleasures in Europe.

II. Literary men, who have no professional pursuits, will often languish in America, from the want of society. Our authors and scholars are generally men of business, and make their literary pursuits subservient to their interests. A lounger in book stores, breakfasting parties for the purpose of literary conversation, and long attic evenings, are as yet but little known in this country. Our companies are generally mixed, and conversation in them is a medley of ideas upon all subjects. They begin as in England with the weather—soon run into politics—now and then diverge into literature—and commonly conclude with facts relative to commerce, manufactures and agriculture, and the best means of acquiring and improving an estate. Men, who are philosophers or poets, without other pursuits, had better end their days in an old country.

III. The United States as yet afford but little encouragement to the professors of most of the fine arts. Painting and sculpture flourish chiefly in wealthy and luxurious countries. Our native American portrait painters who have not sought protection and encouragement in Great Britain, have been obliged to travel occasionally from one State of another in order to support themselves. The teachers of music have been more fortunate in America. A taste for this accomplishment prevails very generally in our large cities: and eminent masters in that art, who have arrived here since the peace, have received considerable sums of money by exercising their profession among us.

I shall now mention those descriptions of people, who may better their condition by coming to America.

I. To the cultivators of the earth the United States open the first asylum in the world. To insure the success and happiness of an European Farmer in our country, it is necessary to advise him either to purchase or to rent a farm which has undergone some improvement.

The business of settling a new tract of land, and that of improving a farm, are of a very different nature. The former must be effected by the native American, who is accustomed to the use of the axe and the grubbing hoe, and who possesses almost exclusively a knowledge of all the peculiar and nameless arts of self-preservation in the woods. I have known many instances of Europeans who have spent all their cash in unsuccessful attempts to force a settlement in the wilderness, and who have afterwards been exposed to poverty and distress at a great distance from friends and even neighbours. I would therefore advise all farmers with moderate capitals, to purchase or rent improved farms in the old settlements of our States. The price and rent of these farms are different in the different parts of the union. In Pennsylvania, the price of farms is regulated by the quality of the land—by the value or the improvements which are erected upon it—by their vicinity to sea ports and navigable water—and by the good or bad state of the roads which lead to them. There is a great variety, of course, in the price of farms: while some of them have been sold for five guineas—others have been sold at lower prices, down to one guinea, and even half a guinea per acre, according as they were varied by the above circumstances.

It is not expected that the whole price of a farm should be paid at the time of purchasing it. An half, a third, or a fourth, is all that is generally required. Bonds and mortgages are given for the remainder, (and sometimes without interest) payable in two, three, five, or even ten years.

The value of these farms has often been doubled and even trebled, in a few years, where the new mode of agriculture has been employed in cultivating them: so that a man with a moderate capital, may, in the course of fifteen years, become an opulent and independent freeholder.

If, notwithstanding what has been said of the difficulties of effecting an establishment in the woods, the low price of the new lands should tempt the European Farmer to settle in them, then let me add, that it can only be done by associating himself in a large company, under the direction of an active and intelligent American farmer. To secure even a company of European settlers from disappointment and want in the woods, it will be necessary to clear a few acres of land the year before, and to sow them with grain, in order to provide subsistance for the company, till they can provide for themselves, by clearing their own farms. The difficulties of establishing this new settlement, will be further lessened, if a few cabins, a grist and a saw mill be erected, at the same time the preparations are made for the temporary subsistance of the company. In this manner, most of the first settlements of the New England men have been made in this country. One great advantage, attending those mode of settling, is, a company may always carry with them a clergyman and a schoolmaster, of the same religion and language with themselves. If a settler in the woods should possess a taste for rural elegance, he may gratify it without any expense, by the manner of laying out his farm. He may shade his house by means of ancient and venerable forrest-trees. He may leave rows of them standing, to adorn his lanes and walks—or clusters of them on the high grounds of his fields, to shade his cattle. If he should fix upon any of those parts of our western country, which are covered with the sugar-trees, he may inclose a sufficient number of them to supply his family with sugar; and may confer upon them at the same time the order and beauty of a fine orchard. In this manner, a highly improved seat may be cut out of the woods in a few years, which will surpass both in elegance and value a farm in an old settlement, which has been for twenty years the subject of improvements in taste and agriculture. To contemplate a dwelling-house—a barn—stables—fields—meadows—an orchard—a garden, &c. which have been produced from original creation by the labour of a single life, is, I am told, to the proprietor of them, one of the highest pleasures the mind of man is capable of enjoying. But how much must this pleasure be increased, when the regularity of art is blended in the prospect, with the wildness and antiquity of nature?

It has been remarked in this country, that clearing the land of its woods, sometimes makes a new settlement unhealthy, by exposing its damp grounds to the action of the sun. To obviate this evil, it will be necessary for the settler either to drain and cultivate his low grounds, as soon as they are cleared, or to leave a body of trees between his dwelling house, and the spots from whence the morbid effluvia are derived. The last of these methods has, in no instance that I have heard of, failed of preserving whole families from such diseases as arise from damp or putrid exhalations.

To country gentlemen, who have been accustomed to live upon the income of a landed estate in Europe, it will be necessary to communicate the following information, viz. that farms, in consequence of the unproductive woodland, which is generally connected with them, seldom yield more than three or four per cent. a year in cash, except in the neighbourhood of large cities. Besides, from the facility with which money enough may be saved in a few years, to purchase land in this country, tenants will not accept of long leases: and hence they are not sufficiently interested in the farms they rent, to keep them in repair. If country gentlemen wish to derive the greatest advantage from laying out their money in lands, they must reside in their vicinity. A capital of five thousand guineas, invested in a number of contiguous farms, in an improved part of our country, and cultivated by tenants under the eye and direction of a landlord, would soon yield a greater income than double that sum would in most parts of Europe. The landlord in this case must frequently visit and inspect the state of each of his farms: and now and then he must stop to repair a bridge or a fence in his excursions through them. He must receive all his rents in the produce of the farms. If the tenant find his own stock, he will pay half of all the grain he raises, and sometimes a certain proportion of vegetables and live stock, to his landlord. The division of the grain is generally made in the field, in sheaves or stacks, which are carried home to be thrashed in the barn of the landlord. An estated gentleman, who can reconcile himself to this kind of life, may be both happy and useful. He may instruct his tenants by his example, as well as precepts in the new modes of husbandry: he may teach them the art and advantages of gardening: he may inspire them with habits of sobriety, industry, and œconomy; and thereby become the father and protector of a dependant and affectionate neighbourhood. After a busy summer and autumn, he may pass his winters in polished society in any of our cities, and in many of our country villages.

But should he be disinclined to such extensive scenes of business, he may confine his purchases and labours to a single farm, and secure his superfluous cash in bonds and mortgages, which will yield him six per cent.

Under this head, it is proper to mention, that the agricultural life begins to maintain in the United States, the same rank that it has long maintained in Great Britain. Many gentlemen of education among us have quitted liberal professions, and have proved, by their success in farming, that philosophy is in no business more useful or profitable, than in agriculture.

II. MECHANICS and MANUFACTURERS, of every description, will find certain encouragement in the United States. During the connection of this country with Great Britain, we were taught to believe that agriculture and commerce should be the only pursuits of the Americans: but experiments and reflexion have taught us, that our country abounds with resources for manufactures of all kinds: and that most of them may be conducted with great advantage in all the states. We are already nearly independent of the whole world for ironwork, paper, and malt liquors: and great progress has been made in the manufacturies of glass, pot-ash, and cloths of all kinds. The commercial habits of our citizens have as yet prevented their employing large capitals in those manufacturies: but I am persuaded that if a few European adventurers would embark in them with capitals equal to the demand for those manufactures, they would soon find an immense profit in their speculations. A single farmer in the state of New York, with a capital of five thousand pounds, has cleared one thousand a year by the manufacture of pot-ash alone.

Those mechanical arts, which are accommodated to the infant and simple state of a country, will bid fairest to succeed among us. Every art, connected with cultivating the earth—building houses and ships, and feeding and clothing the body, will meet with encouragement in this country. The prices of provisions are so different in the different states, and even in the different parts of the same state, and vary so much with the plenty and scarcity of money, that it would be difficult to give you such an account of them as would be useful. I need only remark, that the disproportion between the price of labour and of provisions, is much greater in every part of the United States, than in any part of Europe: and hence our tradesmen every where eat meat and butter every day: and most of them realize the wish of Henry IV. of France, for the peasants of his kingdom, by dining not only once, but two or three times, upon poultry, in every week of the year.

It is a singular fact in the history of the mechanical arts in this country, that the same arts seldom descend from father to son. Such are the profits of even the humblest of them, that the sons of mechanics generally rise from the lower to the more respectable occupations: and thus their families gradually ascend to the first ranks in society among us. The influence, which the prospects of wealth and consequence have in invigorating industry in every line of mechanical business, is very great. Many of the first men in America, are the sons of reputable mechanics or farmers. But I may go farther, and add, that many men, who distinguished themselves both in the cabinet and field, in the late war, had been mechanics. I know the British officers treated the American cause with contempt, from this circumstance: but the event of the war shewed, that the confidence of America was not misplaced in that body of citizens.

III. LABOURERS may depend upon constant employment in the United States, both in our towns and in the country. When they work by the day, they receive high wages: but these are seldom continued through the whole year. A labourer receives annually, with his boarding, washing, and lodging, from fifteen to eighteen guineas, in the middle states. It is agreeable to observe this class of men frequently raised by their industry from their humble stations, into the upper ranks of life, in the course of twenty or thirty years.

IV. PERSONS who are willing to indent themselves as servants for a few years, will find that humble station no obstacle to a future establishment in our country. Many men, who came to America in that capacity, are now in affluent circumstances. Their former situation, where they have behaved well, does not preclude them from forming respectable connections in marriage, nor from sharing, if otherwise qualified, in the offices of our country.

V. The United States continue to afford encouragement to gentlemen of the *learned professions*, provided they be prudent in their deportment, and of sufficient knowledge: for since the establishment of colleges and schools of learning in all our states, the same degrees of learning will not succeed among us, which succeeded fifty years ago.

Several lawyers and physicians, who have arrived here since the peace, are now in good business: and many clergymen, natives of England, Scotland, and Ireland, are comfortably settled in good' parishes. A minister of the gospel in a country place must not expect to have all his salary paid in cash: but he will notwithstanding seldom fail of obtaining a good subsistance from his congregation. They will furnish his table with a portion of all the live stock they raise for their own use: they will shoe his horses—repair his implements of husbandry, and assist him in gathering in his harvests, and in many other parts of the business of his farm. From these aids, with now and then a little cash, a clergyman may not only live well but, in the course of his life, may accumulate an handsome estate for his children. This will more certainly happen, if he can redeem time enough from his parochial duties, and the care of his farm, to teach a school. The people of America are of all sects: but the greatest part of them are of the independent, presbyterian, episcopal, baptist, and methodist denominations. The principles held by each of these societies in America are the same as those which are held by the protestant churches in Europe, from which they derive their origin.

VI. SCHOOLMASTERS of good capacities and fair characters may expect to meet with encouragement in the middle and southern states. They will succeed better, if they confine their instructions to reading, writing, English grammar, and the sciences of number and quantity. These branches of literature are of general necessity and utility: and of course every township will furnish scholars enough for the maintenance of a schoolmaster. Many young men have risen by means of the connexions they have formed in this useful employment, to rank and consequence in the learned professions in every part of this country.

From this account of the United States, you will easily perceive, that they are a hot-bed for industry and genius in almost every human pursuit. It is inconceivable how many useful discoveries necessity has produced within these few years, in agriculture and manufactures, in our country. The same necessity has produced a versatility of genius among our citizens: hence we frequently meet with men who have exercised two or three different occupations or professions in the course of their lives, according to the influence which interest, accident, or local circumstances have had upon them. I know that the peculiarities, which have been mentioned in the American character, strike an European, who has been accustomed to consider man as a creature of habit, formed by long established governments, and hereditary customs, as so many deviations from propriety and order. But a wise man, who knows that national characters arise from circumstances, will view these peculiarities without surprise, and attribute them wholly to the present state of manners, society, and government in America.

From the numerous competitions in every branch of business in Europe, success in any pursuit, may be looked upon in the same light as a prize in a lottery. But the case is widely different in America. Here there is room enough for every human talent and virtue to expand and flourish. This is so invariably true, that I believe there is not an instance to be found, of an industrious, frugal prudent European, with sober manners, who has not been successful in business, in this country.

As a further inducement to Europeans to transport themselves across the Ocean, I am obliged to mention a fact that does little honour to the native American; and that is, in all competitions for business, where success depends upon industry, the European is generally preferred. Indeed, such is the facility with which property is acquired, that where it does not operate as a stimulus to promote ambition, it is sometimes accompanied by a relaxation of industry in proportion to the number of years or generations which interpose between the founder of an American family and his posterity. This preference of European mechanics arises, likewise, from the improvements in the different arts, which are from time to time imported by them into our country. To these facts I am happy in being able to add, that the years of anarchy, which proved so disgusting to the Europeans who arrived among us immediately after the peace, are now at an end, and that the United States have at last adopted a national government which unites with the vigour of monarchy and the stability of aristocracy, all the freedom of a simple republic. Its influence already in invigorating industry, and reviving credit, is universal. There are several peculiarities in this government, which cannot fail of being agreeable to Europeans, who are disposed to settle in America.

1. The equal share of power it holds forth to men of every religious sect. As the first fruits of this perfection in our government, we already see three gentlemen of the Roman Catholic church, members of the legislature of the United States.

2. Birth in America is not required for holding either power or office in the federal government, except that of President of the United States. In consequence of this principle of justice, not only in the national government, but in all our state constitutions, we daily see the natives of Britain, Ireland, Germany, advanced to the most respectable employments in our country.

3. By a late act of congress, only two years residence in the United States are necessary to entitle foreigners of good character to all the privileges of citizenship. Even that short period of time has been found sufficient to give strangers a visible interest in the stability and freedom of our governments.[1]

It is agreeable to observe the influence which our republican governments have already had upon the tempers and manners of our citizens. Amusement is every where giving way to business: and local politeness is yielding to universal civility. We differ about forms and modes in politics: but this difference begins to submit to the restraints of moral and social obligation. Order and tranquility appear to be the natural consequence of a well-balanced republic: for where men can remove the evils of their governments by frequent elections, they will seldom appeal to the less certain remedies

---

[1] By a law passed since the above, five years residence are necessary to entitle a foreigner to citizenship.

of mobs or arms. It is with singular pleasure that I can add further, that notwithstanding the virulence of our dissensions about independence and the federal government, there is now scarcely a citizen of the United States, who is not satisfied with both, and who does not believe this country to be in a happier and safer situation, than it was, in the most flourishing years of its dependence upon Great Britain.

The encouragement held out to European emigrants is not the same in all the states. New England, New York, and New Jersey, being nearly filled with cultivators of the earth, afford encouragement chiefly to mechanicks and labourers. The inhabitants of New England have far surpassed the inhabitants of the other states, in the establishment of numerous and profitable manufactories. These wonderful people discover the same degrees of industry in cultivating the arts of peace, they did of enterprize and perseverance, in the late war. They already export large quantities of wrought iron, hats, women's shoes, cheese, and linen and woolen cloth. The state of New-York has likewise discovered a laudable spirit for manufacturers and domestic improvements. European artists, therefore, cannot fail of meeting with encouragement in each of the above states.

Pennsylvania affords an equal asylum to all the descriptions of people that have been mentioned, under the second head of this letter. Agriculture, manufactures, and many of the liberal arts seem to vie with each other for pre-eminence in this state. Each of them is under the patronage of numerous and respectable societies. No state in the union affords greater resources for ship building, malt liquors, maple sugar, sail cloth, iron work, wooden and linen clothes, potash, and glass. Coal, likewise, abounds on the shores of the Susquehanna, a large river which runs through half the state. The variety of sects and nations, which compose the inhabitants of this state, has hitherto prevented our having any steady traits in our character. We possess the virtues and weaknesses of most of the sects and nations of Europe. But this variety has produced such a collision in opinions and interests, as has greatly favoured the progress of genius in every art and science. We have been accused of being factious by our sister states. This must be ascribed chiefly to our late state constitution, which was established by violence in the beginning of the late war, and which was never assented to by a majority of the people. But that majority have at length asserted their power. A convention, composed of an equal representation of the people, has met and formed a new constitution, which comprehends in it every principle of liberty and just government. From the excellency of this constitution—from the harmony it has restored to our citizens—from the central situation of our state—from the number and courses of our rivers—from the facility with which we are able to draw the resources of the lakes to the Delaware—from the wealth of our capital—and above all, from the industry and sober habits of our citizens—there can be no doubt that Pennsylvania will always maintain the first rank, for national prosperity and happiness, in the United States.

There is one circumstance, peculiar in a great degree to Pennsylvania, which cannot fail of directing the eyes of the inhabitants of several of the European nations to this state—and that is, the natives of Britain, Ireland, Germany, France, Switzerland, and Holland, may here meet with their former fellow subjects, and receive from them that welcome and assistance, which are the natural consequences of the tie of country. So strongly does this principle operate in America, that the natives of Germany and Ireland have formed themselves into societies in the city of Philadelphia, for the express purpose of protecting, advising, and assisting their country-men, as soon as they set their feet upon the shores of Pennsylvania.

It has been said, that the lands in Pennsylvania are dearer than in some of our sister states. They sell, it is true, for a greater nominal sum, than the lands of the neighbouring states: but in the end, they are much cheaper. The soil is deep, rich, and durable, and from the superior industry and skill of our farmers, our lands are more productive than those of our neighbours; hence their higher price; for the price of lands is always in a ratio to their quality, produce and situation: hence likewise, we are able to tell the value of a farm in any part of the state, by first finding out the quantity of grain an acre will produce, and the price of this grain at the nearest mill or store, making some little allowance for the improvements which are connected with the farm. This remark is so universally true, that a farmer never mistakes the application of it in purchasing land. There is a certain instinct, which governs in all purchases and sales of farms, and which arises out of the principle I have mentioned: it is in general as accurate, as if it arose out of the nicest calculation. It is from an ignorance or neglect of this principle, that so many of our citizens have migrated to Kentucky, under a delusive expectation of purchasing lands cheaper than in the old states. They are in fact often much dearer when you estimate their price by the profit of the grain which is cultivated upon them. For instance, an acre of land in Kentucky, which sells for a quarter of a guinea, and yields 30 bushels of corn, at four pence sterling per bushel, is dearer than land of the same quality in Pennsylvania, at a guinea per acre, that yields the same quantity of corn, which can be sold at the nearest mill or store for two shillings sterl. per bushel. To cure this passion for migrating to the waters of the Ohio, there is but one remedy, and that is, to open the navigation of the Mississippi. This, by raising the price of produce, will raise the value of land so high, as to destroy the balance of attraction to that country. This truth is at present a speculative one, but I hope it will be reduced to practice before the waters of the Ohio and Mississippi have been dyed with the blood of two or three hundred thousand men.

The states to the southward of Pennsylvania possess immense resources for political happiness: but while they tolerate negro slavery, they can never be an agreeable retreat for an European. This objection applies chiefly to the sea coasts of those states; for in the western parts of them, the land is cultivated chiefly by freemen. The soil and climate of the extensive western country of those states is kind and mild to a very great degree. There Europeans may prosper and be happy.

Thus, Sir, have I complied in a few words with your request. In communicating many of the facts contained in this letter, I have not considered you simply as a citizen of London, or a subject of the crown of Britain. The whole family of mankind, I know are your brethren; and if men be happy I am sure it is a matter of indifference to you, whether they enjoy their happiness on this side, or on the other side of the Atlantic ocean.

From a review of the facts that have been mentioned, you will perceive that the present is the age of reason and action in America. To our posterity we must bequeath the cultivation of the fine arts and the pleasures of taste and sentiment. The foreigners who have visited and described our country without making allowances for those peculiarities which arise from our present state of society, have done as little honour to their understandings, as they have done to human nature. Nor have those Europeans discovered more wisdom, who have blended with the American character, the accidental disorders, which were the offspring of our late public commotions. They resembled the swelling of the sea, which succeeds a storm. At present, they have as perfectly subsided as the disorders produced by the civil wars in England, in the last century.

It is somewhat remarkable that in every age, great inventions and great revolutions in human affairs have taken place in a quick succession to each other. The many curious machines for lessening labour, which have lately been discovered in Europe, will necessarily throw many thousand artificers out of employment. Perhaps the late successful application of the powers of fire and water to mechanical purposes in your country, was delayed until the present time, only that the sanctuary of our national government might be perfectly prepared to receive and protect those industrious bodies of people, who formerly lived by the labour of their hands, and who might otherwise become a burden to the countries in which they had been deprived of the means of supporting themselves. Perhaps, too, the revolutions, which are now going forward in several of the governments on the continent of Europe, have occurred at the present juncture for a purpose equally wise and benevolent. The first effect of the establishment of freedom in those countries, will be to promote population, by reducing taxes, disbanding standing armies, and abolishing the vows and practices of celibacy: for I take it for granted that military institutions in the time of peace, and monasteries of all kinds, must yield to the present force and cultivated state of human reason, in those countries, which are now the theatres of revolutions in favour of liberty. This increase of population will require an increase of territory, which must be sought for in the United States: for it is not probable that men who have once tasted of the sweets of liberty will ever think of transporting themselves to any other country. This output for supernumerary inhabitants from the nations of Europe, will eventually promote their interests and prosperity: for when a country is so much crouded with people, that the price of the means of subsistence is beyond the ratio of their industry, marriages are restrained: but when emigration to a certain degree takes place, the balance between the means of subsistence and industry is restored, and population thereby revived. Of the truth of this principle there are many proofs in the old counties of all the American states. Population has constantly been advanced in them by the migration of their inhabitants to new or distant settlements.

In spite of all the little systems of narrow politicians, it is an eternal truth, that universal happiness is universal interest. The divine government of our world would admit of a controversy, if men, by acquiring moral or political happiness, in one part, added to the misery of the inhabitants of another part, of our globe.

I shall conclude this long letter by the two following remarks:

I. If freedom, joined with the facility of acquiring the means of subsistence, have such an influence upon population—and if existence be a title to happiness—then think, sir, what an ocean of additional happiness will be created, by the influence which migration to the free and extensive territories of the United States will have, upon the numbers of mankind.

II. If wars have been promoted in all ages and countries, by an over proportion of inhabitants to the means of easy subsistence, then think, sir, what an influence upon the means of supporting human life, migration to America, and the immense increase of the productions of the earth, by the late improvements in agriculture, will probably have, in lessening the temptations and resources of nations to carry on war. The promises of heaven are often accomplished by means in which there is no departure from the common operations of nature. If the events, which have been alluded to, should contribute in any degree to put an end to wars, it will furnish a noble triumph to your society? by shewing how much enlightened policy, and national happiness, are connected with the dictates of christianity.

I am,

Dear sir,

With great respect,

And sincere regard,

Yours very affectionately,

Philadelphia, April 16, 1790.

---

² The gentleman to whom this letter is addressed, is of the society of the people called quakers.

AN ACCOUNT OF THE PROGRESS OF POPULATION, AGRICULTURE, MANNERS, AND GOVERNMENT IN PENNSYLVANIA, IN A LETTER TO A FRIEND IN ENGLAND.

DEAR SIR,

Whatever tends to unfold *facts* in the history of the human species, must be interesting to a curious enquirer.—The manner of settling a new country, exhibits a view of the human mind so foreign to the views of it which have been taken for many centuries in Europe, that I flatter myself the following account of the progress of population, agriculture, manners, and government in Pennsylvania will be acceptable to you. I have chosen to confine myself in the present letter to Pennsylvania only, that all the information I shall give you may be derived from my own knowledge and observations.

The *first* settler in the woods is generally a man who has outlived his credit or fortune in the cultivated parts of the State. His time for migrating is in the month of April. His first object is to build a small cabbin of rough logs for himself and family. The floor of this cabbin is of earth, the roof is of split logs—the light is received through the door, and, in some instances, through a small window made of greased paper. A coarser building adjoining this cabbin affords a shelter to a cow and a pair of poor horses. The labor of erecting these buildings is succeeded by killing the trees on a few acres of ground near his cabbin; this is done by cutting a circle round the trees, two or three feet from the ground. The ground around these trees is then ploughed and Indian-corn planted in it. The season for planting this grain is about the 20th of May—It grows generally on new ground with but little cultivation, and yields in the month of October following, from forty to fifty bushels by the acre. After the first of September it affords a good deal of nourishment to his family, in its green or unripe state, in the form of what is called *roasting ears*. His family is fed during the summer by a small quantity of grain which he carries with him, and by fish and game. His cows and horses feed upon wild grass, or the succulent twigs of the woods. For the first year he endures a great deal of distress from hunger—cold—and a variety of accidental causes, but he seldom complains or sinks under them. As he lives in the neighbourhood of Indians, he soon acquires a strong tincture of their manners. His exertions, while they continue, are violent; but they are succeeded by long intervals of rest. His pleasures consist chiefly in fishing and hunting. He loves spirituous liquors, and he eats, drinks and sleeps in dirt and rags in his little cabbin. In his intercourse with the world he manifests all the arts which characterize the Indians of our country. In this situation he passes two or three years. In proportion as population increases around him, he becomes uneasy and dissatisfied. Formerly his cattle ranged at large, but now his neighbours call upon him to confine them within fences, to prevent their trespassing upon their fields of grain. Formerly he fed his family with wild animals, but these, which fly from the face of man, now cease to afford him an easy subsistence, and he is compelled to raise domestic animals for the support of his family. Above all, he revolts against the operation of laws. He cannot bear to surrender up a single natural right for all the benefits of government,—and therefore he abandons his little settlement, and seeks a retreat in the woods, where he again submits to all the toils which have been mentioned. There are instances of many men who have broken ground on bare creation, not less than four different times in this way, in different and more advanced parts of the State. It has been remarked, that the flight of this class of people is always increased by the preaching of the gospel. This will not surprise us when we consider how opposite its precepts are to their licentious manner of living. If our first settler was the owner of the spot of land which he began to cultivate, he sells it at a considerable profit to his successor; but if (as is oftner the case) he was a tenant to some rich landholder, he abandons it in debt; however, the small improvements he leaves behind him, generally make it an object of immediate demand to a *second* species of settler.

This species of settler is generally a man of some property,—he pays one third or one fourth part in cash for his plantation, which consists of three or four hundred acres, and the rest in gales or instalments, as it is called here; that is, a certain sum yearly, without interest, 'till the whole is paid. The first object of this settler is to build an addition to his cabbin; this is done with hewed logs: and as saw-mills generally follow settlements, his floors are made of boards; his roof is made of what are called clapboards, which are a kind of coarse shingles, split out of short oak logs. This house is divided by two floors, on each of which are two rooms: under the whole is a cellar walled with stone. The cabbin serves as kitchen to this house. His next object is to clear a little meadow ground, and plant an orchard of two or three hundred apple trees. His stable is likewise enlarged; and, in the course of a year or two, he builds a large log barn, the roof of which is commonly thatched with rye straw: he moreover encreases the quantity of his arable land; and, instead of cultivating Indian corn alone, he raises a quantity of wheat and rye: the latter is cultivated chiefly for the purpose of being distilled into whiskey. This species of settler by no means extracts all from the earth, which it is capable of giving. His fields yield but a scanty increase, owing to the ground not being sufficiently ploughed. The hopes of the year are often blasted by his cattle breaking through his half made fences, and destroying his grain. His horses perform but half the labor that might be expected from them, if they were better fed; and his cattle often die in the spring from the want of provision, and the delay of grass. His house, as well as his farm, bear many marks of a weak tone of mind. His windows are unglazed, or, if they have had glass in them, the ruins of it are supplied with old hats or pillows. This species of settler is seldom a good member of civil or religious society: with a large portion of a hereditary mechanical kind of religion, he neglects to contribute sufficiently towards building a church, or maintaining a regular administration of the ordinances of the gospel: he is equally indisposed to support civil government: with high ideas of liberty, he refuses to bear his proportion of the debt contracted by its establishment in our country: he delights chiefly in company—sometimes drinks spirituous liquors to excess—will spend a day or two in every week, in attending political meetings; and, thus, he contracts debts which, (if he cannot discharge in a depreciated paper currency) compel him to sell his plantation, generally in the course of a few years, to the *third* and last species of settler.

This species of settler is commonly a man of property and good character—sometimes he is the son of a wealthy farmer in one of the interior and ancient counties of the state. His first object is to convert every spot of ground, over which he is able to draw water, into meadow: where this cannot be done, he selects the most fertile spots on the farm, and devotes it by manure to that purpose. His next object is to build a barn, which he prefers of stone. This building is, in some instances, 100 feet in front, and 40 in depth: it is made very compact, so as to shut out the cold in winter; for our farmers find that their horses and cattle, when kept warm, do not require near as much food, as when they are exposed to the cold. He uses œconomy, likewise, in the consumption of his wood. Hence he keeps himself warm in winter, by means of stoves, which save an immense deal of labour to himself and his horses, in cutting and hawling wood in cold and wet weather. His fences are every where repaired, so as to secure his grain from his own and his neighbour's cattle. But further, he increases the number of the articles of his cultivation, and, instead of raising corn, wheat and rye alone, he raises oats, buckwheat (the fagopyrum of Linnaeus), and spelts. Near his house, he allots an acre or two of ground for a garden, in which he raises a large quantity of cabbage and potatoes. His newly cleared fields, afford him every year a large increase of turnips. Over the spring which supplies him with water, he builds a milk-house and over this, in some instances, he builds a smoke house; he likewise adds to the number, and improves the quality of his fruit trees:—His sons work by his side all the year and his wife and daughter forsake the dairy and the spinning wheel, to share with him in the toils of harvest. The last object of his industry is to build a dwelling house. This business is sometimes effected in the course of his life, but is oftener bequeathed to his son, or the inheritor of his plantation: and hence we have a common saying among our best farmers, "that a son should always begin where his father left off;" that is, he should begin his improvements, by building a commodious dwelling-house, suited to the improvements and value of the plantation. This dwelling-house is generally built of stone—it is large, convenient, and filled with useful and substantial furniture— It sometimes adjoins the house of the second settler, but is frequently placed at a little distance from it. The horses and cattle of this species of settler, bear marks in their strength, fat and fruitfulness—of their being plentifully fed and carefully kept. His table abounds with a variety of the best provisions—his very kitchen flows with milk and honey—beer, cyder, and home made wine are the usual drinks of his family: the greatest part of the cloathing of his family is manufactured by his wife and daughters:

in proportion as he encreases in wealth, he values the protection of laws: hence he punctually pays his taxes towards the support of government. Schools and churches likewise, as the means of promoting order and happiness in society, derive a due support from him: for benevolence and public spirit, as to these objects, are the natural offspring of affluence and independence. Of this class of settlers are two-thirds of the farmers of Pennsylvania. These are the men to whom Pennsylvania owes her ancient fame and consequence. If they possess less refinement than their southern neighbours, who cultivate their land with slaves, they possess more republican virtue. It was from the farms cultivated by these men, that the American and French armies were chiefly fed with bread during the late revolution; and it was from the produce of these farms, that those millions of dollars were obtained from the Havanna after the year 1780, which laid the foundation of the bank of North America, and which fed and cloathed the American army, till the peace of Paris.—This is a short account of the happiness of a Pennsylvania farmer.—To this happiness our state invites men of every religion and country.

We do not pretend to offer emigrants the pleasures of Arcadia—It is enough if affluence, independence, and happiness are ensured to patience, industry, and labour. The moderate price of land,[1] the credit which arises from prudence, and the safety from our courts of law, of every species of property, render the blessings which I have described, objects within the reach of every man.

---

[1] The unoccupied lands are sold by the state for about six guineas inclusive of all charges, per hundred acres. But as most of the lands that are settled, are procured from persons who had purchased them from the state, they are sold to the first settler for a much higher price. The quality of the soil—its vicinity to mills, court-houses, places of worship, and navigable water: the distance of land-carriage to the sea-ports of Philadelphia or Baltimore, and the nature of the roads, all influence the price of land to the first settler. The quantity of cleared land, and the nature of the improvements, added to all of the above circumstances, influence the price of farms to the second and third settlers. Hence the price of land to the first settlers is from a quarter of a guinea to two guineas per acre; and the price of farms is from one guinea to ten guineas per acre, to the second and third settlers, according as the land is varied by the before-mentioned circumstances. When the first settler is unable to purchase, he often takes a tract of land for seven years on a lease, and contracts instead of paying a rent in cash, to clear 50 acres of land, to build a log cabbin, and a barn, and to plant an orchard on it. This tract, after the expiration of this lease, sells or rents for a considerable profit.

From a review of the three different species of settlers, it appears, that there are certain regular stages which mark the progress from the savage to civilized life. The first settler is nearly related to an Indian in his manners—In the second, the Indian manners are more diluted: It is in the third species of settlers only, that we behold civilization completed—It is to the third species of settlers only, that it is proper to apply the term of *farmers*. While we record the vices of the first and second settlers, it is but just to mention their virtues likewise.—Their mutual wants produce mutual dependence: hence they are kind and friendly to each other—their solitary situation makes visitors agreeable to them;—hence they are hospitable to strangers: their want of money, (for they raise but little more than is necessary to support their families) has made it necessary for them to associate for the purposes of building houses, cutting their grain, and the like:—This they do in turns for each other, without any other pay than the pleasures which usually attend a country frolic—Perhaps what I have called virtues are rather *qualities*, arising from necessity, and the peculiar state of society in which these people live.—Virtue should, in all cases, be the offspring of principle.

I do not pretend to say, that this mode of settling farms in Pennsylvania is universal—I have known some instances where the first settler has performed the improvements of the second, and yielded to the third. I have known a few instances likewise, of men of enterprizing spirits, who have settled in the wilderness, and who, in the course of a single life, have advanced through all the intermediate stages of improvement that I have mentioned and produced all those conveniences which have been ascribed to the third species of settlers; thereby resembling, in their exploits, not only the pioneers and light-infantry, but the main body of an army. There are instances likewise, where the first settlement has been improved by the same family, in hereditary succession, 'till it has reached the third stage of cultivation. There are many spacious stone houses and highly cultivated farms in the neighbouring counties of the city of Philadelphia, which are possessed by the grandsons and great-grandsons of men who accompanied William Penn across the ocean, and who laid the foundation of the present improvements of their posterity, in such cabbins as have been described.

This passion for migration which I have described, will appear strange to an European. To see men turn their backs upon the houses in which they drew their first breath—upon the church in which they were dedicated to God—upon the graves of their ancestors—upon the friends and companions of their youth—and upon all the pleasures of cultivated society, and exposing themselves to all the hardships and accidents of subduing the earth, and thereby establishing settlements in a wilderness, must strike a philosopher on your side the water, as a picture of human nature that runs counter to the usual habits and principles of action in man. But this passion, strange and new as it appears, is wisely calculated for the extention of population in America: and this it does, not only by promoting the increase of the human species in new settlements, but in the old settlements likewise. While the degrees of industry and knowledge in agriculture, in our country, are proportioned to farms of from 75 to 300 acres, there will be a languor in population, as soon as farmers multiply beyond the number of farms of the above dimensions. To remove this languor, which is kept alike by the increase of the price, and the division of farms, a migration of part of the community becomes absolutely necessary. And as this part of the community often consists of the idle and extravagant, who eat without working, their removal, by increasing the facility of subsistence to the frugal and industrious who remain behind, naturally increases the number of people, just as the cutting off the suckers of an apple-tree increases the size of the tree, and the quantity of fruit.

I have only to add upon this subject, that the migrants from Pennsylvania always travel to the southward. The soil and climate of the western parts of Virginia, North and South-Carolina, and Georgia, afford a more easy support to lazy farmers, than the stubborn but durable soil of Pennsylvania.—Here, our ground requires deep and repeated plowing to render it fruitful—there, scratching the ground once or twice affords tolerable crops. In Pennsylvania, the length and coldness of the winter make it necessary for the farmers to bestow a large share of their labour in providing for and feeding their cattle; but in the southern states, cattle find pasture during the greatest part of the winter, in the fields or woods. For these reasons, the greatest part of the western counties of the States, that have been mentioned, are settled by original inhabitants from Pennsylvania. During the late war, the militia of Orange county, in North Carolina, were enrolled, and their number amounted to 3,500, every man of whom had migrated from Pennsylvania. From this you will see, that our State is the great outport of the United States for Europeans; and that, after performing the office of a sieve by detaining all those people who possess the stamina of industry and virtue, it allows a passage to the rest, to those States which are accommodated to their habits of indolence.

I shall conclude this letter by remarking, that in the mode of extending population and agriculture, which I have described, we behold a new species of war. The *third* settler may be viewed as a conqueror. The weapons with which he atchieves his conquests, are the implements of husbandry: and the virtues which direct them, are industry and economy. Idleness—extravagance—and ignorance fly before him. Happy would it be for mankind, if the kings of Europe would adopt this mode of extending their territories: it would soon put an end to the dreadful connection, which has existed in every age, between war and poverty, and between conquest and desolation.

> With great respect,
> I have the honor to be,
> Sir,
> Your most obedient
> humble servant.

AN ACCOUNT OF THE MANNERS OF THE GERMAN INHABITANTS OF PENNSYLVANIA.

THE state of Pennsylvania is so much indebted for her prosperity and reputation, to the German part of her citizens, that a short account of their manners may, perhaps, be useful and agreeable to their fellow citizens in every part of the United States.

The aged Germans, and the ancestors of those who are young, migrated chiefly from the Palatinate; from Alsace, Swabia, Saxony, and Switzerland: but natives of every principality and dukedom, in Germany, are to be found in different parts of the state. They brought but little property with them. A few pieces of gold or silver coin, a chest filled with clothes, a bible, and a prayer or an hymn book constituted the whole stock of most of them. Many of them bound themselves, or one or more of their children, to masters after their arrival, for four, five, or seven years, in order to pay for their passages across the ocean. A clergyman always accompanied them when they came in large bodies.

The principal part of them were farmers; but there were many mechanics, who brought with them a knowledge of those arts which are necessary and useful in all countries. These mechanics were chiefly weavers, taylors, tanners, shoemakers, comb-makers, smiths of all kinds, butcherrs, papermakers, watch makers and sugar bakers. I shall begin this account of the German inhabitants of Pennsylvania, by describing the manners of the German farmers.

This body of citizens are not only industrious and frugal, but skilful cultivators of the earth. I shall enumerate a few particulars, in which they differ from most of the other farmers of Pennsylvania.

1st. In settling a tract of land, they always provide large and suitable accommodations for their horses and cattle, before they lay out much money in building a house for themselves. The barn and the stables are generally under one roof, and contrived in such a manner as to enable them to feed their horses and cattle, and to remove their dung, with as little trouble as possible. The first dwelling house upon this farm is small, and built of logs. It generally lasts the life time of the first settler of a tract of land; and hence they have a saying, that "a son should always begin his improvements where his father left off,"—that is, by building a large and convenient stone house.

2d. They always prefer good land or that land on which there is a large quantity of meadow ground. From an attention to the cultivation of grass, they often double the value of an old farm in a few years, and grow rich on farms, on which their predecessors of whom they purchased them, have nearly starved. They prefer purchasing farms with some improvements to settling on a new tract of land.

3d. In clearing new land, they do not girdle the trees simply, and leave them to perish in the ground, as is the custom of their English or Irish neighbours; but they generally cut down and burn them. In destroying under-wood and bushes, they generally grub them out of the ground; by which means a field is as fit for cultivation the second year after it is cleared, as it is in twenty years afterwards. The advantages of this mode of clearing, consist in the immediate product of the field, and in the greater facility with which it is ploughed, harrowed and reaped. The expense of repairing a plough, which is often broken two or three times in a year by small stumps concealed in the ground, is often greater than the extraordinary expense of grubbing the same field completely, in clearing it.

4th. They feed their horses and cows, of which they keep only a small number, in such a manner, that the former perform twice the labour of those horses, and the latter yield twice the quantity of milk of those cows, that are less plentifully fed. There is great œconomy in this practice, especially in a country where so much of the labour of a farmer is necessary to support his domestic animals. A German horse is known in every part of the state: indeed he seems to "feel with his lord, the pleasure and the pride" of his extraordinary size or fat.

5th. The fences of a German farm are generally high, and well built; so that his fields seldom suffer from the inroads of his own or his neighbours, horses, cattle, hogs, or sheep.

6th. The German farmers are great œconomists of their *wood*. Hence they burn it only in stoves, in which they consume but a 4th. or 5th. part of what is commonly burnt in ordinary open fire places: besides, their horses are saved by means of this œconomy, from that immense labour, in hauling wood in the middle of winter, which fre-

quently unfits the horses of their neighbours for the toils of the
ensuing spring. Their houses are, moreover, rendered so comfortable, at all times, by large close stoves, that twice the business is
done by every branch of the family, in knitting, spinning, and
mending farming utensils, that is done in houses where every
member of the family crouds near to a common fire-place, or shivers
at a distance from it,—with hands and fingers that move, by reason
of the cold, with only half their usual quickness.

They discover œconomy in the preservation and increase of
their wood in several other ways. They sometimes defend it, by high
fences, from their cattle; by which means the young forest trees are
suffered to grow, to replace those that are cut down for the necessary
use of the farm. But where this cannot be conveniently done, they
surround the stump of that tree which is most useful for fences, viz.
the chestnut, with a small triangular fence. From this stump a
number of suckers shoot out in a few years, two or three of which
in the course of five and twenty years, grow into trees of the same
size as the tree from whose roots they derived their origin.

7th. They keep their horses and cattle as warm as possible in
winter, by which means they save a great deal of their hay and grain;
for those animals, when cold, eat much more than when they are
in a more comfortable situation.

8th. The German farmers live frugally in their families, with
respect to diet, furniture and apparel. They sell their most profitable
grain, which is wheat; and eat that which is less profitable, but more
nourishing, that is rye or Indian corn. The profit to a farmer, from
this single article of œconomy, is equal, in the course of a life time,
to the price of a farm for one of his children. They eat sparingly of
boiled animal food, with large quantities of vegetables, particularly
sallad, turnips, onions, and cabbage, the last of which they make
into *sour crout*. They likewise use a large quantity of milk and cheese
in their diet. Perhaps the Germans do not proportion the quantity
of their animal food, to the degrees of their labour; hence it has
been thought, by some people, that they decline in strength sooner
than their English or Irish neighbours. Very few of them ever use
distilled spirits in their families: their common drinks are cyder,
beer, wine, and simple water. The furniture of their house is plain
and useful. They cover themselves in winter with light feather beds
instead of blankets: in this contrivance there is both convenience,

and œconomy, for the beds are warmer than blankets, and they are made by themselves. The apparel of the German farmers is usually *home spun*. When they use European articles of dress, they prefer those which are of the best quality, and of the highest price. They are afraid of debt, and seldom purchase any thing without paying cash for it.

9th. The German farmers have large or profitable gardens near their houses. These contain little else but useful vegetables. Pennsylvania is indebted to the Germans for the principal part of their knowledge in horticulture. There was a time when turnips and cabbage were the principal vegetables that were used in diet by the citizens of Pennsylvania. This will not surprise those persons, who know that the first English settlers in Pennsylvania left England while horticulture was in its infancy in that country. It was not till the reign of William III. that this useful and agreeable art was cultivated by the English nation. Since the settlement of a number of German gardeners in the neighbourhood of Philadelphia, the tables of all classes of citizens have been covered with a variety of vegetables, in every season of the year; and to the use of these vegetables, in diet, may be ascribed the general exemption of the citizens of Philadelphia from diseases of the skin.

10th. The Germans seldom *hire* men to work upon their farms. The feebleness of that authority which masters possess over hired servants, is such that their wages are seldom procured from their labour, except in harvest, when they work in the presence of their masters. The wives and daughters of the German farmers frequently forsake, for a while, their dairy and spinning-wheel, and join their husbands and brothers in the labour of cutting down, collecting and bringing home the fruits of their fields and orchards. The work of the gardens is generally done by the women of the family.

11th. A large and strong waggon covered with linen cloth, is an essential part of the furniture of a German farm. In this waggon, drawn by four or five large horses of a peculiar breed: they convey to market over the roughest roads, between 2 or 3 thousand pounds weight of the produce of their farms. In the months of September and October, it is no uncommon thing, on the Lancaster and Reading roads, to meet in one day from fifty to an hundred of these waggons, on their way to Philadelphia, most of which belong to German farmers.

12th. The favourable influence of agriculture, as conducted by the Germans in extending human happiness, is manifested by the joy they express upon the birth of a child. No dread of poverty, nor distrust of Providence from an encreasing family, depress the spirits of these industrious and frugal people. Upon the birth of a son, they exult in the gift of a ploughman or a waggoner; and upon the birth of a daughter, they rejoice in the addition of another spinster, or milkmaid to their family. Happy state of human society! what blessings can civilization confer, that can atone for the extinction of the ancient and patriarchal pleasure of raising up a numerous and healthy family of children, to labour for their parents, for themselves, and for their country; and finally to partake of the knowledge and happiness which are annexed to existence! The joy of parents upon the birth of a child is the grateful echo of creating goodness. May the mountains of Pennsylvania be for ever vocal, with songs of joy upon these occasions! They will be the infallible signs of innocence, industry, wealth and happiness in the state.

13th. The Germans take great pains to produce, in their children, not only *habits* of labour, but a *love* of it. In this they submit to the irreversible sentence inflicted upon man, in such a manner, as to convert the wrath of heaven into private and public happiness. "To fear God, and to love work," are the first lessons they teach their children. They prefer industrious habits to money itself; hence, when a young man asks the consent of his father to marry the girl of his choice, he does not enquire so much whether she be rich or poor? or whether she possesses any personal or mental accomplishments—as whether she be industrious, and acquainted with the duties of a good house-wife?

14th. The Germans set a great value upon patrimonial property. This useful principle in human nature prevents much folly and vice in young people. It moreover leads to lasting and extensive advantages, in the improvement of a farm; for what inducement can be stronger in a parent to plant an orchard, to preserve forest-trees or to build a commodious and durable house, than the idea, that they will all be possessed by a succession of generations, who shall inherit his blood and name.

15th. The German farmers are very much influenced in planting and pruning trees, also in sowing and reaping, by the age and appearances of the moon. This attention to the state of the moon has been ascribed to superstition; but if the facts related by Mr. Wilson in his observations upon climates are true, part of their success in agriculture must be ascribed to their being so much influenced by it.

16th. From the history that has been given of the German agriculture, it will hardly be necessary to add that a German farm may be distinguished from the farms of the other citizens of the state, by the superior size of their barns; the plain, but compact form of their houses; the height of their enclosures; the extent of their orchards; the fertility of their fields; the luxuriance of their meadows, and a general appearance of plenty and neatness in everything that belongs to them.

The German mechanic possesses some of the traits of the character that has been drawn of the German farmer. His first object is to become a freeholder; and hence we find few of them live in rented houses. The highest compliment that can be paid to them on entering their houses is to ask them, "is this house your own." They are industrious, frugal, punctual and just. Since their settlement in Pennsylvania, many of them have acquired a knowledge of those mechanical arts, which are more immediately necessary and useful in a new country; while they continue at the same time, to carry on the arts they imported from Germany, with vigour and success.

But the genius of the Germans of Pennsylvania, is not confined to agriculture and the mechanical arts. Many of them have acquired great wealth by foreign and domestic commerce. As merchants they are candid and punctual. The bank of North America has witnessed, from its first institution, their fidelity to all their pecuniary engagements.

Thus far have I described the *individual* character of several orders of the German citizens of Pennsylvania. I shall now take notice of some of their manners in a collective capacity. All the different sects among them are particularly attentive to the religious education of their children, and to the establishment and support of the christian religion. For this purpose they settle as much as possible together—and make the erection of a school house and a place of worship the first object of their care. They commit the education and instruction of their children in a peculiar manner to the ministers and officers of their churches;—hence they grow up with prejudices in favour of public worship, and of the obligations of christianity. Such has been the influence of a pious education among the German Lutherans in Pennsylvania, that in the course of nineteen years only one of them has ever been brought to a place of public shame on punishment.

As members of civil government, the Germans are peaceable and exact in the payment of their taxes. Since they have participated in the power of the state, many of them have become sensible and enlightened in the science of legislation. Pennsylvania has had the speaker's chair of her assembly, and the vice-president's office of her council, filled with dignity by gentlemen of German families. The same gentlemen have since been advanced to seats in the house of representatives, under the new constitution of the United States. In the great controversy about the national government, a large majority of the Germans in Pennsylvania decided in favour of its adoption, notwithstanding the most popular arts were used to prejudice them against it.

The Germans are but little addicted to convivial pleasures.

They seldom meet for the simple purpose of eating and drinking in what are justly called "feeding parties"; but they are not strangers to the virtue of hospitality.—The hungry or benighted traveller, is always sure to find a hearty welcome under their roofs. A gentleman of Irish extraction, who lost his way in travelling through Lancaster county, called late at night at the door of a German farmer. He was kindly received and entertained with the best of every thing the house afforded. The next morning, he offered to pay his host for his lodging and other accommodations: "No" said the friendly German, in broken English—"I will take nothing from you. I was once lost, and entertained, as you have been, at the house of a stranger who would take no pay from me for his trouble. I am therefore now only discharging that debt:—do you pay your debt to me in the same way to somebody else."—

They are extremely kind and friendly as neighbours. They often assist each other by loans of money for a short time, without interest, when the purchase of a plantation makes a larger sum necessary than is commonly possessed by a single farmer. To secure their confidence, it is necessary to be punctual. They never lend money a second time, to a man who has once disappointed them in paying what he had borrowed agreeably to his promise or obligations. It was remarked, during the late war, that there were very few instances of any of them discharging a bond or a debt, with depreciated paper money.

It has been said, that the Germans are deficient in learning; and that in consequence of their want of more general and extensive education, they are much addicted to superstition, and are frequently imposed upon in the management of their affairs. Many of them have lost valuable estates by being unacquainted with the common forms of law, in the most simple transactions; and many more of them have lost their lives, by applying to quacks in sickness: but this objection to the Germans will soon cease to have any foundation in Pennsylvania. Several young men, born of German parents, have been educated in law, physic and divinity, who have demonstrated by their abilities and knowledge, that the German genius for literature has not depreciated in America. A college has lately been founded by the state of Lancaster,[1] and committed chiefly to the care of the Germans of all sects, for the purpose of diffusing learning among their children. In this college they are to be taught the German and English languages, and all those branches of literature which are usually taught in the colleges of Europe and America. The principal of this college is a native of Pennsylvania, of German parentage.[2] His extensive knowledge and taste in the arts and sciences, joined with his industry in the discharge of the duties of his station, have afforded to the friends of learning in Pennsylvania, the most flattering prospects of the future importance and usefulness of this institution.

Both sexes of the Germans discover a strong propensity to vocal and instrumental music. They excel, in psalmody, all the other religious societies in the state.

The freedom and toleration of the government has produced a variety of sects, among the Germans in Pennsylvania. The Lutherans compose a great proportion of the German citizens of the state. Many of their churches are large and splendid. The German Presbyterians are the next to them in numbers. Their churches are likewise large and furnished, in many places, with organs. The

---

[1] This college is called after Dr. FRANKLIN, who was president of the state at the time it was founded, and who contributed very liberally to its funds.

[2] The Reverend Dr. Henry Muhlenberg.

clergy, belonging to these churches, have moderate salaries, but they are punctually and justly paid. In the country they have glebes which are stocked and occasionally worked by their congregations. The extra expences of their ministers, in all their excursions to their ecclesiastical meetings, are borne by their respective congregations. By this means the discipline and general interests of their churches are preserved and promoted. The German Lutherans and Presbyterians live in great harmony with each other, insomuch that they often preach in each other's churches, and in some instances unite in building a church, in which they both worship at different times. This harmony between two sects, one so much opposed to each other, is owing to the relaxation of the Presbyterians in some of the peculiar doctrines of Calvanism. I have called them Presbyterians, because most of them object to being designated by the name of Calvanists. The Menonists, the Moravians, the Swingfielders, and the Catholics, compose the other sects of the German inhabitants of Pennsylvania. The Menonists hold war and oaths to be unlawful. They admit the sacraments of baptism, by *sprinkling*, and the supper. From them a sect has arisen, who hold, with the above principles and ceremonies, the necessity of *immersion baptism*; hence they are called *Dunkers* or Baptists. Previously to their partaking of the sacrament of the supper, they wash each other's feet, and sit down to a love-feast. They practice these ceremonies of their religion with great humility and solemnity. They, moreover, hold the doctrine of universal salvation. From this sect there have been several seceders, one of whom devoted themselves to perpetual celibacy. They have exhibited for many years, a curious spectacle of pious mortification, at a village called Ephrata, in Lancaster county. They are at present reduced to fourteen or fifteen members. The *Separatists* who likewise dissented from the Dunkers, reject the ordinances of baptism and the sacrament; and hold the doctrine of the *Friends* concerning the internal revelation of the gospel. They hold, with the Dunkers, the doctrine of universal salvation. The singular piety, and exemplary morality of these sects, have been urged, by the advocates for the salvation of all mankind, as a proof that the belief of that doctrine is not so unfriendly to morals, and the order of society, as has been supposed. The Dunkers and Separatists agree in taking no interest upon money, and in not applying to law to recover their debts.

The German Moravians are a numerous and respectable body of

christians in Pennsylvania. In their village of Bethlehem, there are two large stone buildings, in which the different sexes are educated in habits of industry in useful manufactures. The sisters (for by that epithet the women are called) all sleep in two large and neat apartments. Two of them watch over the rest, in turns, every night, to afford relief from those sudden indispositions which sometimes occur, in the most healthy persons, in the hours of sleep. It is impossible to record this fact, without pausing a moment to do homage to that religion, which produces so much union and kindness in human souls. The number of women, who belong to this sequestered female society, amounts sometimes to 120, and seldom to less than 100. It is remarkable that notwithstanding they lead a sedentary life, and set constantly in close stove-rooms in winter, that not more than one of them, upon an average, dies in a year. The disease which generally produces this annual death, is the consumption. The conditions and ages of the women of the village, as well as of the society that has been mentioned, are distinguished by ribbons of a peculiar kind which they wear on their cap: the widows, by white; the married women, by blue; the single women, above 18 years of age, by pink; and those under that age, by a ribbon of a cinnamon colour. Formerly this body of Moravians held all their property in common in imitation of the primitive christians; but, in the year 1760, a division of the whole of it took place, except a tavern, a tan-yard, 2000 acres of land near Bethlehem, and 5000 acres near Nazareth, a village in the neighbourhood of Bethlehem. The profits of these estates are appropriated to the support and propagation of the gospel. There are many valuable manufactures carried on at Bethlehem. The inhabitants possess a gentleness in their manners, which is peculiarly agreeable to strangers. They inure their children, of five and six years old, to habits of early industry. By this means they are not only taught those kinds of labor which are suited to their strength and capacities, but are preserved from many of the hurtful vices and accidents to which children are exposed.

The Swingfielders are a small society. They hold the same principles as the Friends, but they differ from them in using psalmody in their worship.

The German Catholics are numerous in Philadelphia, and have several small chapels in other parts of the state.

There is an incorporated charitable society of Germans in Philadelphia, whose objects are their poor and distressed countrymen.

There is likewise a German society of labourers and journeymen mechanics, who contribute 2s 6d eight times a year, towards a fund, out of which they allow 30s a week to each other's families, when the head of it is unable to work; and 7£10s to his widow, as soon as he is taken from his family by death.

The Germans of Pennsylvania, including all the sects that have been mentioned, compose nearly one third part of the whole inhabitants of the state.

The intercourse of the Germans with each other, is kept up chiefly in their own language; but most of their men, who visit the capital, and the trading or country towns of the state, speak the English language. A certain number of the laws of the state are now printed in German, for the benefit of those of them who cannot read English. A large number of German news-papers are likewise circulated through the state, through which knowledge and intelligence have been conveyed, much to the advantage of the government. There is scarcely an instance of a German, of either sex, in Pennsylvania, that cannot *read*; but many of the wives and daughters of the German farmers cannot *write*. The present state of society among them renders this accomplishment of little consequence to their improvement or happiness.

If it were possible to determine the amount of all the property brought into Pennsylvania by the present German inhabitants of the state, and their ancestors, and then compare it with the present amount of their property, the contrast would form such a monument of human *industry* and *œconomy* as has seldom been contemplated in any age or country.

I have been informed that there was an ancient prophecy which foretold, that "God would bless the Germans in foreign countries." This prediction has been faithfully verified in Pennsylvania. They enjoy here every blessing that liberty, toleration, independence, affluence, virtue and reputation, can confer upon them.

How different is their situation here; from what it was in Germany! Could the subjects of the princes of Germany, who now groan away their lives in slavery and unprofitable labour, view from an eminence, in the month of June, the German settlements of Stratsburg, or Manheim in Lancaster county, or of Lebanon or Bethlehem in the counties of Dauphin and Northampton; could they be accompanied on this eminence, by a venerable German farmer, and be told by him that many of those extensive fields of grain, full-fed herds, luxuriant meadows, orchards, promising loads of fruit, together with the spacious barns—and commodious stone-dwelling houses, which compose the prospects that have been mentioned, were all the product of the labour of a single family, and of *one* generation; and that they were all secured to the owners of them by *certain* laws; I am persuaded, that no chains would be able to detain them from sharing in the freedom of their Pennsylvania friends and former fellow-subjects. "We will assert our dignity— (would be their language) we will be men—we will be free—we will enjoy the fruits of our own labours—we will no longer be bought and sold to fight battles—in which we have neither interest nor resentment—we will inherit a portion of that blessing which God has promised to the Germans in foreign countries—we will be Pennsylvanians."

I shall conclude this account of the manners of the German inhabitants of Pennsylvania by remarking that if I have failed in doing them justice, it has not been the fault of my subject. The German character once employed the pen of one of the first historians of antiquity. I mean the elegant and enlightened Tacitus. It is very remarkable that the Germans in Pennsylvania retain in a great degree all the virtues, which this author ascribes to their ancestors in his treatise "*de moribus Germanorum*".—They inherit their integrity—fidelity—and chastity—but christianity has banished from them, their drunkenness, idleness, and love of military glory. There is a singular trait in the features of the German character in Pennsylvania, which shews how long the most trifling customs may exist among a people who have not been mixed with other nations. Tacitus describes the manner in which the ancient Germans build their villages in the following words. "*Suam quisque domum spatiis circumdat sive adversus casus ignis remedium, sive inscitia ædificandi.*"[3] Many of the German villages in Pennsylvania are constructed in the same manner. The small houses are composed of a mixture, of wood, brick and clay, neatly united together. The large

---

[3] Each man leaves a space between his house, and those of his neighbours, either to avoid the danger from fire, or form unskilfulness in architecture.

houses are built of stone, and many of them after the English fashion. Very few of the houses in Germantown are connected together.—Where the Germans connect their houses in their villages, they appear to have deviated from one of the customs they imported from Germany.

CITIZENS of the United States learn from the account that has been given of the German inhabitants of Pennsylvania, to prize knowledge and industry in agriculture and manufactures, as the basis of domestic happiness and national prosperity.

LEGISLATORS of the United States, learn from the wealth, and independence of the German inhabitants of Pennsylvania, to encourage by your example, and laws, the republican virtues of industry and œconomy. They are the only pillars which can support the present constitution of the United States.

LEGISLATORS of Pennsylvania,—learn from the history of your German fellow citizens that you possess an inexhaustible treasure in the bosom of the state, in their manners and arts. Continue to patronize their newly established seminary of learning and spare no expense in supporting their public free-schools. The vices which follow the want of religious instruction, among the children of poor people, lay the foundation of most of the jails, and places of public punishment in the state. Do not contend with their prejudices in favour of their language. It will be the channel through which the knowledge and discoveries of one of the wisest nations in Europe, may be conveyed into our country. In proportion as they are instructed and enlightened in their own language, they will become acquainted with the language of the United States. Invite them to share in the power and offices of government: it will be the means of producing an union in principle and conduct between them, and those of their enlightened fellow-citizens who are descended from other nations. Above all, cherish with peculiar tenderness, those sects among them who hold war to be unlawful.—Relieve them from the oppression of absurd and unnecessary militia laws. Protect them as the repositories of a truth of the gospel, which has existed in every age of the church, and which must spread hereafter over every part of the world.

The opinions respecting the commerce and slavery of the Africans, which have nearly produced a revolution in their favour, in some of the European governments, were transplanted from a

sect of christians in Pennsylvania. Perhaps those German sects of christians among us, who refuse to bear arms for the purpose of shedding human blood, may be preserved by divine providence, as the centre of a circle, which shall gradually embrace all the nations of the earth in a perpetual treaty of friendship and peace.

THOUGHTS ON COMMON SENSE.

THE human mind in common with other branches of philosophy, has become the subject of attention in the present age of free and general enquiry. While new faculties are discovering in it, it will conduce equal to our acquiring a perfect knowledge of its powers, to detect and remove such *supposed* faculties as do not belong to it.

I have long suspected the term *common sense* to be applied improperly to designate a faculty of the mind. I shall not repeat the accounts which have been given of it by Cicero—Buffier—Berkely—Shaftesbury—Bentley—Fenelon—Locke—Hume—Hobs—Priestly and others, all of whom agree in describing it as a *faculty* or *part* of a faculty, possessing a quick and universal perception of *right* and *wrong*, *truth* and *error*, and of *propriety* and *impropriety* in human affairs.

I shall copy, as the substance of all that those authors have said upon this subject, Dr. Reid's account of common sense, published in the 2d. chapter of the sixth number of his Essays on the intellectual powers of man.—"It is absurd to conceive (says the Doctor) that there can be any opposition between reason and common sense. It is the first born of reason, and, as they are commonly joined together in speech and writing, they are inseparable in their nature."

"We ascribe to reason two offices or two degrees. The first is to judge of things self-evident; the second is to draw conclusions that are not self-evident from things that are. The first of these is the province, and the sole province, of common sense, and therefore it *coincides* with reason in its *whole* extent, and is only *another* name for one *branch* or one *degree* of reason."

"There is an obvious reason why this degree of reason should have a name appropriated to it, and that is, that in the greatest part of mankind no other degree of reason is to be found. It is this degree of reason that entitles them to the denomination of reasonable creatures."

"These two degrees of reason differ in other respects, which would be sufficient to entitle them to distinct names. The first is the gift of heaven—the second is learned by practice and rules, when the first is not wanting."—Thus far Dr. Reid.

It is with great diffidence that I object to any thing that comes from a gentleman from whose writings I have derived so much entertainment and instruction, and who has done so much towards removing the rubbish that has for many ages obscured the science of metaphysicks. This diffidence to offer a single objection to Dr. Reid's opinion upon the subject under consideration, is increased by the group of popular and respectable names under which he has supported it.

The idea which I have adopted of common sense is plain and simple. I consider it as the perception of things as they appear to the *greatest* part of mankind. It has no relation to their being *true* or *false*, *right* or *wrong*, *proper* or *improper*. For the sake of perspicuity, I shall define it to be, *Opinions and Feelings in unison with the Opinions and Feelings of the bulk of mankind*.

From this definition it is evident that common sense must necessarily differ in different ages and countries and, in both, must vary with the progress of taste, science, and religion. In the uncultivated state of reason, the opinions and feelings of a majority of mankind will be *wrong*, and, of course, their common or universal sense will partake of their errors. In the cultivated state of reason, *just* opinions and feelings will become general, and the common sense of the majority will be in unison with truth. I beg leave to illustrate what I mean by a few examples.

1. There are many things which were contrary to common sense in former ages, both in philosophy and religion, which are now universally believed, insomuch that to call them in question is to discover a want of judgment, or a defective education.

2. It is contrary to common sense to speak or write in favour of republicanism, in several European countries; and it is equally contrary to it to speak or write in favour of monarchy, in the United States of America.

3. The common sense of the planters in Jamaica, is in favour of the commerce and slavery of the Africans.—In Pennsylvania, reason, humanity, and common sense, have universally declared against them.

4. In Turkey, it is contrary to the common sense of delicacy which prevails in that country for a gentleman to dance with a lady. No such common sense prevails in any of the western countries of Europe, or in the States of Amercia.

5. It is contrary to the common sense of many numerous sects to believe that it is possible for men to go to heaven, who do not embrace their principles, or mode of worship.—Among rational men, this common sense is contrary to truth and christian religion.

6. The common sense of mankind has generally been in favour of established modes and habits of practice, in medicine. Opium, bark, mercury and the lancet have all forced their way into general use, contrary to this common sense. Their utility is a proof how little common sense accords with the decisions of reason, and how improperly it is supposed to be a part of that noble power of the mind.

7. It is agreeable to the common sense of a great part of mankind, to revenge public and private injuries by wars and duels, and yet no wise or just reason has ever been given to justify the practice of either of them.

8. The common sense of the bulk of the inhabitants of the British Dominions, and of the United States, is in favour of boys spending four or five years in learning the Latin and Greek languages, in order to qualify them to understand the English language. Those persons who recollect that the most perfect language in the world, viz. the Greek, was learned without the medium or aid of a dead or foreign language, consider the above practice (founded in common sense) as contrary to right reason and productive of many evils in education. But further, under this head. The common sense of the same immense proportion of people, is in favour of teaching boys *words*, before they are taught *ideas*. Now nature and right reason both revolt at this absurd practice.

9. The common sense of nearly all nations, is in favour of preventing crimes by the punishment of death, but right reason, policy, and the experience of a wise and enlightened prince,[1] all concur in proving that the best means of preventing crimes, is by *living* and not by *dead* examples.

In the perfection of knowledge, common sense and truth will be in unison with each other. It is *now more* related to error than to truth, and in the sense in which I have described it, it implies more praise than censure to want it.

To say that a man has common sense, is to say that he thinks with his age or country, in their *false*, as well as their *true* opinions;

---

[1] Leopold, Emperor of Germany.

and the greater the proportion of people, he acts and thinks with, the greater share he possesses of this common sense.—After all that has been said in its favour, I cannot help thinking that it is the characteristic only of common minds.

To think and act with the majority of mankind, when they are *right*, and differently from them, when they are *wrong*, constitutes in my opinion, the perfection of human wisdom and conduct.

The *feelings* and *opinions* of mankind are often confounded; but they are widely different from each other. There may be *just* feelings connected with *erroneous* opinions and conduct. This is often the case in religion and government—But, in general, opinions and feelings are just and unjust in equal degrees, according to the circumstance of age, country, and the progress of knowledge before mentioned.

Had this common sense depended upon the information of any one of the *five external* senses, I should have had no difficulty in admitting Dr. Reid's account of it, inasmuch as the perceptions they afford are the *same*, in their nature, in all healthy men, and in all ages and countries. But to suppose it to be an inferior degree, or the *first* act of reason, and afterwards to suppose it to be *universal*, is to contradict every thing that history and observation teach us of human nature.[2]

In matters addressed to our reason, the principal business of reason is to correct the evidence of our *senses*. Indeed, the perception of truth, in philosophy, seems to consist in little else than in the refutation of the ideas acquired from the testimony of our senses. In the progress of knowledge, when the exact connection between the senses and reason is perfectly understood, it is probable that the senses and reason will be in unison with each other, and that mankind will as suddenly connect the evidence of all the senses with the decisions of reason, as they now connect, with certainty, the distance of objects with the evidence of the eyes. This general unison between the senses and reason, as in the case of vision, must be the result only of experience and habit.

I cannot dismiss this subject without adding the following remark.

---

[2] The King of Prussia, in his posthumous works, says, "Reason never did any thing great," by which he must have meant the *common* degree of it, or what is called, by Dr. Reid, *common sense*.

Mankind are governed, says Mr. Bayle, by their prejudices, and not by their principles. To do them good, we must, in some measure, conform to those prejudices;—hence we find the most acceptable men in practical society, have been those who have never shocked their contemporaries, by opposing popular or common opinions. Men of opposite characters, like objects placed too near the eye, are seldom seen distinctly by the age in which they live. They must content themselves with the prospect of being useful to the distant and more enlightened generations which are to follow them. Galileo, who asked pardon of the Pope, on his knees, for contradicting the *common sense* of the church, respecting the revolution of the earth, and Dr. Harvey, who lost all his business by refuting the *common sense* of former ages, respecting the circulation of the blood, now enjoy a reputation for their opinions and discoveries, which has in no instance ever been given to the cold blood of common sense.

April 3d. 1791.

AN ACCOUNT OF THE VICES PECULIAR TO THE INDIANS OF NORTH AMERICA.

IT has become fashionable of late years for the philosophers of Europe to celebrate the virtues of the savages of America. Whether the design of their encomiums was to expose christianity, and to depreciate the advantages of civilization, I know not; but they have evidently had those effects upon the minds of weak people. Without contradicting the accounts that have been published by those gentlemen, of the virtues of the Indians in North America, I shall briefly add an account of some of their vices, in order to complete their natural history. My information shall be taken from the travels of Charlevoix—Hennepen—Carver—Romans and Bartram, and from conversations with persons of veracity who have resided among them.

The first vice I shall name, that is universal among our savages, is UNCLEANNESS. They are, in general, strangers to the obligations both of morality and decency, as far as they relate to the marriage bed.—The exceptions to this remark, have been produced among those nations chiefly, who have had an occasional intercourse with civilized nations.

2. NASTINESS is another Indian vice. This is exemplified in their food—drinks—dress—persons—and above all, in their total disregard to decency in the *time—place*—and *manner* of their natural evacuations.

3. DRUNKENNESS is a more general vice among savages than among civilized nations.—Whole Indian tribes have been destroyed by it. Indeed they glory in their fondness for strong liquors, and consider it as a part of their character. A country man who had dropt from his cart a keg of rum, rode back a few miles in hopes of finding it. On his way he met an Indian who lived in his neighbourhood, whom he asked if he had seen his keg of rum on the road? The Indian laughed in his face, and addressed him in the following words. "What a fool you are to ask an Indian such a question. Don't you see I am sober? Had I met with your keg, you would have found it empty on one side of the road, and Indian Tom drunk and asleep on the other."

4. GLUTTONY is very common among Indians. To this their long abstinence, produced by their idleness, naturally tempts them.—It is very common to see them stretch themselves on the ground after a full meal, and grunt there for several hours till they recover from the effects of their intemperance. Mr. Bartram tells us, that they sometimes rise in the middle of the night, in order to gratify their appetites for eating.

5. TREACHERY is another Indian vice. Who ever trusted to an Indian treaty?—They generally begin their wars, with professions of peace and perpetual friendship.

6. The CRUELTY of Indians is well known. They consider compassion as a mark of effeminacy. Their treatment of their prisoners, shews them to possess a spirit of revenge, which places them upon a footing with infernal spirits.

7. IDLENESS is the universal vice of savages. They are not only too lazy to work, but even to think. Nothing but the powerful stimulus of hunger, or revenge, is sufficient to rouse them into action.

8. THEFT is an Indian vice. The Indians not only steal from their civilized neighbours, but from each other. A horse—a gun—or spirits, have charms in the eyes of an Indian that no restraints can prevent his stealing, whenever they come in his way.

9. GAMING belongs in an eminent degree to the Catalogue of Indian vices.

10. But the infamy of the Indian character is completed by the low rank to which they degrade their women. It is well known that their women perform all their work. They not only prepare their victuals, but plant, hoe and gather their corn and roots. They are seldom admitted to their feasts, or share in their conversation. The men oblige them to lie at their feet, when they sleep *without* fire; and at their backs when they sleep *before* a fire. They afford them no assistance in the toil of tending, feeding, and carrying their children. They are even insensible of the dangers to which their women are often exposed in travelling with them. A gentleman from Northumberland county, informed me, that he once saw a body of Indian men and women wading across the river Susquehannah. The men arrived first on the opposite shore, and pursued their journey along the river. The women, some of whom had children on their backs, upon coming to a deep and rapid current, suddenly cried out for help, and made signs to their husbands and

fathers to come to their assistance. The men stood for a few minutes—and after attentively surveying their distress, bursted out a laughing, and then with a merry indifference, walked from them along the shore.

This is a short nomenclature of the vices of the Indians of North America. If it were necessary, I would quote the chapters and pages of the authors who have established, by their observations, the truth of the character I have given of them. I am not disposed to enter into an examination of their virtues, but I cannot help supposing them to be rather the *qualities of necessity*, than the offspring of feeling, or principle. Their hospitality—their friendships—their patience—and their fidelity to engagements, are the effects of necessity, and are as essential to their existence, as honesty is to a band of associated robbers. Their politeness in never contradicting any person, I believe is the effect of indolence, for I know of nothing that lazy people dislike more than to dispute, even where truth is on their side, or where victory is certain.—Where is the man that in a lazy fit (to which all men at times are subject) has not heard false and absurd opinions advanced in company, without contradicting them?

The taciturnity of the Indians which has been so much celebrated, as a mark of their wisdom. is the effect of their wants of ideas. Except in cases of extraordinary pride, I believe taciturnity, in nine cases out of ten, in civilized company, is the effect of stupidity. I will make one more exception to this true, and that is in favour of those people who are in the habits of communicating their thoughts, by writing for the public, or by corresponding with their friends. Ideas, whether acquired from books, or by reflection, produce a plethora in the mind, which can only be relieved by depletion from the pen, or tongue.

But what shall we say to the encomiums that have been lavished upon the love of liberty which characterizes our savage neighbours?—Why—that they arise from an ignorance of the influence of property, upon the human mind.—Property, and a regard for law, are born together in all societies. The passion for liberty, is as different from the passion for it in a civilized republican, as the impurity of lust, is, from the delicacy of love. There is a certain medium to be observed between an affection for law, and for liberty. An excess of the former has sometimes led to tyranny, while an excess of the former has sometimes led to tyrany, while an excess of the latter, leads to idleness and vice. The Athenians appear to have been intoxicated with an excess of liberty when they spent their whole time in hearing and telling news. There is always an excess of law or liberty in a community whose poor men are idle, or where vices of any kind are suffered with impunity.

The only reflections that I shall add upon this subject, shall be, how are the blessings of civil government which exterpates, restrains, or punishes the vices that have been mentioned! and how great is the efficacy of christianity, which, by purifying the heart, renders the practice of the contrary virtues natural and agreeable?

OBSERVATIONS UPON THE INFLUENCE OF THE HABITUAL USE OF TOBACCO UPON HEALTH, MORALS, AND PROPERTY.

WERE it possible for a being who had resided upon our globe, to visit the inhabitants of a planet, where reason governed, and to tell them that a vile weed was in general use among the inhabitants of the globe it had left, which afforded no nourishment—that this weed was cultivated with immense care—that it was an important article of commerce—that the want of it produced real misery—that its taste was extremely nauseous, that it was unfriendly to health and morals, and that its use was attended with a considerable loss of time and property, the account would be thought incredible, and the author of it would probably be excluded from society, for relating a story of so improbable a nature. In no one view, is it possible to contemplate the creature man in a more absurd and ridiculous light, than in his attachment to TOBACCO.

This weed is of a stimulating nature whether it be used in smoaking, chewing or in snuff. Like opium and spirituous liquors, it is sought for in all those cases where the body is debilitated *indirectly* by intemperance in eating, or by excessive application to study, or business, or *directly* by sedative passions of the mind, particularly by grief and fear. Persons after losing relations or friends by death, often resort to it. One of the greatest snuffers I ever knew, used it for the first time, in order to console her under a presentiment she entertained, that she should die in childbed. Fear creates a desire for Tobacco. Hence it is used in a greater quantity by soldiers and sailors than by other classes of people. It is used most profusely by soldiers when they act as picket guards, or centinels, and by sailors in stormy weather. Persons labouring under that state of madness which is accompanied with a sense of misery, are much devoted to it, hence the tenants of mad-houses often accost their attendants and visitors, with petitions for TOBACCO.

The progress of habit in the use of Tobacco is exactly the same as in the use of spirituous liquors. The slaves of it begin, by using it only after dinner—then during the whole afternoon and evening, afterwards before dinner, then before breakfast, and finally during the whole night. I knew a lady who had passed through all these stages, who used to wake regularly two or three times every night to compose her system with fresh doses of snuff. Again—the progress in the decay of the sensibility of the nose, to the stimulus of snuff is analogous to the decay of sensibility of the stomach, to the stimulus of spirituous liquors. It feels for a while the action of Rappee; next it requires Scotch snuff, afterwards Irish-blackguard—and finally it is affected only by a composition of Tobacco and ground glass. This mixture is to the nose, what Cayenne pepper and Jamaica spirits are to the stomachs of habitual dram drinkers.

The appetite for Tobacco is wholly artificial. No person was ever born with a relish for it. Even in those persons who are much attached to it, nature frequently recovers her disrelish to it. It ceases to be agreeable in every febile indisposition. This is so invariably true, that a disrelish to it is often a sign of an approaching, and a return of the appetite for it, a sign of a departing fever.

In considering the pernicious effects of Tobacco, I shall begin agreeably to the order I have laid down, by taking notice of its influence upon health; and here I shall mention its effects not only upon the body, but upon the mind.

1. It impairs the appetite. Where it does not produce this effect,

2. It prevents the early and complete digestion of the food, and thereby induces distressing, and incurable diseases not only of the stomach, but of the whole body. This effect of Tobacco is the result of the waste of the saliva in chewing, and smoking, or of the Tobacco insinuating itself into the stomach, when used in chewing, or snuffing.—I once lost a young man of 17 years of age, of a pulmonary consumption, whose disorder was brought on by the intemperate use of segars.

3. It produces many of those diseases which are supposed to be seated in the nerves. The late Sir John Pringle was subject in the evening of his life to tremors in his hands. In his last visit to France, a few years before he died, in company with Dr. Franklin, he was requested by the Doctor to observe, that the same disorder was very common among those people of fashion who were great snuffers. Sir John was led by this remark to suspect that his tremors were occasioned by snuff which he took in large quantities. He immediately left off taking it, and soon afterwards recovered the perfect use of his hands. I have seen head-ache, vertigo, and epilepsy produced by the use of Tobacco. A Physician in Connecticut has remarked that

it has in several instances produced palsy and apoplexy; and Dr. Tissot ascribes sudden death in one instance, to the excessive use of it in smoking.

4. A citizen of Philadelphia lost all his teeth by drawing the hot smoke of Tobacco into his mouth by means of a short pipe, and I have been informed of a cancer on the lip, which terminated fatally from the same cause, in a farmer in Northumberland county in this state. The acrid nature of the matter which is mixed with the smoke of the Tobacco may easily be discovered by the taste or smell of a pipe stem that has been in use for two or three weeks.

5. Tobacco when used in the form of snuff seldom fails of impairing the voice by obstructing the nose. It moreover imparts to the complexion a disagreeable dusky colour.

I have thus briefly enumerated the morbid effects of Tobacco upon the human body. It remains under this head to mention, that the want of it is a source of uneasiness more distressing than many bodily disorders. This uneasiness in persons who have long been accustomed to the use of Tobacco has in some instances produced an agitation of mind that has bordered upon distraction. Colonel Burr informed me that the greatest complaints, dissatisfaction and suffering that he heard the soldiers who accompanied General Arnold in his march from Boston to Quebec through the wilderness, in the year 1775, were from the want of Tobacco. This was the more remarkable, as they were so destitute of provisions as to be obliged to kill, and eat their dogs. The Persians, we are told by travellers, expatriate themselves, when they are forbidden the use of Tobacco, in order to enjoy it in a foreign country. These facts will not surprise those persons who have been accustomed to view our appetites when perverted to such things as artificial and disagreeable, to be much more ungovernable than the appetite for things that are originally natural and agreeable.

But the use of Tobacco has been known to produce a more serious effect upon the mind than the distress that has been mentioned. Sir John Pringle's memory was impaired by snuff. This was proved by his recovering the perfect exercise of it after he left off taking snuff agreeably to the advice of his friend Dr. Franklin. Dr. Masillac informed me that his father lost his memory at forty years of age by the excessive use of snuff. He took for several years two ounces of it every day.

In answer to these observations upon the morbid effects of Tobacco it has been said,

1. That it possesses many medical virtues. I grant it, and the facts which establish its utility in medicine furnish us with additional arguments against the *habitual* use of it. How feeble would be the effects of opium and bark upon the body, if they constituted a part of the condiments of our daily food;—While I admit the efficacy of tobacco as a medicine, I cannot help adding, that some of the diseases, or symptoms of diseases which it relieves, are evidently induced by the habit of using it. Thus a dram of ardent spirits suspends, for a while, a vomiting and tremors of the hands, but who does not know that those complaints, are the effects of the intemperate and habitual use of spirituous liquors?

2. The advocates for Tobacco, tell us that smoking and snuff relieve that uneasiness which succeeds a plentiful meal. I admit that the stimulars of the Tobacco restores the system from the indirect weakness which is induced by intemperance in eating, but the relief which is thus obtained, illy compensates for the waste of the saliva in smoking, at a time when it is most wanted, or for the mixture of a portion of the tobacco with the aliment in the stomach by means of snuffing. But why should we cure one evil by producing another? Would it not be much better to obviate the necessity of using Tobacco by always eating a moderate meal? The recollection of the remedy probably disposes to that intemperance in eating which produces the uneasiness that has been mentioned.

3. We are sometimes told that Tobacco is a preservative from contagious diseases. But many facts contradict this assertion. Mr. Howard informs us that it had no efficacy in checking the contagion of the plague, and repeated experience in Philadelphia has proved, that it is equally ineffectual in preserving those who use it, from the Influenza and Yellow Fever.

4. It has been further said that chewing and smoking Tobacco assist the intellectual operations. So do wine, and distilled spirits, but shall we upon that account, have recourse to those liquors when we wish to stimulate our thinking faculties? Tea ad Coffee are to be preferred, when we wish to stimulate the mind. Mr. Pope recommends a trotting horse for the same purpose. Rousseau excited his invention by walking backwards and forwards in his room. I suspect that Tobacco is often used, rather to supply the *want*

of ideas than to *collect*, or excite them. The absence of sensation, whether of external impressions upon the body, or of the reaction of the mind in thought, is always accompanied with misery. The Indians afford a striking proof of this remark—hence they spend whole days and even weeks in smoking, in order to relieve themselves from the anguish which attends the inactivity and vacuum of their minds.

We proceed next to mention the influence of the habitual use of Tobacco upon morals.

1. One of the usual effects of smoaking and chewing is thirst. This thirst cannot be allayed by water, for no sedative or even insipid liquor will be relished after the mouth and throat have been exposed to the stimulus of the smoke, or juice of Tobacco. A desire of course is excited for strong drinks, and these when taken between meals soon lead to intemperance and drunkenness. One of the greatest sots I ever knew, acquired a love for ardent spirits by swallowing cuds of Tobacco, which he did, to escape detection in the use of it, for he had contracted the habit of chewing, contrary to the advice and commands of his father. He died of a Dropsy under my care in the year 1780.

2. The use of Tobacco, more especially in smoking, disposes to idleness, and idleness has been considered as the root of all evil. "An idle man's brain, (says the celebrated and original Mr. Bunyan) is the Devil's work shop."

3. The use of Tobacco is necessarily connected with the neglect of cleanliness. The influence of this neglect upon morals has been happily pointed out in an extract from captain Cook's journal, which is published by Sir John Pringle in one of his Orations before the Royal Society of London.

4. Tobacco, more especially when used in smoking, is generally *offensive* to those people who do not use it. To smoke in company under such circumstances, is a breach of good manners; now, manners have an influence upon morals. They may be considered as the out post of virtue. A habit of offending the senses of friends or strangers, by the use of Tobacco, cannot therefore be indulged with innocence. It produces a want of respect for our fellow creatures, and this always disposes to unkind and unjust behaviour towards them. Who ever knew a rude man compleatly, or uniformly moral?

The methodists forbad the use of Tobacco in the infancy of their society. The prohibition discovered a high and just sense of the self-denial, decency, and universal civility which are required by the gospel. What reception may we suppose would the apostles have met with, had they carried into the cities and houses to which they were sent, snuff-boxes, pipes, segars, and bundles of cut, or rolls of hog, or pigtail Tobacco? Such a costly and offensive apparatus for gratifying their appetites, would have furnished solid objections to their persons and doctrines, and would have been a just cause for the clamours and contempt which were excited against them. It is agreeable to observe that a regard to good manners, upon this subject, has at last awakened in some parts of the world. In England smoking is not permitted in taverns and coffee-houses until after 10 o'clock at night, and in France snuffing is becoming unfashionable and vulgar. How much is it to be lamented that while the use of Tobacco is declining in two of the most enlightened countries in Europe, it is becoming more general in America. Who can see groups of boys of six or eight years old in our streets smoking segars, without anticipating such a depreciation of our posterity in health and character, as can scarcely be contemplated at this distance of time without pain and horror!

It remains now that I briefly point out the influence of the use of tobacco upon time and property. Snuffing makes a great inroad upon time. A man who takes a pinch of snuff every twenty minutes, (which most habitual snuffers do) and snuffs fifteen hours in four and twenty, (allowing him to consume not quite half a minute every time he uses his box,) will waste about five whole days of every year of his life in this useless, and unwholesome practice. But when we add to the profitable use to which this time might have been applied, the expences of Tobacco, pipes, snuff and spitting boxes— and of the injuries which are done to the cloathing, during a whole life, the aggregate sum would probably amount to several hundred dollars. To a labouring man this would be a decent portion for a son or daughter, while the same sum, saved by a man in affluent circumstances, would have enabled him by a contribution to a public charity to have lessened a large portion of the ignorance, or misery of mankind.

In reviewing the account that has been given of the disagreeable and mischievous effects of Tobacco, we are led to enquire, what are its uses upon our globe,—for we are assured that nothing, exists in vain. Poison is a relative term, and the most noxious plants have been discovered to afford sustenance to certain animals. But what animal besides man, will take Tobacco into its mouth? Horses, Cows, Sheep, Cats, Dogs, and even Hogs refuse to taste it. Flies, Musquetoes, and the Moth are chased from our cloaths by the smell of it. But let us not arraign the wisdom and œconomy of nature in the production of this plant. Modern Travellers have at last discovered that it constitutes the food of a solitary and filthy wild beast, well known in the deserts of Africa, by the name of the ROCK GOAT.

I shall conclude these observations by relating an Anecdote of the late Dr. Franklin. A few months before his death, he declared to one of his friends that he had never used Tobacco in any way in the course of his long life, and that he was disposed to believe there was not much advantage to be derived from it, for that he had never met with a man who used it, who advised him to follow his example.

AN ACCOUNT OF THE SUGAR MAPLE-TREE OF THE UNITED STATES; IN A LETTER TO THOMAS JEFFERSON, ESQ., THEN SECRETARY OF STATE OF THE UNITED STATES, AND ONE OF THE VICE PRESIDENTS OF THE AMERICAN PHILOSOPHICAL SOCIETY.

DEAR SIR,

In obedience to your request, I have sat down to communicate to our society, through the medium of a letter to you, a short account of the *Sugar Maple-tree* of the United States, together with such facts and remarks as I have been able to collect, upon the methods of obtaining sugar from it, and upon the advantages both public and private, of this Sugar.

The *Acer Sacharinum* of Linnaeus, or the Sugar Maple-tree, grows in great quantities in the western counties of all the Middle States of the American Union. Those which grow in New-York and Pennsylvania yield the sugar in a greater quantity than those which grow on the waters of the Ohio.—These trees are generally found mixed with the Beech (a), Hemlock (b), White and water Ash (c), the Cucumber tree (d), Linden (e), Aspen (f), Butter Nut (g), and Wild Cherry trees (h). They sometimes appear in groves covering five or six acres in a body, but they are more commonly interspersed with some, or all of the forest trees which have been mentioned. From 30 to 50 trees are generally found upon an acre of ground. They grow only in the richest soils and frequently in stony ground. Springs of the purest water abound in their neighbourhood. They are, when fully grown, as tall as the white and black oaks, and from two to three feet in diameter.[1] They put forth a beautiful white

---

Fagus Ferruginea (a), *Pinus abies* (b), *Fraxinus Americana* (c), *Magnolia acuminata* (d), *Tilia Americana* (e), *Populus tremula* (f), *Juglans alba (oblonga)* (g), *Prunus Virginiana, of Linnaeus* (h).

[1] Baron La Hontan, in his voyage to North America, gives the following account of the Maple-tree in Canada. After describing the black Cherry-tree, some of which he says are as tall as the loftiest oaks, and as big as a hogs-head, he adds, "The Maple-tree is much of the same height and bulk. It bears no resemblance to that sort we have in Europe."

blossom in the Spring before they show a single leaf. The colour of the blossom distinguishes them from the *acer rubrum*, or the common maple, which affords a blossom of a red colour. The wood of the Sugar Maple-tree is extremely inflammable, and is prefered upon that account by hunters and surveyors for fire wood. Its small branches are so much impregnated with sugar as to afford support to the cattle, horses, and sheep of the first settlers during the winter, before they are able to cultivate forage for that purpose. Its ashes afford a great quantity of pot ash, exceeded by few, or perhaps by none of the trees that grow in the woods of the United States.

The tree is supposed to arrive at its full growth in the woods in twenty years.

It is not injured by tapping; on the contrary, the oftner it is tapped, the more syrup is obtained from it. In this respect it follows a law of animal secretion. A single tree has not only survived, but flourished after *forty-two* tappings in the same number of years. The effects of a yearly discharge of sap from the tree in improving and increasing the sap, is demonstrated from the superior excellence of those trees which have been perforated in an hundred places, by a small wood-pecker which feeds upon the sap. These trees after having been wounded in this way, distil the remains of their juice on the ground, and afterwards acquire a black colour. The sap of these trees is much sweeter to the taste than that which is obtained from trees which have not been previously wounded, and it affords more sugar.

From twenty-three gallons and one quart of sap procured in twenty hours from only two of these dark coloured trees, Arthur Noble, Esq. of the state of New-York, obtained four pounds and thirteen ounces of good grained sugar.

A tree of an ordinary size yields in a good season from twenty to thirty gallons of sap, from which are made from five to six pounds of sugar. To this there are sometimes remarkable exceptions. Samuel Low, Esq. a Justice of Peace in Montgomery county, in the state of New-York, informed Arthur Noble, Esq. that he had made twenty pounds and one ounce of sugar between the 14th and 23rd of April, in the year 1789, from a single tree that had been tapped for several successive years before.

From the influence which culture has upon forest and other trees, it has been supposed, that by transplanting the Sugar Maple-Tree into a garden, or by destroying such other trees as shelter it from the rays of the Sun, the quantity of the sap might be increased; and its quality much improved. I have heard of one fact which favours this opinion. A farmer in Northampton county, in the state of Pennsylvania, planted a number of these trees above twenty years ago in his meadow from *three* gallons of the sap of which he obtains every year a pound of sugar. It was remarked formerly that it required *five* or *six* gallons of the sap of the trees which grow in the woods, to produce the same quantity of sugar.

The sap distils from the *wood* of the tree. Trees which have been cut down in the winter for the support of the domestic animals of the new settlers, yield a considerable quantity of sap as soon as their trunks and limbs feel the rays of the Sun in the spring of the year.

It is in consequence of the sap of these trees being equally diffused through every part of them, that they live three years after they are *girdled*, that is, after a circular incision is made through the bark into the substance of the tree for the purpose of destroying it.

It is remarkable that grass thrives better under this tree in a meadow, than in situations exposed to the constant action of the Sun.

The season for tapping the trees is in February, March, and April, according to the weather which occurs in these months.

Warm days and *frosty* nights are most favourable to a plentiful discharge of sap.[2] The quantity obtained in a day from a tree, is from five gallons to a pint, according to the greater or less heat of the air. Mr. Low, informed Arthur Noble, Esq. that he obtained near three and twenty gallons of sap in one day (April 14, 1789.) from the single tree which was before mentioned. Such instances of a profusion of sap in single trees are however not very common.

There is always a suspension of the discharge of sap in the night if a frost succeed a warm day. The perforation in the tree is made with an axe or an auger. The latter is prefered from experience of its advantages. The auger is introduced about three-quarters of an

---

[2] The influence of the weather in increasing and lessening the discharge of the sap from trees is very remarkable.

Dr. Tongue supposed, long ago, (Philosophical Transactions, No. 68) that changes in the weather of every kind might be better ascertained by the discharges of sap from trees than by weather glasses. I have seen a journal of the effects of heat, cold, moisture, drought and thunder upon the discharges from the sugar trees, which disposes me to believe there is some foundation for Dr. Tongue's opinion.

inch, and in an ascending direction (that the sap may not be frozen in a slow current in the mornings or evenings) and is afterwards depened gradually to the extent of two inches. A spout is introduced about half an inch into the hole, made by this auger, and projects from three to twelve inches from the tree. The spout is general made of the Sumach (a) or Elder (b), which commonly grow in the neighbourhood of the sugar trees. The tree is first tapped on the *South* side; when the discharge of its sap begins to lessen, an opening is made on its *North* side, from which an increased discharge takes place. The sap flows from four to six weeks, according to the temperature of the weather. Troughs large enough to contain three or four gallons made of white pine, or white ash, or of dried water ash, aspen, linden, poplar (c), or common maple, are placed under the spout, to receive the sap, which is carried every day to a large receiver, made of either of the trees before mentioned. From this receiver it is conveyed, after being strained, to the boiler.

To preserve the sap from rain and inpurities of all kinds, it is a good practice to cover the troughs with a concave board, with a hole in the middle of it.

It remains yet to be determined whether some artificial heat may be applied so as to increase the quantity and improve the quality of the sap. Mr. Noble informed me, that he saw a tree, under which a farmer had accidently burnt some brush, which dropped a thick heavy syrup resembling molasses. This fact may probably lead to something useful hereafter.

During the remaining part of the spring months, as also in the Summer, and in the beginning of Autumn, the Maple Tree yields a thin sap, but not fit for the manufactory of sugar. It affords a pleasant drink in harvest, and has been used instead of rum, in some instances by those farmers in Connecticut, whose ancestors have left to them here, and there, a sugar maple tree, (probably to shade their cattle,) in all their fields. Mr. Bruce describes a drink, of the same kind prepared by the inhabitants of Egypt, by infusing the sugar cane in water, which he declares to be "the most refreshing drink in the world."[3]

(a) *Rhus.* (b) *Sambucus canadensis.* (c) *Liriodendron Tulipifera.*

[3] Baron La Hontan, gives the following account of the sap of the sugar-maple tree, when used as a drink, and of the manner of obtaining it. "The tree yields a sap which has a much pleasanter taste than the best lemonade or cherry water, and

There are three methods of reducing the sap to sugar.

1. By *freezing* it; this method has been tried for many years, by Mr. Obediah Scott, a farmer in Luzerne county in this state, with great success. He says that one half of a given quantity of sap reduced in this way, is better than one-third of the same quantity reduced by boiling. If the frost should not be intense enough, to reduce the sap to the graining point, it may afterwards be exposed to the action of the fire for that purpose.

2. By *spontaneous evaporation*. The hollow stump of a maple-sugar tree, which had been cut down in the spring, and which was found sometime afterwards filled with sugar, first suggested this method of obtaining sugar to our farmers. So many circumstances of cold and dry weather, large and flat vessels, and above all so much time are necessary to obtain sugar, by either of the above methods, that the most general method among our farmers is to obtain it.

3. By *boiling*. For this purpose the following facts which have been ascertained by many experiments, deserve attention.

(1) The sooner the sap is boiled, after it is collected from the tree, the better. It should never be kept longer than twenty four hours, before it is put over the fire.

(2) The larger the vessel in which the sap is boiled, the more sugar is obtained from it.

(3) A copper vessel affords a sugar of a fairer colour than an iron vessel.

The sap flows into wooden troughs from which it is carried and poured into stone troughs or large cisterns in the shape of a canoe or large manger made of white ash, linden, bass wood, or white

---

makes the wholesomest drink in the world. This liquor is drawn by cutting the tree two inches deep in the wood, the cut being made sloping to the length of ten or twelve inches; at the lower end of this gash, a knife is trust into the tree slopingly, so that the water runs along the cut or gash, as through a gutter and falls upon the knife, which has some vessels placed underneath to receive it. Some trees will yield five or six bottles of this water in a day, and some inhabitants of Canada might draw twenty hogsheads of it in one day, if they would thus cut and notch all the maple trees of their respective plantations. The gash does no *harm to the tree*. Of this sap they make sugar and syrup which is so valuable that there can be no better remedy for fortifying the stomach. 'Tis but a few of the inhabitants that have the patience to make them, for as common things are slighted, so there are scarce any body, but children that give themselves the trouble of gashing these trees."

pine, from which it is conveyed to the kettle in which it is to be boiled. These cisterns, as well as the kettle, are generally covered by a shed to defend the sap from the rain. The sugar is improved by straining the sap through a blanket or cloth, either before or after it is half boiled. Butter, hogslard, or tallow are added to the sap in the kettle to prevent its boiling over, and lime, eggs or new milk are mixed with it in order to clarify it. I have seen clear sugar made without the addition of either of them. A spoonful of slack lime, the white of one egg, and a pint of new-milk are the usual proportions of these articles which are mixed with fifteen gallons of sap. In some samples which I have lately seen of maple-sugar clarified with each of the above articles, that, in which milk alone was used, had an evident superiority over the others, in point of colour.

The sugar after being sufficiently boiled, is *grained* and *clayed*, and afterwards *refined*, or converted into loaf sugar. The methods of conducting each of these processes is so nearly the same with those which are used in the manufactory of West-India sugar, and are so generally known, that I need not spend any time in describing them.

It has been a subject of enquiry whether the maple sugar might not be improved in its quality and increased in its quantity by the establishment of boiling houses in the sugar maple country to be conducted by *associated* labor. From the scattered situation of the trees, the difficulty of carrying the sap to a great distance, and the many expenses which must accrue from supporting labourers and horses in the woods in a season of the year in which nature affords no sustenance to man or beast, I am disposed to believe, that the most productive method, both in quantity and profit, of obtaining this sugar will be by the labour of private families. For a great number of years many hundred private families in New-York and Pennsylvania have supplied themselves plentifully with this sugar during the whole year. I have heard of many families who have made from two to four hundred pounds in a year; and of one man who sold six hundred pounds, all made with his own hands in one season.[4]

---

[4] The following receipts published by William Cooper, Esq. in the Albany Gazette, fully establishes this fact.

"Received, Cooper's Town, April 30th, 1790, of William Cooper, sixteen pounds,

Not more knowledge is necessary for making this sugar than is required to make soap, cyder, beer, sour-crout, &c. and yet one or all of these are made in most of the farm houses of the United States. The kettles and other utensils of a farmer's kitchen, will serve most of the purposes of making sguar, and the time required for the labor, (if it deserves that name) is at a season when it is impossible for the farmer to employ himself in any species of agriculture. His wife and all his children above ten years of age, moreover may assist him in this business, for the profit of the weakest of them is nearly equal to that of a man, when hired for that purpose.

A comparative view of this sugar has been frequently made with the sugar which is obtained from the West-India sugar cane, with respect to its *quality*, *price*, and the possible or probable *quantity* that can be made of it in the United States, each of which I shall consider in order.

1. The *quality* of this sugar is necessarily better than that which is made in the West Indies. It is prepared in a season when not a single insect exists to feed upon it, or to mix its excretions with it, and before a particle of dust or of the pollen of plants can float in the air. The same observation cannot be applied to the West India sugar. The insects and worms which prey upon it, and of course mix with it, compose a page in a nomenclature of natural history. I shall say nothing of the hands which are employed in making sugar in the West Indies, but, that men who work for the exclusive benefit of others, are not under the same obligations to keep their persons clean while they are employed in this work, that men women and children are, who work exclusively for the benefit of *themselves*, and who have been educated in the habits of cleanliness. The superior purity of the maple sugar is farther proved by its leaving a less sediment, when dissolved in water, than the West India sugar.

---

for six hundred and forty pounds of sugar made with *my own* hands, without any assistance in less than four weeks, besides attending to the other business of my farm, as providing fire wood, taking care of the cattle, & signed John Nicholls. Witness R. Smith."

A single family, consisting of a man and his two sons, on the maple sugar lands between the Delaware and Susquehannah made 180 lb. of maple sugar in one season.

It has been supposed that the maple sugar is inferior to the West India sugar in *strength*. The experiments which led to this opinion, I suspect have been inaccurate, or have been made with maple sugar, prepared in a slovenly manner. I have examined equal quantities, by weight, of both the grained and the loaf sugar, in hyson tea, and in coffee, made in every respect equal by the minutest circumstances that could effect the quality or taste of each of them, and could perceive no inferiority in the strength of the maple sugar. The liquors which decided this question were examined at the same time, by Alexander Hamilton, Esq. Secretary of the Treasury of the United States, Mr. Henry Drinker, and several Ladies, who all concurred in the above opinion.

2. Whoever considers that the gift of the sugar maple trees is from a benevolent Providence, that we have many millions of acres in our country covered with them, that the tree is improved by repeated tappings, and that the sugar is obtained by the frugal labour of a farmer's family, and at the same time considers the labour of cultivating the sugar cane, the capitals sunk in sugar works, the first cost of slaves and cattle, the expenses of provisions for both of them, and in some instances the additional expence of conveying the sugar to a market, in all the West India islands, will not hesitate in believing that the maple sugar may be manufactured much cheaper, and sold at a *less price* than that which is made in the West Indies.

3. The resources for making a sufficient *quantity* of this sugar not only for the consumption of the United States, but for exportation, will appear from the following facts. There are in the states of New-York and Pennsylvania alone at least ten millions of acres of land which produce the sugar maple-tree, in the proportion of thirty trees to one acre. Now, supposing all the persons capable of labour in a family to consist of three, and each person to attend 150 trees and each tree to yield 5lbs. of sugar in a season, the product of the labour of 60,000 families would be 135,000,000 pounds of sugar, and allowing the inhabitants of the United States to compose 600,000 families, each of which consumed 200 pounds of sugar in a year, the whole consumption would be 120,000,000 pounds in a year, which would leave a balance of 15,000,000 pounds for exportation. Valuing the sugar at 6-90 of a dollar per pound, the sum saved to the United States would be 8,000,000 dollars by home consumption,

and the sum gained by exportation would be 1,000,000 dollars. The only part of this calculation that will appear improbable is, the number of families supposed to be employed in the manufactory of the sugar, but the difficulty of admitting this supposition will vanish when we consider, that double that number of families are employed every year, in making cyder, the trouble, risks and expences of which are all much greater than those of making maple-sugar.

But the profit of the maple tree is not confined to its sugar. It affords a most agreeable molasses, and an excellent vinegar. The sap which is suitable for these purposes is obtained after the sap which affords the sugar has ceased to flow, so that the manufactories of these different products of the maple tree, by *succeeding*, do not interfere with each other. The molasses may be made to compose the basis of a pleasant summer beer. The sap of the maple is moreover capable of affording a spirit, but we hope this precious juice will never be prostituted by our citizens to this ignoble purpose. Should the use of sugar in diet become more general in our country, it may tend to lessen the inclination or supposed necessity for spirits, for I have observed a relish for sugar in diet to be seldom accompanied by a love for strong drink. It is the sugar which is mixed with tea which makes it so generally disagreeable to drunkards. But a diet, consisting of a plentiful mixture of sugar has other advantages to recommend it, which I shall briefly enumerate:

1. Sugar affords the greatest quantity of nourishment in a given quantity of matter of any substance in nature; of course it may be preserved in less room in our houses, and may be consumed in less time, than more bulky and less nourishing aliment. It has this peculiar advantage over most kinds of aliment, that it is not liable to have its nutritious qualities affected by time or the weather; hence it is preferred by the Indians in their excursions from home. They mix a certain quantity of maple sugar, with an equal quantity of Indian corn, dried and powdered, in its milky state. This mixture is packed in little baskets, which are frequently wetted in travelling, without injuring the sugar. A few spoons full of it mixed with half a pint of spring water, afford them a pleasant and strengthening meal. From the degrees of strength and nourishment, which are conveying into animal bodies by a small bulk of sugar, I conceive it might be given to horses with great advantage, when they are used

in circumstances which make it difficult or expensive to support them, with more bulky or weighty aliment. A pound of sugar with grass or hay, I have been told, has supported the strength and spirits of an horse, during a whole day's labour in one of the West-India Islands. A larger quantity given alone, has fattened horses and cattle, during the war before last in Hispaniola, for a period of several months, in which the exportation of sugar, and the importation of grain, were prevented by the want of ships.

2. The plentiful use of sugar in diet, is one of the best preventives that had ever been discovered of the diseases which are produced by worms. The Author of Nature seems to have implanted a love for this aliment in all children, as if it were on purpose to defend them from those diseases. I know a gentleman in Philadelphia, who early adopted this opinion, and who by indulging a large family of children, in the use of sugar, has preserved them all from the diseases usually occasioned by worms.

3. Sir John Pringle has remarked, that the plague has never been known in any country where sugar composes a material part of the diet of the inhabitants. I think it probable, that the frequency of malignant fevers of all kinds has been lessened by this diet, and that its more general use would defend that class of people, who are most subject to malignant fevers, from being so often affected by them.

4. In the numerous and frequent disorders of the breast, which occur in all countries, where the body is exposed to a variable temperature of weather, sugar affords the basis of many agreeable remedies. It is useful in weakness, and acrid defluxions upon other parts of the body. Many facts might be adduced in favour of this assertion. I shall mention only one, which from the venerable name of the person, whose case furnished it, cannot fail of commanding attention and credit. Upon my enquiring of Dr. Franklin, at the request of a friend, about a year before he died, whether he had found any relief from the pain of the stone, from the Blackberry-Jam, of which he took large quantities, he told me that he had, but that he believed the medicinal part of the jam, resided wholly in the sugar, and as a reason for thinking so, he added, that he often found the same relief, by taking about half a pint of a syrup, prepared by boiling a little brown sugar in water, just before he went to bed, that he did from a dose of opium. It has been supposed by some of the early physicians of our country, that the sugar obtained from the

maple tree, is more medicinal, than that obtained from the West-India sugar cane, but this opinion I believe is without foundation. It is preferrable in its qualities to the West-India sugar only from its superior *cleanliness*.

Cases may occur in which sugar may be required in medicine, or in diet, by persons who refuse to be benefited, even indirectly by the labour of slaves. In such cases, the innocent maple sugar will always be preferred.[5]

It has been said, that sugar injures the teeth, but this opinion now has so few advocates, that it does not deserve a serious refutation.

To transmit to future generations, all the advantages which have been enumerated from the maple tree, it will be necessary to protect it by law, or by a bounty upon the maple sugar, from being destroyed by the settlers in the maple country, or to transplant it from the woods, and cultivate it in the old and improved parts of the United States. An orchard consisting of 200 trees, planted upon a common farm would yield more than the same number of apple trees, at a distance from a market town. A full grown tree in the woods yields five pounds of sugar a year. If a greater exposure of a tree to the action of the sun, has the same effects upon the maple, that it has upon other trees, a larger quantity of sugar might reasonably be expected from each tree planted in an orchard. Allowing it to be only seven pounds, then 200 trees will yield 1400 pounds of sugar, and deducting 200 from the quantity, for the consumption of the family, there will remain for sale 1200 pounds which at 6-90 of a dollar per pound will yield an annual profit to the farmer of 80 dollars. But if it should be found that the shade of the maple does not check the growth of grain any more than it does of grass, double or treble that number of maple trees may be planted on

---

[5] Dr. Knowles, a physician of worthy character in London, had occasion to recommend a diet to a patient, of which sugar composed a material part. His patient refused to submit to his prescription, and gave as a reason for it, that he had witnessed so much of the oppression and cruelty which were exercised upon the slaves, who made the sugar, that he had made a vow never to taste the product of their misery as long as he lived.

every farm, and a profit proportioned to the above calculation be derived from them. Should this mode of transplanting the means of obtaining sugar be successful, it will not be a new one. The sugar cane of the West-Indies, was brought originally from the East-Indies, by the Portuguese, and cultivated at Madeira, from whence it was transplanted directly or indirectly, to all the sugar Islands of the West-Indies.

It were to be wished, that the settlers upon the sugar maple lands, would spare the sugar tree in clearing their lands. On a farm of 200 acres of land, according to our former calculation, there are usually 6,000 maple trees. If only 2,000 of those original and ancient inhabitants of the woods, were suffered to remain, and each tree were to afford only five pounds of sugar, the annual profit of such a farm in sugar alone, at the price formerly mentioned, would amount to 666 dollars, 150 dollars of which would probably more than defray all the expences of making it, and allow a plentiful deduction for family use.

According to the usual annual profit of a sugar maple tree, each tree is worth to a farmer, two dollars and 2-3 of a dollar; exclusive therefore of the value of his farm, the 2,000 sugar maple trees alone confer a value upon it of 5,330 dollars and 33-90 of a dollar.

It is said, that the sugar trees when deprived of the shelter and support they derive from other forest trees, are liable to be blown down, occasioned by their growing in a rich, and of course, a loose soil. To obviate this, it will only be necessary to cut off some of their branches, so as to alter its center of gravity, and to allow the high winds to have an easy passage through them. Orchards of sugar maple trees, which grow with an original exposure of all their parts to the action of the sun, will not be liable to this inconvenience.

In contemplating the present opening prospects in human affairs, I am led to expect that a material share of the happiness, which Heaven seems to have prepared for a part of mankind, will be derived from the manufactory and general use of maple sugar, for the benefits which I flatter myself are to result from it, will not be confined to our own country. They will, I hope, extend themselves to the interests of humanity in the West-Indies. With this view of the subject of this letter, I cannot help contemplating a sugar maple tree with a species of affection and even veneration, for I have persuaded myself, to behold in it the happy means of rendering the commerce and slavery of our African brethern, in the sugar Islands as unnecessary, as it has always been inhuman and unjust.

From, dear Sir, your sincere friend,

BENJAMIN RUSH

July 10th, 1791.

AN ACCOUNT OF THE LIFE AND DEATH OF EDWARD DRINKER, WHO DIED ON THE 17TH. OF NOVEMBER, 1782, IN THE 103RD. YEAR OF HIS AGE.

EDWARD DRINKER was born on the 24th. of December, 1680, in a small cabbin, near the present corner of Walnut and Second-streets, in the city of Philadelphia. His parents came from a place called Beverly, in the state of Massachusetts. The banks of the Delaware, on which the city of Philadelphia now stands, were inhabited, at the time of his birth, by Indians, and a few Swedes and Hollanders. He often talked to his companions of picking whortle berries and catching rabbits, on spots now the most improved and populous in the city. He recollected the second time William Penn came to Pennsylvania, and used to point to the place where the cabbin stood, in which he, and his friends, that accompanied him, were accommodated upon their arrival. At twelve years of age, he went to Boston, where he served his apprenticeship to a cabinet maker. In the year 1745, he returned to Philadelphia, with his family, where he lived until the time of his death. He was four times married, and had eighteen children, all of whom were by his first wife. At one time of his life, he sat down, at his own table, with fourteen children. Not long before his death he heard of a grand-child, to one of his grand-children, the fifth in succession to himself.

He retained all his faculties till the last year of his life. Even his memory, so early and so generally diminished by age was but little impaired. He not only remembered the incidents of his childhood and youth,[1] but the events of latter years; and so faithful was his memory to him, that his son has informed me he never heard him tell the same story twice, but to different persons, and in different

---

[1] It is remarkable that the incidents of childhood and youth are seldom remembered or called forth until old age. I have sometimes been led, from this and other circumstances, to suspect that nothing is ever lost that is lodged in the memory, however it may be buried for a time by a variety of causes. How often do we find the transactions of early life, which we had reason to suppose were lost from the mind for ever, revived in our memories by certain accidental sights or sounds,

companies. His eye-sight failed him, many years before his death, but his hearing was uniformly perfect and unimpaired. His appetite was good till within a few days before his death. He generally ate a hearty breakfast of a pint of tea or coffee, as soon as he got out of his bed, with bread and butter in proportion. He ate likewise at eleven o'clock, and never failed to eat plentifully at dinner of the grossest solid food. He drank tea, in the evening, but never ate any supper: he had lost all his teeth thirty years before his death, which was occasioned, his son says, by drawing excessive hot smoke of tobacco into his mouth: but the want of suitable mastication of his food, did not prevent its speedy digestion, nor impair his health. Whether the gums, hardened by age, supplied the place of his teeth in a certain degree, or whether the juices of the mouth and stomach became so much more acrid by time, as to perform the office of dissolving the food more speedily and more perfectly, I know not, but I have often observed, that old people are most disposed to excessive eating, and that they suffer fewest inconveniences from it. He was inquisitive after news in the last years of his life. His education did not lead him to increase the stock of his ideas any other way. But it is a fact well worth attending to, that old age, instead of diminishing, always increases the desire of knowledge. It must afford some consolation to those who expect to be old, to discover, that the infirmities to which the decays of nature expose the human body, are rendered more tolerable by the enjoyments that are to be derived from the appetite for sensual and intellectual food.

He was remarkably sober and temperate. Neither hard labour,

---

particularly by certain notes or air in music. I have known a young man speak French fluently when drunk, that could not put two sentences of that language together, when sober. He had been taught it perfectly, when a boy, but had forgotten it from disuse. A French countess was nursed by a Welsh woman, from whom she learned to speak her language, which she soon forgot, after she had acquired the French, which was her mother tongue. In the delirium of a fever many years afterwards, she was heard to mutter words which none of her family or attendants understood. An old Welsh woman came to see her, who soon perceived that the sounds which were so unintelligible to the family, were the Welsh language. When she recovered, she could not recollect a single word of the language, she had spoken in her sickness. I can conceive great advantages may be derived from this retentive power in our memories, in the advancement of the mind towards perfection in knowledge (so essential to its happiness) in a future world.

nor company, nor the usual afflictions of human life, nor the wastes of nature, ever led him to an improper or excessive use of strong drink. For the last twenty-five years of his life, he drank twice every day of toddy, made with two table spoonfuls of spirits, in half a pint of water. His son, a man of fifty-nine years of age, told me that he had never seen him intoxicated. The time and manner in which he used spiritous liquors, I believe, contributed to lighten the weight of his years, and probably to prolong his life. "Give wine to him that is of a heavy heart, and strong drink to him that is ready to perish with age, as well as with sickness. Let him drink and forget his sorrow, and remember his misery no more."

He enjoyed an uncommon share of health, insomuch that in the course of his long life he never was confined more than three days to his bed. He often declared that he had no idea of that most distressing pain called the head ache. His sleep was interrupted a little in the last years of his life with a defluxion on his breast, which produced what is commonly called the old man's cough.

The character of this aged citizen was not summed up in his negative quality of temperance: he was a man of the most amiable temper: old age had not curdled his blood; he was uniformly cheerful and kind to every body; his religious principles were as steady as his morals were pure. He attended public worship about thirty years in the Rev. Dr. Sproat's church, and died in a full assurance of a happy immortality. The life of this man is marked with several circumstances, which perhaps have seldom occurred in the life of an individual. He saw and heard more of those events which are measured by time, than have ever been seen or heard by any name since the age of the patriarchs; he saw the same spot of earth, which at one period of his life, was covered with wood and bushes, and the receptacle of beasts and birds of prey, afterwards become the seat of a city not only the first in wealth and arts in the new, but rivalling in both, many of the first cities in the old world. He saw regular streets where he once pursued a hare: he saw churches rising upon morasses, where he had often heard the croaking of frogs; he saw wharfs and ware-houses, where he had often seen Indian savages draw fish from the river for their daily subsistence; and he saw ships of every size and use in those streams, where he had often seen nothing but Indian canoes; he saw a stately edifice filled with legislators, astonishing the world with their wisdom and virtue, on the same spot, probably, where he had seen an Indian council fire; he saw the first treaty ratified between the newly confederated powers of America and the ancient monarchy of France, with all the formalities of parchment and seals, on the same spot, probably, where he once saw William Penn ratify his first and last treaty with the Indians, without the formality of pen, ink or paper; he saw all the intermediate states through which a people pass, from the most simple to the highest degrees of civilization. He saw the beginning and end of the empire of Great-Britain, in Pennsylvania. He had been the subject of seven successive crowned heads, and afterwards became a willing citizen of a republic; for he embraced the liberties and independence of America in his withered arms, and triumphed in the last years of his life in the salvation of his country.

Remarkable Circumstances in the Constitution and Life of Ann Woods, an Old Woman of 96 Years of Age.

In the summer of the year 1788, while I was engaged in collecting the facts upon the subject of old age, which I have since published,[1] a poor woman came to my house to beg for cold victuals. Perceiving by her countenance, and the stoop in her walk, that she was very old, I requested her to sit down by me, while I recorded the following information, which I received from her, and which was confirmed to me a few days afterwards, by one of her daughters with whom she lived. Her name was Ann Woods. Her age at that time was 96. She was born in Herefordshire, in England, and came to this city when she was but ten years old, where she had lived ever since. She had been twice married. By her first husband, William Dickson, she had nine children, four of whom were then living. By her second husband, Joseph Woods, whom she married after she was sixty years old, she had one child, born within ten months after her marriage. There were intervals of two and nearly three years between each of her children. Three died soon after weaning them at the usual age in which children are taken from the breast. This led her to suckle her other children during the whole time of her pregnancy, and in several instances, she suckled two of them, born in succession to each other, at the same time. One of her children by her first husband, sucked until it was five years old. Her menses appeared between her nineteenth and twentieth years and continued without any intermission, except during her pregnancy and eleven months after the birth of each of her children, until she was eighty years of age. At the time I saw her, she heard tolerably well, but her sight was lost in one eye, and was weak in the other. She lost all her teeth when she was between fifty and sixty years of age. Her hair became grey when she was between forty and fifty. Her sleep was not sound, owing to her having been afflicted with the Rheumatism, a disease which was brought on her by the alternate heat and cold to which she had exposed herself, by following the business of a washer woman for many years. She had had several

---

[1] Medical Enquiries and Observations. Vol. 2.

attacks of the Intermitting Fever and of the Pleurisy, in the course of her life, and was much afflicted with the Head-Ache, after her menses ceased. She had been frequently bled while afflicted with the above diseases. Her diet was simple, consisting chiefly of weak tea, milk, cheese, butter and vegetables. Meat of all kinds, except veal, disagreed with her stomach. She found great benefit from frequently changing her aliment. Her drinks were water, cyder and water, molasses and vinegar in water. She had never used spirits. Her memory was but little impaired. She was cheerful and thankful that her condition in life was happier than hundreds of other old people.

From the history of this old woman's constitution and manner of life, the following observations will naturally occur to the reader.

1. That there is a great latitude in the time in which the menses cease. It is more common for them in their excentricities, to disappear at the usual time, and to return in extreme old age. In the year 1795, I saw a case of this kind in a woman of seventy years of age in the Pennsylvania Hospital.

2. There is a great latitude in the time in which women bear children. Many children are born between fifty and sixty, but very few I believe beyond sixty.

3. It appears from the history that has been given, that acute and chronic diseases if opposed by temperance and suitable remedies, do not necessarily shorten the duration of human life.

4. That child-bearing, and suckling children, do not materially affect health, or longevity, where their effects are opposed by temperance and moderate labour.

5. That the evils of life are seldom so numerous, as not to leave room for thankfulness for an exemption from a great deal of misery. This poor woman did not complain of her weakness, pains or poverty. On the contrary, she appeared thankful under all the afflictions of her life. While the indolent are commanded by the wise man to go to the ant to learn industry, those persons who abound with all the external means of happiness, and at the same time complain of the moral government of our world, may be invited to sit down by the side of Ann Woods, and learn from the example of her gratitude to heaven, for a single drop of divine goodness, to render unceasing thanks for the ocean of blessings they derive from the same source.

BIOGRAPHICAL ANECDOTES OF BENJAMIN LAY.

THERE was a time when the name of this celebrated Christian Philosopher, was familier to every man, woman and to nearly every child, in Pennsylvania.—His size, which was not much above four feet, his dress, which was always the same, consisting of light coloured plain clothes, a white hat, and half-boots;—his milk- white beard, which hung upon his breast; and, above all, his peculiar principles and conduct, rendered him to many, an object of admiration, and to all, the subject of conversation.—

He was born in England, and spent the early part of his life at sea. His first settlement was in Barbadoes, as a merchant, where he was soon convinced of the iniquity of the slave trade. He bore an open testimony against it, in all companies, by which means he rendered himself so unpopular, that he left the island in disgust, and settled in the then province of Pennsylvania. He fixed his home at Abington, ten miles from Philadelphia, from whence he made frequent excursions to the city, and to different parts of the country.—

At the time of his arrival in Pennsylvania, he found many of his brethren, the people called Quakers, had fallen so far from their original principles, as to keep negro slaves. He remonstrated with them, both publickly and privately, against the practice; but frequently with so much indiscreet zeal, as to give great offence. He often disturbed their public meetings, by interrupting or opposing their preachers, for which he was once carried out of a meeting-house, by two or three friends.—Upon this occasion he submitted with patience to what he considered a species of persecution.—He lay down at the door of the meeting-house, in a shower of rain, till divine worship was ended; nor could he be prevailed upon to rise, till the whole congregation had stepped over him in their way to their respective homes.—

To shew his indignation against the practice of slave-keeping, he once carried a bladder filled with blood into a meeting; and, in the presence of the whole congregation, thrust a sword, which he had concealed under his coat, into the bladder, exclaiming, at the same time, "Thus shall God shed the blood of those persons who enslave their fellow creatures." The terror of this extravagant and unexpected act, produced swoonings in several of the women of the congregation.—

He once went into the house of a friend in Philadelphia, and found him seated at breakfast, with his family around him. Being asked by him to sit down and breakfast with them, he said, "Dost thou keep slaves in thy house?" Upon being answered in the affirmative, he said, "Then I will not partake with thee, of the fruits of thy unrighteousness."

He took great pains to convince a farmer and his wife, in Chester county, of the iniquity of keeping negro slaves, but to no purpose. They not only kept their slaves, but defended the practice. One day he went into their house, and after a short discourse with them upon the wickedness, and particularly the inhumanity of separating children from their parents, which was involved in the slave trade, he seized the only child of the family, (a little girl about three years old) and pretended to run away with her.—The child cried bitterly, "I will be good,—I will be good," and the parents shewed signs of being alarmed. Upon observing this scene, Mr. Lay said, very emphatically,—"You *see,* and *feel* now, a little of the distress you occasion every day, by the inhuman practice of slave-keeping."

This singular philosopher did not limit his pious testimony against vice, to slave-keeping alone. He was opposed to every species of extravagance. Upon the introduction of tea, as an article of diet, into Pennsylvania, his wife bought a small quantity of it, with a sett of cups and saucers, and brought them home with her. Mr. Lay took them from her, brought them back again to the city, and from the balcony of the courthouse scattered the tea, and broke the cups and saucers, in the presence of many hundred spectators, delivering, at the same time, a striking lecture upon the folly of preferring that foreign herb, with its expensive appurtenances, to the simple and wholesome diet of our country.

He possessed a good deal of wit, and was quick at repartee. A citizen of Philadelphia, who knew his peculiarities, once met him in a croud, at a funeral, in Germantown. Being desirous of entering into a conversation with him that should divert the company, the citizen accosted him, with the most respectful ceremony, and declared himself to be "his most humble servant." "Art thou my servant." said Mr. Lay,—"Yes—I am" said the citizen. "Then, said Mr. Lay, (holding up his foot towards him,) clean this shoe."—This unexpected reply turned the laugh upon the citizen. Being desirous of recovering himself in the opinion of the company, he asked him to instruct him in the way to heaven. "Dost thou indeed wish to be taught," said Mr. Lay. "I do," said the citizen. "Then," said Mr. Lay, "Do justice—love mercy, and walk humbly with thy God."

He wrote a small treatise upon negro-slavery, which he brought to Dr. Franklin to be printed. Upon looking over it, the Doctor told him that it was not paged, and that there appeared to be no order or arrangement in it. "It is no matter said Mr. Lay—print any part thou pleasest first."—This book contained many pious sentiments, and strong expressions against negro slavery; but even the address and skill of Dr. Franklin were not sufficient to connect its different parts together, so as to render it an agreeable or useful work. This book is in the library of the city of Philadelphia.

Mr. Lay was extremely attentive to young people. He took great pleasure in visiting schools, where he often preached to the youth. He frequently carried a basket of religious books with him, and distributed them as prizes, among the scholars.

He was fond of reading. In the print of him, which is to be seen in many houses in Philadelphia, he is represented with "Tryon on Happiness" in his hand, a book which he valued very much, and which he frequently carried with him in his excurions from home.

He was kind and charitable to the poor, but had no compassion for beggars. He used to say, "there was no man or woman, who was able to go abroad to beg, that was not able to earn *four pence* a day, and this sum, he said, was enough to keep any person above want, or dependence, in this country."

His humanity was as ingenious as it was extensive, and embraced the sufferings which arise from even the common inconveniences of life. One, among many instances that might be mentioned of this species of humanity, was his advising the farmers who lived near to public roads to plant fruit trees along them, in order "to protect the weary traveller by their shade, and to refresh him with their fruits."

He was a severe enemy to idleness, insomuch that when he could not employ himself out of doors, or when he was tired of reading, he used to spend his time in spinning. His common sitting room was hung with skains of threads, spun entirely by himself. All his clothes were of his own manufactory.

He was extremely temperate in his diet, living chiefly upon

vegetables.—Turnips boiled, and afterwards roasted, were his favourite dinner. His drink was pure water. From a desire of imitating our Saviour, in every thing, he once attempted to fast for forty days. This experiment, it is said had nearly cost him his life. He was obliged to desist from it, long before the forty days were expired; but the fasting, it was said, so much debilitated his body, as to accelerate his death. He lived above eighty years, and died in his own house in Abington, about thirty years ago.

In reviewing the history of this extraordinary man, we cannot help absolving him of his weaknesses, when we contemplate his many active virtues. He was the pioneer of that war, which has since been carried on, so successfully, against the commerce and slavery of the negroes.—Perhaps the turbulence and severity of his temper were necessary to rouse the torpor of the human mind, at the period in which he lived, to this interesting subject. The meekness and gentleness of Anthony Benezet, who compleated what Mr. Lay began would probably have been as insufficient for the work performed by Mr. Lay, as the humble piety of De Renty, or of Thomas a' Kempis, would have been to accomplish the works of the zealous Luther, or the intrepid Knox in the sixteenth century.

The success of Mr. Lay, in sowing the seeds of a principle which bids fair to produce a revolution in morals—commerce—and government, in the new and in the old world, should teach the benefactors of mankind not to despair, if they do not see the fruits of their benevolent propositions, or undertakings, during their lives.—No one seed of truth or virtue ever perished.—Wherever it may be sowed, or even scattered, it will preserve and carry with it the principle of life.—Some of these seeds produce their fruits in a short time, but the most valuable of them, like the venerable oak— are centuries in growing; but they are unlike the pride of the forests, as well as all other vegetable productions, in being incapable of a decay;

They exist and bloom for ever.

February 10th. 1790.

BIOGRAPHICAL ANECDOTES OF ANTHONY BENEZET.

THIS excellent man was placed by his friends in early life in a counting-house, but finding commerce opened temptations to a worldly spirit, he left his master, and bound himself as an apprentice to a cooper. Finding this business too laborious for his constitution, he declined it, and devoted himself to schoolkeeping; in which useful employment, he continued during the greatest part of his life.

He possessed uncommon activity and industry in every thing he undertook. He did every thing as if the words of his Saviour were perpetually sounding in his ears, "wist ye not, that I must be about my Father's business?"

He used to say, "the highest act of charity in the world was to bear with the *unreasonableness* of mankind."

He generally wore plush clothes, and gave as a reason for it, that after he had worn them for two or three years, they made comfortable and decent garments for the poor.

He once informed a young friend, that his memory began to fail him; "but this," said he, "gives me one great advantage over thee— for thou canst find entertainment in reading a good book only *once*—but I enjoy that pleasure as often as I read it; for it is always new to me."

He published several valuable tracts in favor of the emancipation of the blacks, and of the civilizing and christianizing the Indians. He also published a pamphlet against the use of ardent spirits. All these publications were circulated with great industry, and at his own expense, throughout every part of the United States.

He wrote letters to the queen of Great-Britain, and to the queen of Portugal to use their influence with their respective courts to abolish the African trade. He accompanied his letter to the queen of Great-Britain with a present of his works. The queen received them with great politeness, and said after reading them, "that the author appeared to be a very good man."

He also wrote a letter to the King of Prussia, in which he endeavoured to convince him of the unlawfulness of war.

During the time the British army was in possession of the city of Philadelphia, he was indefatigable in his endeavours to render the situation of the persons who suffered from captivity as easy as possible. He knew no fear in the presence of his fellow men, however dignified they were by titles or station, and such were the propriety and gentleness of his manners in his intercourse with the gentlemen who commanded the British and German troops, that when he could not obtain the objects of his requests, he never failed to secure their civilities, and frequently their esteem.

So great was his sympathy with every thing that was capable of feeling pain, that he resolved towards, the close of his life, to [me] eat no animal food. Upon coming into his brother's house one day, when his family was dining upon poultry, he was asked by his brother's wife, to sit down and dine with them. "What!" (said he,) "would you have eat my neighbours?"

This misapplication of a moral feeling, was supposed to have brought on such a debility in his stomach and bowels, as produced a disease in those parts of which he finally died.

Few men, since days of the apostles, ever lived a more disinterested life. And yet, upon his death bed, he said, he wished to live a little longer, that "he might bring down SELF."

The last time he ever walked across his room, was to take from his desk six dollars, which he gave to a poor widow whom he had long assisted to maintain.

He bequeathed after the death of his widow, a house and lot in which consisted his whole estate, to the support of a school for the education of negro children, which he had founded and taught for several years before his death.

He died in May 1784, in the 71st year of his age.

His funeral was attended by persons of all religious denominations, and by many hundred black people.

Colonel J——n, who had served in the American army, during the late war, in returning from the funeral, pronounced an eulogium upon him. It consisted only of the following words: "I would rather," said he, "be Anthony Benezet in that coffin, than George Washington with all his fame."

July 15, 1788.

PARADISE OF NEGRO SLAVES.—A DREAM.

SOON after reading Mr. Clarkson's ingenious and pathetic essay on the slavery and commerce of the human species, the subject made so deep an impression upon my mind, that it followed me in my sleep, and produced a dream of so extraordinary a nature, that I have yielded to the importunities of some of my friends, by communicating it to the public. I thought I was conducted to a country, which in point of cultivation and scenery, far surpassed any thing I had ever heard, or read of in my life. This country, I found, was inhabited only by negroes. They appeared cheerful and happy. Upon my approaching a beautiful grove, where a number of them were assembled for religious purposes, I perceived at once a pause in their exercises, and an appearance of general perturbation. They fixed their eyes upon me—while one of them, a venerable looking man, came forward, and in the name of the whole assembly, addressed me in the following language:

"Excuse the panic which you have spread through this peaceful and happy company: we perceive that you are a *white man*.—That colour which is the emblem of innocence in every other creature of God, is to us a sign of guilt in man. The persons whom you see here, were once dragged by the men of your colour from their native country, and consigned by them to labour—punishment—and death.—We are here collected together, and enjoy an ample compensation in our present employments for all the miseries we endured on earth. We know that we are secured by the Being whom we worship, from injury and oppression. Our appearance of terror, therefore, was entirely the sudden effect of habits which have not yet been eradicated from our minds."

"Your apprehensions of danger from the sight of a white man," said I, "are natural. But in me—you behold a friend. I have been your advocate—and."—Here, he interrupted me, and said, "Is not your name—?" I answered in the affirmative. Upon this he ran up and embraced me in his arms, and afterwards conducted me into the midst of the assembly, where, after being introduced to the principal characters, I was seated upon a bank of moss; and the following account was delivered to me by the venerable person who first accosted me.

"The place we now occupy, is called the *paradise of negro slaves.* It is destined to be our place of residence 'till the general judgement; after which time, we expect to be admitted into higher and more perfect degrees of happiness. Here we derive great pleasure from con-templating the infinite goodness of God, in alloting to us our full proportion of misery on earth; by which means we have escaped the punishments, to which the free and happy part of mankind too often expose themselves after death. Here we have learned to thank God, for all the afflictions our task-masters heaped on us; inasmuch, as they were the means of our present happiness. Pain and distress are the unavoidable portions of all mankind. They are the only possible avenues that can conduct them to peace and felicity. Happy are they, who partake of their proportion of both upon the earth." Here he ended.—

After a silence of a few minutes, a young man, who bore on his head the mark of a wound, came up to me and asked "If I knew any thing of Mr. —, of the Island of—" I told him "I did not." "Mr. —," said he, "was my master. One day, I mistook his orders and saddled his mare instead of his horse, which provoked him so much, that he took up an axe which laid in his yard, and with a stroke on my head dismissed me from life.

"I long to hear, whether he has repented of this unkind action. Do, sir, write to him, and tell him, his sin is not too great to be forgiven, tell him, his once miserable slave, Scipio, is not angry at him—he longs to bear his prayers to the offended majesty of heaven—and—when he dies—Scipio will apply to be one of the con-voy, that shall conduct his spirit to the regions of bliss appointed for those who repent of their iniquities."

Before I could reply to this speech, an old man came and sat down by my side. His wool was white as snow. With a low, but gentle voice, he thus addressed me.

"Sir, I was the slave of Mr. —, in the Island of—I served him faithfully upwards of sixty years. No rising sun ever caught me in my cabin—no setting sun ever saw me out of the sugar field, except on Sundays and holydays. My whole subsistence never cost my master more than forty shillings a year. Herrings and roots were my only food. One day, in the eightieth year of my age, the overseer saw me stop to rest myself against the side of a tree, where I was at work. He came up to me, and beat me, 'till he could endure the fatigue and heat occasioned by the blows he gave me, no longer.

Nor was this all—he complained of me to my master, who instantly
set me up at public vendue, and sold me for two guineas to a tavern-
keeper, in a distant parish. The distress I felt, in leaving my children,
and grandchildren (28 of whom I left on my old master's plantation)
soon put an end to my existence, and landed me upon these happy
shores. I have now no wish to gratify but one—and that is to be permitted to visit my old master's family. I long to tell my master, that
his wealth cannot make him happy.—That the sufferings of a single
hour in the world of misery, for which he is preparing himself, will
overbalance all the pleasures he ever enjoyed in his life—and that
for every act of unnecessary severity he inflicts upon his slaves, he
shall suffer tenfold in the world to come."

He had hardly finished his tale, when a decent looking woman
came forward, and addressed me in the following language.—

Sir,

"I was once the slave of Mr. —, in the state of—. From the
healthiness of my constitution, I was called upon to suckle my
Master's eldest son. To enable me to perform this office more effectually, my own child was taken from my breast, and soon afterwards
died. My affections in the first emotions of my grief, fastened
themselves upon my infant master. He thrived under my care and
grew up a handsome young man. Upon the death of his father, I
became his property.—Soon after this event, he lost £100 at cards.
To raise this money I was sold to a planter in a neighbouring state.
I can never forget the anguish, with which my aged father and
mother followed me to the end of the lane, when I left my master's
house, and hung upon me, when they bid me farewell."

"My new master obliged me to work in the field; the consequence of which was, I caught a fever which in a few weeks ended
my life. Say, my friend, is my first young master still alive?—If he
is—go to him, and tell him, his unkind behaviour to me is upon
record against him. The gentle spirits in heaven, whose happiness
consists in expressions of gratitude and love, will have no fellowship
with him. His soul must be melted with pity, or he can never escape
the punishment which awaits the hard-hearted, equally with the
impenitent, in the regions of misery."

As soon as she had finished her story, a middle aged woman
approached me, and after a low and respectful curtsey, thus
addressed me.

"Sir I was born and educated in a christian family in one of the southern states of America. In the thirty-third year of my age, I applied to my master to purchase my freedom. Instead of granting my request, he conveyed me by force on board of a vessel and sold me to a planter in the island of Hispaniola. Here it pleased God."—Upon pronouncing these words, she paused and a general silence ensued.—All at once, the eyes of the whole assembly were turned from me, and directed towards a little white man who advanced towards them, on the opposite side of the grove, in which we were seated. His face was grave, placid, and full of benignity. In one hand he carried a subscription paper and a petition—in the other, he carried a small pamphlet, on the unlawfulness of the African slave-trade, and a letter directed to the King of Prussia, upon the unlaw-fulness of war. While I employed in contemplating this venerable figure—suddenly I beheld the whose assembly running to meet him—the air resounded with the clapping of hands—and I awoke from my dream, by the noise of a general acclamation of—ANTHONY BENEZET!

AN INQUIRY INTO THE CAUSES OF PREMATURE DEATHS.

THE frequency of death in infancy, childhood, and middle life, and the immense disproportion between the number who die in those periods, and of those who die in old age, have often been urged as arguments against the wisdom and goodness of the divine government. The design of this inquiry is to shew that, in the present state of the world those supposed evils, or defects, are blessing in disguise, and a part of a wise and extensive system of goodness to the children of men.

The reasons for this opinion are:

1. Did all the people who are born, live to be seventy or eighty years of age, the population of the globe would soon so far surpass its present cultivation, that millions would perish yearly from the want of food.

2. Did all the men and women who come into the world, live to be old, how miserable would be the condition of most of them, from weakness, sickness, and pain! Unable to assist each other, and neglected or deserted by their children, or friends, they would perish from want, or perhaps putrify above ground. This view of the consequences of universal longevity is not an exaggerated one. A tribe of northern Indians, Mr. Hearnes says, always leave their parents, when they become old and helpless, to die alone with hunger. They meet death, he adds, with resignation, from an idea of its necessity, and from the recollection of their having treated their parents in the same manner. In support of the remark, under this head, let us recollect how many old people in humble life, are maintained by the public, and how few parents in genteel life, after they have exhausted their liberality upon their children, receive from them a due porportion of gratitude or respect.

3. In the present depraved state of human nature, how great would be the mass of vice in the world, if old age were universal? If avarice in an individual strikes a whole city with surprise and horror, how great would be the mass of this vice in a city that contained 30 or 40,000 old people, all equally absorbed in the love of money? Again, what would be the extent and degrees of ambition, malice and cruelty, nurtured and cherished for 70 or 80 years in the same

number of human beings? But, to do justice to this part of our subject, let us view the effects of universal longevity upon another and
greater scale. Suppose Alexander, Caesar, Nero, Caligula, and many
others of the conquerors and tyrants of the ancient worlds, had
lived to be old men with the ambition and love of power that have
been ascribed to them, growing with their years, how much more
accumulated would have been their crimes, and how much more
distressing would have been the history of the nations which were
conquered and enslaved by them! The same Alexander, who at
thirty years of age, only demanded divine homage from his captives,
would probably at seventy have exacted human sacrifices to satisfy
his assumed divinity; and the same Nero, who, when a young man,
only fiddled at the sight of the houses of Rome in a blaze, had he
lived to be old, would probably have danced at the sight of all the
inhabitants of that city perishing in its general conflagration. But
I will not rely upon mere supposition, to evince the pernicious influence which universal longevity has upon morals. The inhabitants
of the antediluvian world exhibited a memorable instance of it.
Their wickedness is characterized by the sacred historian in the
following words. "And God saw that the wickedness of man was
great in the earth, and that every imagination of the thoughts of his
heart was only evil, continually. The earth also was corrupt before
God: and the earth was filled with violence." Gen. vi. 6 & 11. The
extent of the wickedness among the antediluvians may easily be
conceived from the two following circumstances.

1. The small number of those persons who escaped the general
depravity of morals which had overspread the world, being *eight*
only; and that at a time when the world was probably more
populous than it has ever been since.

2. The abortive issue of the means that God employed to reform
them. Noah preached to them several hundred years, and probably
during that long period, travelled over a great portion of the world,
and yet not a single person was converted, or saved from destruction by his ministry, except the members of his own family.

It was from a review of this wickedness, by the Supreme Being,
that life was shortened, as if in mercy to prevent a similar accumula-
tion of it in any future age of the world. "And the Lord said, my
breath shall not always remain in these men because they are flesh,

yet shall their days be one hundred and twenty years."[1] For the same reason they were afterwards reduced to seventy, or a few more years, as is obvious from the 10th verse of the 90th Psalm.

4. The mass of vice is not only lessened by the small proportion of the human race who live to be old, but the mass of virtue is thereby greatly increased. The death of persons who have filled up the measure of their days, and who descend to the grave in a good old age, seldom excites a serious reflection; but every death that occurs in early or middle life, has a tendency to damp the ardor of worldly pursuits, to weaken the influence of some sinful passion, and to produce some degrees of reverence for that religion which opens prospects of life and happiness beyond the grave.

5. If vice, as we are taught to believe, will be punished, according to its degrees, in a future state of existence, how much greater would be the mass of misery hereafter, if the whole human race lived to be old, and with increasing habits of wickedness, than it will be in the present contracted duration of human life? It is therefore no less an act of mercy, than justice, that the "wicked live not out half their days."

6. If old age were universal, how difficult and severe would be the conflicts of virtue! To be exposed to the malignant passions of bad men, or, what is often worse, to contend with our own evil propensities for seventy or eighty years, would render the warfare of good men much more perilous, and their future happiness much more precarious, than it is at present. How few persons who live to be old, escape the idolatrous passion of covetousness? Were old age universal, this passion would probably exclude one half of them from the kingdom of heaven.

---

[1] This translation of the verse is copied from the ROMANS lxx. whose version is justified by all the circumstances of the case. The creator had breathed into man's nostrils the breath of life, (Gen. ii. 7.) and a continuance in life was promised him during his continuance in innocence; but upon his transgression he became mortal; and upon an increase of wickedness, human life was proportionably shortened. It was for this reason (Gen. vi. 13) that God determined to destroy the old world; and this occasioned the above declaration; the punctuality with which it was verified deserves particular notice; for Noah was employed 120 years in building the ark; and at the expiration of that time the flood came, and destroyed "all in whose nostrils was the *breath of life*, of all that was in the dry land." Gen. vii. 22.

7. Did all men live to be old, it would render knowledge stationary. Few men alter their opinions, or admit new truths, after they are forty years of age. None of the contemporary physicians of Dr. Harvey, who had passed that age, admitted his discovery of the circulation of the blood. Now considering that nearly all discoveries in science are made by men under forty, and considering the predominating influence and authority which accompany the hostility of old men to new truths, discoveries made by young men could never acquire belief, or an establishment in the world. They owe both, to the small number of philosophers who live to be seventy or eighty years of age.

8. Were longevity universal, with all the deformity from wrinkles, baldness, and the loss of teeth and complexion, that are usually connected with it, what a gloomy and offensive picture would the assemblies of our fellow-creatures exhibit? In the present small proportion of old people to the young and middle aged, they seem like shades in painting, or like a few decayed trees near a highly cultivated garden, filled with blooming and fragrant flowers, to exhibit the charms of youth and beauty to greater advantage. From an assembly composed exclusively of old men and women, we should turn our eyes with pain and disgust.

If the causes of premature deaths which have been assigned, be correct, instead of complaining of them, it becomes us, in the present state of the cultivation, population, government, religion, morals, and knowledge in the world, to consider them as subjects for praise and thanksgiving to the wise and benevolent Governor of the Universe.

While we thus do homage to the divine wisdom and goodness, let us look forward to the time when the improvements in the physical, moral, and political condition of the world, predicted in the Old Testament, shall render the early and distressing separation of parents and children, and of husbands and wives, wholly unnecessary; when the physical and moral sources of those apparent evils shall be removed by the combined influence of philosophy and religion, and when old age shall be the only outlet of human life. The following verses taken from the 65th chapter of the prophecy of Isaaih, justify a belief in an order of things, such as has been mentioned: "There shall be no more thence an infant of days," [or an infant that has lived but a few days] "nor an old man that hath not filled his days, for the child shall die an hundred years old. And they shall build houses, and inhabit them, and they shall plant vineyards, and eat the fruit of them. They shall not build, and another inhabit, they shall not plant, and another eat, for as the days of a tree, are the days of my people, and mine elect shall long enjoy the work of their hands."

AN EULOGIUM UPON DR. WILLIAM CULLEN, PROFESSOR OF THE PRACTICE OF PHYSIC, IN THE UNIVERSITY OF EDINBURGH; DELIVERED BEFORE THE COLLEGE OF PHYSICIANS OF PHILADELPHIA, ON THE 9TH OF JULY, AGREEABLY TO THEIR VOTE OF THE 4TH OF MAY, 1790, AND AFTERWARDS PUBLISHED AT THEIR REQUEST.

MR. President and Gentlemen,

By your unanimous vote, to honor with an Eulogium, the character of the late DR. WILLIAM CULLEN, Professor of medicine in the University of Edinburgh, you have done equal homage to science and humanity. This illustrious Physician was the Preceptor of many of us:—He was moreover a distinguished citizen of the republic of medicine, and a benefactor to mankind; and although, like the sun, he shone in a distant hemisphere, yet many of the rays of his knowledge have fallen upon this quarter of the globe. I rise, therefore, to mingle your grateful praises of him, with the numerous offerings of public and private respect which have been paid to his memory in his native country. Happy will be the effects of such acts of distant sympathy, if they should serve to unite the influence of science with that of commerce, to lessen the prejudices of nations against each other, and thereby to prepare the way for the operation of that divine system of morals, whose prerogative alone it is, to teach mankind that they are brethren, and to make the name of a fellow-creature, in every region of the world, a signal for brotherly affection.

In executing the task you have imposed upon me, I shall confine myself to such parts of Dr. Cullen's character as came within the compass of my own knowledge, during two years residence in Edinburgh.—To his fellow citizens in Great Britain, who were more intimately acquainted with him, we must resign the history of his domestic character, as well as the detail of all those steps which, in early life, led him to his unparalleled height of usefulness and fame.

Dr. Cullen possessed a great and original genius. By genius, in the present instance, I mean a power in the human mind of discovering the relation of distant truths, by the shortest train of intermediate propositions. This precious gift of Heaven, is composed of a vigorous imagination, quick sensibility, a talent for extensive and accurate observation, a faithful memory, and a sound judgment. These faculties were all united in an eminent degree in the mind of Dr. Cullen. His imagination surveyed all nature at a glance, and, like a camera obscura, seemed to produce in his mind a picture of the whole visible creation. His sensibility was so exquisite that the smallest portions of truth acted upon it. By means of his talent for observation he collected knowledge from every thing he heard, saw, or read, and from every person with whom he conversed. His memory was the faithful repository of all his ideas, and appeared to be alike accurate upon all subjects. Over each of these faculties of his mind a sound judgement presided, by means of which he discovered the relation of ideas to each other, and thereby produced those new combinations which constitute principles in science. This process of the mind has been called invention, and is totally different from a mere capacity of acquiring learning, or collecting knowledge from the discoveries of others. It elevates man to a distant resemblance of his Maker; for the discovery of truth, is the perception of·things as they appear to the Divine Mind.

In contemplating the human faculties, thus exquisitely formed, and exactly balanced, we feel the same kind of pleasure which arises from a view of a magnificent palace, or an extensive and variegated prospect; but with this difference, that the pleasure, in the first instance, is as much superior to that which arises from contemplating the latter objects, as the mind of man is superior, in its importance, to the most finished productions of nature or of art.

Dr. Cullen possessed not only the genius that has been described, but an uncommon share of learning, reading, and knowledge.

His learning was of peculiar and useful kind—He appeared to have overstepped the slow and tedious forms of the schools, and, by the force of his understanding, to have seized upon the great ends of learning, without the assistance of many of those means which were contrived for the use of less active minds. He read the ancient Greek and Roman writers only for the sake of the knowledge which they contained, without wasting any of the efforts of his genius in attempting to imitate their style. He was intimately acquainted with modern languages, and through their means, with the improvements of medicine in every country in Europe. Such was the facility with which he acquired a language, and so great was his enterprise in his researches in medicine, that I once heard him speak of learning the Arabic for the sake of reading Avicenna in the original, as if it were a matter of as little difficulty to him, as it was to compose a lecture, or to visit a patient.

Dr. Cullen's reading was extensive, but it was not confined wholly to medicine. He read books upon all subjects; and he had a peculiar art of extracting something from all of them which he made subservient to his profession. He was well acquainted with ancient and modern history, and delighted in the poets, among whom Shakespeare was his favourite. The history of our globe, as unfolded by books of geography and travels, was so familiar to him that strangers could not converse with him, without supposing that he had not only travelled, but that he had lived every where. His memory had no rubbish in it. Like a secretory organ, in the animal body, it rejected every thing in reading that could not be applied to some useful purpose. In this he has given the world a most valuable lesson, for the difference between error and useless truth is very small; and a man is no wiser for knowledge, which he cannot apply, than he is rich from possessing wealth, which he cannot spend.

Dr. Cullen's knowledge was minute in every branch of medicine. He was an accurate anatomist, and an ingenious physiologist. He enlarged the boundaries, and established the utility of Chemistry, and thereby prepared the way for the discoveries and fame of his illustrious pupil Dr. Black. He stripped Materia Medica, of most of the errors that had been accumulating in it for two thousand years, and reduced it to a simple and practical science. He was intimately acquainted with all the branches of natural history and philosophy. He had studied every ancient and modern system of physic. He found the system of Dr. Boerhave universally adopted when he accepted a chair in the University of Edinburgh. This system was founded chiefly on the supposed presence of certain acrid particles in the fluids, and in the departure of these, in point of consistency, from a natural state. Dr. Cullen's first object was to expose the errors of this pathology; and to teach his pupils to seek for the causes of diseases in the solids. Nature is always coy. Ever since she was driven from the heart, by the discovery of the circulation of the blood, she has concealed herself in the brain and nerves. Here she has been pursued by Dr. Cullen; and if he has not dragged her to public view, he has left us a clue which must in time conduct us to her last recess in the human body. Many, however, of the operations of nature in the nervous system have been explained by him; and no candid man will ever explain the whole of them, without acknowledging that the foundation of his successful inquiries was laid by the discoveries of Dr. Cullen.

He was intimately acquainted with the histories and distinctions of the diseases of all countries, ages, stations, occupations, and states of society. While his great object was to explode useless remedies, he took pains to increase the influence of diet, dress, air, exercise, and the action of the mind, in medicine. In a word he was a great practical physician; and he has left behind him as many monuments of his success in curing diseases, as he has of accuracy and ingenuity in describing their symptoms and explaining their causes.

But his knowledge was not confined wholly to those sciences which are intimately connected with medicine. His genius was universal, as to natural and artificial subjects. He was minutely acquainted with the principles and practices of all the liberal, mechanical, and chemical arts; and tradesmen were often directed by him to new objects of observation and improvement in their respective occupations. He delighted in the study of agriculture, and contributed much to excite that taste for agricultural science, which has of late years so much distinguished the men of genius and leisure in North-Britain. I have been informed, that he yielded at last to that passion for rural improvements, which is common to all men, and amused himself in the evening of his life by cultivating a farm in the neighbourhood of Edinburgh. Happy would it be for the interests of agriculture, if physicians in all countries, would imitate Dr. Cullen by an attachment to this noble science; for their previous studies are of such a nature as frequently to enable them to arrive at improvements in it without experiments, and to apply the experiments of others, in the most extensive and profitable manner.

Dr. Cullen's publications were few in number compared with his discoveries. They consist of his Elements of Physiology, his

Nosologia Methodica, his First Lines of the Practice of Physic, an Essay upon the Cold produced by Evaporation, published in the second volume of the Physical and Literary Essays of Edinburgh, a Letter to Lord Cathcart upon the method of recovering persons supposed to be dead from drowning, and a system of the Materia Medica. These are all the works which bear his name; but the fruits of his inquiries are to be found in most of the medical publications that have appeared in Great-Britain within the last thirty years. Many of the Theses, published in Edinburgh during his life, were the vehicles of his opinions or practice in medicine: and few of them contained an important or useful discovery, which was not derived from hints thrown out in his lectures.

As a TEACHER of medicine, Dr. Cullen possessed many peculiar talents. He mingled the most agreeable eloquence with the most profound disquisitions. He appeared to *lighten* upon every subject upon which he spoke. His language was simple, and his arrangement methodical, by which means he was always intelligible. From the moment he ascended his chair, he commanded the most respectful attention from his pupils, insomuch that I never saw one of them discover a sign of impatience during the time of any of his lectures.

In the investigation of truth, he sometimes ventured into the regions of conjecture. His imagination was an hot-bed of hypotheses, which led him to constant observation and experiment. These often proved the seeds of subsequent discoveries. It was thus Sir Isaac Newton founded an empire in science; for most of his discoveries were the result of preconceived hypotheses. In delivering new opinions, Dr. Cullen preserved the strictest integrity. I have known him more than once, refute the opinions which he had taught the preceding year, even before the fallacy of them had been suspected by any of his pupils. Such instances of candor often pass with the vulgar for instability; but they are the truest characteristics of a great mind. To be unchangeable, supposes perpetual error, or a perception of truth without the use of reason; but this sublime act of intuition belongs only to the Deity.

There was no tincture of credulity in the mind of Dr. Cullen. He taught his pupils the necessity of acquiring "the slow consenting academic doubt." I mention these words of the poet with peculiar pleasure, as I find them in my notes of one of his lectures, in which

he has delivered rules for judging of the truth of things related as facts: for he frequently remarked that there were ten false facts (if the expression can be allowed) to one false opinion in medicine. His Materia Medica abounds with proofs of the truth of this part of his character. With how much caution does he admit the efficacy of medicines, as related in books, or as suggested by his own experience. Who could have expected to have found so much modesty in the writings of a physician in the 77th year of his age? But let it be remembered, that physician was Dr. Cullen: and that he always preferred utility to novelty, and loved truth, more than fame.

He took great pains to deliver his pupils from the undue influence which antiquity and great names are apt to have upon the human mind. He destroyed the superstitious veneration which had been paid for many ages to the names of Hippocrates, Galen, and other ancient authors, and inspired his pupils with a just estimate of the writings of modern physicians. His constant aim was to produce in their minds a change from a passive to an active state; and to force upon them such habits of thinking and observation, as should enable them to instruct themselves.

As he admitted no truth without examination, so he submitted to no custom in propagating it that was not reasonable. He had a principal share in the merit of delivering medicine from the fetters of the Latin, and introducing the English language, as the vehicle of public instruction in the university of Edinburgh. Much of the success of the revolution he effected in medicine, I believe, may be ascribed to this circumstance. Perhaps the many improvements which have lately been made in medicine, in the British dominions, may likewise be ascribed to the present fashionable custom of communicating medical knowledge in the English language. By this means, our science has excited the notice and inquiries of ingenious and observing men in all professions, and thereby a kind of galaxy has been created in the hemisphere of medicine. By assuming an English dress, it has moreover been prepared more easily to associate with other sciences; from each of which it has received assistance and support.

In his intercourse with his pupils Dr. Cullen was truly kind and affectionate. Never have I known a man who possessed in a higher degree those qualities which seize upon every affection of the heart. He knew the rare and happy arts, as circumstances required, of being affable without being sociable; sociable without being familiar; and familiar, without losing a particle of respect. Such was the interest he took in the health, studies, and future establishment of all his pupils, that each of them believed that he possessed a pre-eminence in his friendship; while the equal diffusion of his kind offices proved that he was the common friend and father of them all. Sometimes he would lay aside the distance, without lessening the dignity of the professor, and mix with his pupils at his table upon terms of the most endearing equality. Upon these occasions his social affections seemed to have an influence upon his mind. Science, sentiment, and convivial humor, appeared for hours together to strive which should predominate in his conversation. I appeal to you, gentlemen, who have shared in the pleasure which I have described, for the justice of the picture which I have drawn of him at his hospitable table. You will recollect, with me, how agreeably he accommodated himself to our different capacities and tempers; how kindly he dissipated our youthful blushes, by inviting us to ask him questions; and how much he taught us, by his inquiries, of the nature of the soil, climate, products, and diseases of even our own country.

From the history that has been given of Dr. Cullen, we shall not be surprised at the reputation which he gave to the university of Edinburgh, for upwards of thirty years. The city of Edinburgh during his life became the very atmosphere of medicine. But let me not here be unjust to the merits of his illustrious colleagues. The names of Whytt, Rutherford, the Monroes, Black, the Gregories, Hope, and Home, will always be dear to the lovers of medical science. May every healing plant bloom upon the graves of those of them who are departed! and may those who have survived him together with their new associate, the learned and excellent Dr. Duncan, long continue to maintain the honor of that justly celebrated school of medicine!

It remains now that I add a short account of Dr. Cullen's conduct as a physician and a man.

In his attendance upon his patients, he made their health his first object, and thereby confirmed a line between the mechanical and liberal professions; for while wealth is pursued by the former, as the end of labour, it should be left by the latter, to follow the more noble exertions of the mind. So gentle and sympathizing was

Dr. Cullen's manner in a sick room, that pain and distress seemed to be suspended in his presence. Hope followed his footsteps, and death appeared frequently to drop his commission in a combat with his skill. He was compassionate and charitable to the poor; and from his pupils, who consulted him in sickness, he constantly refused to receive any pecuniary satisfaction for his services.

In his intercourse with the world he exhibited the manners of a well-bred gentleman. He exercised upon all occasions the agreeable art, in which true politeness is said to consist, of speaking with civility, and listening with attention to every body. His conversation was at all times animated, agreeable and instructing. Few persons went into his company without learning something; and even a common thought, by passing through his mind, received an impression, which made it ever afterwards worth of being preserved.

He was a strict economist of time. He seldom went out of his house in his carriage, or a sedan chair, without a book in his hand; and he once told me, that he frequently employed one of his sons to read to him after he went to bed, that he might not lose that portion of time which passes between lying down, and falling asleep.

He was remarkably punctual to all his professional engagements. He appeared to consider time as a species of property which no man had a right to take from another without his consent.

It was by means of his economy and punctuality in the use of time, that he accomplished so much in his profession. I have read of some men who have spent more time in their closets, and of others who have done more business; but I have never read, nor heard of a man, who mingled more study and business together. He lived by rule, without subjecting himself to the slavery of forms. He was always employed, but never in a hurry; and amidst the numerous and complicated avocations of study and business, he appeared to enjoy the pleasure of society, as if company-keeping and conversation were the only business of his life.

I shall mention but one more trait in the character of Dr. Cullen, and that is, that he was distinguished by no one singularity of behaviour from other men. It is true he stood alone; but this singularity was occasioned, not by his quitting the society of his fellow-men by walking on their left, or right side, but by his walking before them. Eccentricities in behaviour are the offspring of a lively fancy only, but order is inseparably connected with real genius. The actions of the former may be compared to the crooked flash of distant lightning, while the latter resembles in its movements the steady revolutions of the heavenly bodies.

In reviewing the character which has been given of Dr. Cullen, I am forced to make a short digression, while I do homage to the profession of physic by a single remark. So great are the blessings which mankind derive from it, that if every other argument failed to prove the administration of a providence in human affairs, the profession of medicine alone would be sufficient for that purpose. Who can think of the talents, virtues, and services of Dr. Cullen, without believing that the Creator of the world delights in the happinesss of his creatures, and that his tender mercies are over all his works!

For the information of such of the members of our college as have not seen Dr. Cullen, it may not be improper to add the following description of his person. He was tall, slender, and had a stoop in his shoulders; his face was long; his under lip protruded a little beyond the upper; his nose was large, and inclined to a point downwards; his eye, which was of a blue colour, was penetrating, but soft; and over his whole face was diffused an air of mildness and thought, which was strongly characteristic of the constant temper and operations of his mind.

It pleased God to prolong his life to a good old age. He lived near 78 years. He lived to demonstrate how much the duration of all the faculties of the mind depends upon their constant exercise. He lived to teach his brethren by his example, that the obligations to acquire and communicate knowledge, should cease only with health and life; and lastly, he lived to reap the fruits of his labours in the most extensive fame; for not only his pupils, and his works, had conveyed his reputation; but canvass, paper, and clay, had borne even the image of his person to every quarter of the globe.

The public papers, as well as private letters, inform us, that he survived his usefulness but a few months. He resigned his professorship in the autumn of 1789, on account of bodily weakness, and died in the month of January of the present year; a year fatal to the pride of man; for this year Franklin and Howard, as well as Cullen, have mingled with the dust. During the interval between his resignation and his death he received the most affectionate marks of public and private respect. The city of Edinburgh voted him their thanks, and presented him with a piece of plate. This instance of public gratitude deserves our particular attention, as it is more common for cities to treat their eminent literary characters with neglect during their lives, and centuries afterwards to contend for the honor of having given them birth. The different medical societies of Edinburgh followed him to his chamber with addresses full of gratitude and affection. In mentioning these facts, I am led to contemplate the venerable subject of our praises in a situation truly solemn and interesting. How pregnant with instruction is the deathbed of a physician, who has spent a long life in extensive and successful practice! If the sorrows we have relieved are the surest support in our own, how great must have been the consolation which Dr. Cullen derived, in his last hours, from a review of his active and useful life! How many fathers and mothers, husbands and wives, brothers and sisters, whose tears he had wiped away by averting the stroke of death from the objects of their affections, must have presented themselves to his imagination, and soothed his soul with grateful prayers for his eternal welfare! But the retrospect of the services he had rendered to his fellow-creatures, was not confined to the limits of his extensive business in the city of Edinburgh. While the illustrious actions of most men may be viewed with a naked eye, the atchievements of Dr. Cullen in the distant regions of humanity and science, can only be perceived by the help of a telescope. Let us apply this instrument to discover his exploits of beneficence in every quarter of the world. He had filled the capitals, and most of the towns of Great-Britain and Ireland with eminent physicians. Many of his pupils had arrived at the first honors in their profession in the principal cities on the continent of Europe. Many of them had extended the blessings of his impróvements in the principles and practice of medicine, to every British settlement in the East and West Indies, and to every free state in America. But the sum of his usefulness did not end here. He had taught the different Professors in the University of Pennsylvania, the art of teaching others the most successful methods of curing diseases, and thereby he had conveyed the benefits of his discoveries into every part of the United States. How great was the mass of such accumulated beneficence! and how sublime must have been the pleasure which the review of it created in his mind! Had it been possible for the merit of such extensive and complicated services to mankind to have rescued one mortal from the grave, Dr. Cullen had never died. But the decree of death is universal, and even the healing art, is finally of no effect in saving the lives of those who have exercised it with the most success in saving the lives of others.

Dr. Cullen is now no more. What a blank has been produced by his death in the great volume of science! Behold! The Genius of Humanity weeping at his feet, while the Genius of Medicine lifts up the key, which fell from his hand with his last breath, and with inexpressible concern, cries out, "to whom shall I give this instrument? Who now will unlock for me the treasures of universal nature?"

Venerable Shade, adieu! What though thy American pupils were denied the melancholy pleasure of following thee from thy Professor's-chair to thy sick bed, with their effusions of gratitude, and praise! What though we did not share in the grief of thy funeral obsequies, and though we shall never bedew with our tears the splendid monument which thy affectionate and grateful British pupils have decreed for thee in the metropolis of thy native country; yet the remembrance of thy talents and virtues, shall be preserved in each of our bosoms, and never shall we return in triumph from beholding the efficacy of medicine in curing a disease, without feeling our obligations for the instructions we have derived from thee!

I repeat it again, Dr. Cullen is now no more—No more, I mean, a pillar and ornament of an ancient seat of science—no more, the delight and admiration of his pupils—no more the luminary of medicine to half the globe—no more the friend and benefactor of mankind.—But I would as soon believe that our solar system was created only to amuse and perish like a rocket, as believe that a mind endowed with such immense powers of action and contemplation had ceased to exist. Reason bids us hope that he will yet *live*—And Revelation enables us to say, with certainty and confidence, that he shall again *live*—Fain would I lift the curtain which separates eternity from time, and inquire—But it is not for mortals to pry into the secrets of the invisible world.

Such was the man whose memory we have endeavoured to celebrate. He lived for our benefit. It remains only that we improve the event of his death in such a manner, that he may die for our benefit likewise. For this purpose I shall furnish our Eulogium with the following observations.

I. Let us learn from the character of Dr. Cullen duly to estimate our profession. While Astronomy claims a Newton, and Electricity a Franklin, Medicine has been equally honoured by having employed the genius of a Cullen. Whenever therefore we feel ourselves disposed to relax in our studies, to use our profession for selfish purposes, or to neglect the poor, let us recollect how much we lessen the dignity which Dr. Cullen has conferred upon our profession.

II. By the death of Dr. Cullen the republic of medicine has lost one of its most distinguished and useful members. It is incumbent upon us therefore to double our diligence in order to supply the loss of our indefatigable fellow-citizen. That physician has lived to little purpose, who does not leave his profession in a more improved state than he found it. Let us remember, that our obligations to add something to the capital of medical knowledge, are equally binding with our obligations to practise the virtues of integrity and humanity in our intercourse with our patients. Let no useful fact therefore, however inconsiderable it may appear, be kept back from the public eye; for there are mites in science as well as in charity, and the remote consequences of both are often alike important and beneficial. Facts are the morality of medicine. They are the same in all ages and in all countries. They have preserved the works of the immortal Sydenham from being destroyed by their mixture with his absurd theories; and under all the revolutions in systems that will probably take place hereafter, the facts which are contained in Dr. Cullen's works, will constitute the best security for their safe and grateful reception by future ages.

III. Human nature is ever prone to extremes. While we celebrate the praises of Dr. Cullen, let us take care lest we check a spirit of free inquiry, by too great a regard for his authority in medicine. I well remember an observation suited to our present purpose which he delivered in his introduction to a course of lectures on the Institutes of Medicine in the year 1766. After speaking of the long continued and extensive empire of Galen in the schools of physic, he said, "It is a great disadvantage to any science to have been improved by a great man. His authority imposes indolence, timidity, or idolatry upon all who come after him."—Let us avoid these evils in our veneration for Dr. Cullen. To believe in great men, is often as great an obstacle to the progress of knowledge, as to believe in witches and conjurers. It is the image worship of science; for error is as much an attribute of man, as the desire of happiness; and I think I have observed, that the errors of great men partake of the dimensions of their minds, and are often of a greater magnitude than the errors of men of inferior understanding. Dr. Brown has proved the imperfection of human genius, by extending some parts of Dr. Cullen's system of physic, and by correcting some of its defects. But he has left much to be done by his successors. He has even bequeathed to them the labor of removing the errors he has introduced into medicine by his neglect of an important principle in the animal economy, and by his ignorance of the histories and symptoms of diseases. Perhaps no system of medicine can be perfect, while there exists a single disease which we do not know, or cannot cure. If this be true, then a complete system of medicine cannot be formed, till America has furnished descriptions and cures of all her peculair diseases. The United States have improved the science of civil government. The freedom of our constitutions, by imparting vigor and independence to the mind, is favourable to bold and original thinking upon all subjects. Let us avail ourselves therefore of this political aid to our researches, and endeavor to obtain histories and cures of all our diseases, that we may thereby contribute our part towards the formation of a complete system of medicine. As a religion of some kind is absolutely necessary to promote morals; so systems of medicine of some kind, are equally necessary to produce a regular mode of practice. They are not only necessary, but unavoidable in medicine; for no physician, nay more, no empire, practices without them.

The present is an age of great improvement. While the application of reason to the sciences of government and religion, is daily meliorating the condition of mankind, it is agreeable to observe the influence of medicine, in lessening human misery, by abating the mortality or violence of many diseases. The decrees of heaven appear to be fulfilling by natural means; and if no ancient prophecies had declared it, the late numerous discoveries in medicine would authorize us to say, that the time is approaching, when not only tyranny, discord and superstition shall cease from our world, but when diseases shall be unknown, or cease to be incurable; and when old age shall be the only outlet of human life,

"Thus heaven-ward all things tend."

In that glorious aera, every discovery in medicine shall meet with its full reward; and the more abundant gratitude of posterity to the name of Dr. Cullen; shall then bury in oblivion the feeble attempt of this day to comply with your vote to perpetuate his fame.

An Eulogium upon David Rittenhouse, Late President of the American Philosophical Society; Delivered before the Society in the First Presbyterian Church in High-Street, Philadelphia, on the 17th December, 1796, Agreeably to Appointment, and Publsihed at the Request of the Society.

GENTLEMEN of the Philosophical Society, Friends and Colleagues, We are assembled this day upon a mournful occasion. Death has made an inroad upon our Society. Our illustrious and beloved PRESIDENT is no more. RITTENHOUSE, the ingenious, the modest and the wise—Rittenhouse, the friend of God and man, is now no more!—For this, the temple of science is hung in mourning—for this our eyes now drop a tributary tear. Nor do we weep alone.—The United States of America sympathize in our grief, for his name gave a splendor to the American character, and the friends of humanity in distatnt parts of the world, unite with us in lamenting our common loss—for he belonged to the whole human race.

By your vote to perpetuate the memory of this great and good man, you have made a laudable attempt to rescue philosophers from their humble rank in the history of mankind. It is to them we owe our knowledge and possession of most of the necessaries and conveniences of life. To procure these blessings for us, "they trim their midnight lamp, and hang o'er the sickly taper." For us, they traverse distant regions, expose themselves to the inclemencies of the weather, mingle with savages and beasts of prey, and in some instances, evince their love of science and humanity by the sacrifice of their lives.

The amiable philosopher whose talents and virtues are to be the subject of the following eulogium, is entitled to an uncommon portion of our gratitude and praise. He acquired his knowledge at the expense of uncommon exertions, he performed services of uncommon difficulty, and finally he impaired his health, and probably shortened his life, by the ardor of his studies and labors for the benefit of mankind.

In attempting to discharge the difficult and painful duty you have assigned to me, it will be necessary to give a short account of the life of Mr. Rittenhouse, insomuch as several of the most interesting parts of his character are intimately connected with it.

The village of Germantown in the neighbourhood of this city, had the honor of giving birth to this distinguished philosopher on the 8th day of April, in the year 1732. His ancestors migrated from Holland about the beginning of the present century. They were distinguished, together with his parents, for probity, industry, and simple manners. It is from sourses thus pure and retired, that those talents and virtues have been chiefly derived, which have in all ages enlightened the world. They prove by their humble origin, that the Supreme Being has not surrendered up the direction of human affairs to the advantages acquired by accident or vice, and they bear a constant and faithful testimony of his impartial goodness, by their necessary and regular influence in equalizing the condition of mankind. This is the divine order of things, and every attempt to invert it, is a weak and unavailing effort to wrest the government of the world from the hands of God.

The early part of the life of Mr. Rittenhouse was spent in agricultural employments under the eye of his father, in the county of Montgomery, twenty miles from Philadelphia, to which place he removed during the childhood of his son. It was at this place his peculiar genius first discovered itself. His plough, the fences, and even the stones of the field in which he worked, were frequently marked with figures which denoted a talent for mathematical studies. Upon finding that the native delicacy of his constitution unfitted him for the labors of husbandry, his parents consented to his learning the trade of a clock and mathematical instrument maker. In acquiring the knowledge of these useful arts, he was his own instructor.—They afforded him great delight inasmuch as they favoured his disposition to inquire into the principles of natural philosophy.—Constant employment of any kind, even in the practice of mechanical arts has been found, in many instances, to administer vigor to human genius. Franklin studied the laws of nature, while he handled his printing types. The father of Rousseau, a jeweller at Geneva, became acquainted with the principles of national jurisprudence, by listening to his son while he read to him in his shop, the works of Grotius and Puffendorf; and Herschel conceived the great idea of a new planet, while he exercised the humble office of a musician to a marching regiment.

It was during the residence of our ingenious philosopher with his father in the country, that he made himself master of Sir Isaac Newton's principia, which he read in the English translation of Mr. Mott. It was here likewise he became acquainted with the science of fluxions, of which sublime invention he believed himself for a while to be the author, nor did he know for some years afterwards, that a contest had been carried on between Sir Isaac Newton and Liebnitz, for the honor of that great and useful discovery. What a mind was here!—Without literary friends or society, and with but two or three books, he became, before he reached his four and twentieth year, the rival of the two greatest mathematicians in Europe!

It was in this retired situation, and while employed in working at his trade, that he planned and executed an orrery, in which he represented the revolutions of the heavenly bodies in a manner more extensive and complete, than had been done by any former astronomers. A correct description of this orrery drawn up by the Rev. Dr. Smith, is published in the first volume of our Transactions. This master-piece of ingenious mechanism was purchased by the college of New-Jersey. A second was made by him, after the same model, for the use of the college of Philadelphia. It now forms part of the philosophical apparatus of the University of Pennsylvania, where it has for many years commanded the admiration of the ingenious and the learned, from every part of the world.

The reputation he derived from the construction of this orrery, as well as his general character for mathematical knowledge, attracted the notice of his fellow-citizens in Pennsylvania, and in several of the neighbouring states, but the discovery of his uncommon merit belonged chiefly to his brother-in-law, the Rev. Mr. Barton, Dr. Smith, and the late Mr. John Lukens, an ingenious mathematician of this city. These gentlemen fully appreciated his talents, and united in urging him to remove to Philadelphia, in order to enlarge his opportunities of improvement and usefulness. He yielded with reluctance to their advice, and exchanged his beloved retirement in the country for this city, in the year, 1770. Here he continued for several years, to follow his occupation of a clock and mathematical instrument maker. He excelled in both branches of that business. His mathematical instruments have been esteemed by good judges to be superior in accuracy and workmanship to any of the same kind that have been imported from Europe.

About the time he settled in Philadelphia, he became a member of our Society. His first communication to the Society was a calculation of the transit of Venus as it was to happen on the 3d of June, 1769, in 40 degrees north latitude, and 5 hours west longitude from Greenwich. He was one of a committee appointed by the Society to observe, in the township of Norrington, this rare occurence in the revolution, of that planet, and bore an active part in the preparations which were made for that purpose. Of this Dr. Smith who was likewise of the committee, has left an honourable record in the history of that event which is published in the first volume of the transacitons of our Society. "As Mr. Rittenhouse's dwelling (says the Doctor) is about twenty miles north west from Philadelphia; our other engagements did not permit Mr. Lukens or myself to pay much attention to the necessary preparations; but we knew that we had intrusted them to a gentleman on the sport [meaning Mr. Rittenhouse] who had, joined to a complete skill in mechanics, so extensive and astronomical, and mathematical knowledge, that the use, management and even construction of the apparatus were perfectly familiar to him. The laudable pains he had taken in these material articles will best appear from the work itself, which he hath committed into my hands, with a modest introduction, giving me a liberty with them, which his own accuracy, taste and abilities leave no room to exercise."

We are naturally led here to take a view of our philosopher with his associates in their preparations to observe a phaenomenon which had never been seen but twice before by any inhabitant of our earth, which would never be seen again by any person then living, and on which depended very important astronomical consequences. The night before the long expected day, was probably passed in a degree of solicitude which precluded sleep. How great must have been their joy when he beheld the morning sun, "and the whole horizon without a cloud;" for such is the description of the day given by Mr. Rittenhouse in the report referred to by Dr. Smith. In pensive silence, and trembling anxiety they waited for the predicted moment of observation; it came, and brought with it all that had been wished for and expected by those who saw it. In our philosopher, it excited in the instant of one of the contacts of the planet with the sun, an emotion of delight so exquisite and powerful, as to induce fainting. This will readily be believed by those who have known the extent of that pleasure which attends the discovery, or first perception of truth. Soon after this event, we find him acting as one of a committee appointed to observe the transit of Mercury on the 9th of November in the same year. This was likewise done at Norrington. An account of it was drawn up, and published at the request of the committee by Dr. Smith. A minute history of the whole of these events, in which Mr. Rittenhouse continued to act a distinguished part, is given in our transactions. It was received with great satisfaction by the astronomers of Europe, and contributed much to raise the charter of our then infant country for astronomical knowledge.

In the year 1775, he was appointed to compose and deliver the annual oration before our society. The subject of it, was the history of astronomy. The language of this oration is simple. but the sentiments contained in it are ingenious, original, and in some instances, sublime. It was delivered in a feeble voice, and without any of the advantages of oratory, but it commanded, notwithstanding, the most profound attention, and was followed by universal admiration and applause from a crowded and respectable audience.

From the contents of this oration, it appears that Astronomy was the favourite object of his studies.

Attempts have been made to depreciate this branch of natural philosophy, by denying its utility, and application to human affairs.—The opinion is an unjust one, and as it tends to convey a limited idea of the talents of Mr. Rittenhouse, I hope I shall be excused in saying a few words in favour of this science.

It is to astronomy we are indebted for our knowledge of navigation, by which means the different parts of our globe have been discovered, and afterwards cemented together by the mutual wants and obligations of commerce.

It was astronomy that taught mankind the art of predicting and explaining eclipses of the Sun and Moon, and thereby delivered them from the superstition which in the early ages of the world, was connected with those phaenomena of nature.

We are taught by astronomy to correct our ideas of the visible heavens, and thus by discovering the fallacy of the simple evidence of our senses, to call to their aid, the use of our reason, in deciding upon all material objects of human knowledge.

Astronomy delivers the mind from a groveling attachment to the pursuits and pleasure of this world. "Take the miser (says our philosopher in his oration) from the earth, if it be possible to disengage him—he whose nightly rest has been long broken by the loss of a single foot of it, useless perhaps to him; and remove him to the planet Mars, one of the least distant from us—Persuade the ambitious monarch to accompany him, who has sacrificed the lives of thousands of his subjects to an imaginary property in certain small portions of the earth, and point out this earth to them, with all its kingdoms and wealth, a glittering star, close by the moon, the latter scarce visible, and the former, less bright than our evening star.—They would turn away their disgusted sight from it, not thinking it worth their smallest attention, and seek for consolation in the gloomy regions of Mars."

Once more—the study of astronomy has the most friendly influence upon morals, and religion. "Yes," (says our philosopher in another part of his oration) "The direct tendency of this science is to dilate the heart with universal benevolence, and to enlarge its views. It flatters no princely vice, nor national depravity. It encourages not the libertine by relaxing any of the precepts of morality, nor does it attempt to undermine the foundations of religion. It denies none of those attributes, which the wisest and best of mankind have in all ages ascribed to the Deity. Nor does it degrade the human mind from that dignity which is ever necessary to make it contemplate *itself* with complacency. None of these things does astronomy pretend to, and if these things merit the name of philosophy, and the encouragement of a people, then let scepticism flourish, and astronomy lie neglected. Let the names of Barkley and Hume become immortal, and that of Newton be lost in oblivion."—

The following is a list of such of Mr. Rittenhouse's other publications as are contained in the three volumes of our transactions.

Observations of the comet which appeared in June and July 1770, with the elements of its motion and the trajectory of its path in a letter to Dr. William Smith.

An easy method of deducing the true time of the sun's passing the meridian, by means of a clock, from a comparison of four equal attitudes, observed on two succeeding days, without the help of the equation tables, communicated by Dr. William Smith.

An explanation of an opticle deception, namely, that the surfaces of bodies viewed through the double microscope, sometimes appear to be reversed, that is, those parts which are elevated seem depressed, and the contrary.

An account of a remarkable meteor observed at Philadelphia on the 31st of October, 1775, with some conjectures relative to the theory of meteors, in answer to a letter from John Page, Esq. giving an account of the same meteor seen in many distant places in Virginia.

Conjectures, corroborated by experiments, relative to a new theory of magnetism; in a letter to John Page, Esq. of Virginia.

A new method of placing a meridian mark for a transit instrument within a few feet of the observatory, so as to have all the advantages of one placed at a great distance; in a letter to the Rev. Dr. John Ewing.

Observations on a comet discovered in the month of January 1784.

An explanation of a curious optical phaenomenon, namely, if a candle or other luminous body be viewed through a silk umbrella, handkerchief or the like, the luminous body will appear to be doubled; in a letter to Francis Hopkinson, Esq.

A series of observations made at sundry times in the years 1784, 85, and 86 on the new planet, or Georgium Sidus, also an observation of the transit of Mercury over the Sun's disk on the 12th of November 1782.

An account of three horses in Philadelphia struck with lightning on the 7th of June, 1789.

An account of the effects of a stroke of lightning upon a house furnished with two metallic conductors on the 17th of August, 1789; in a letter to Mr. Robert Patterson.

Astronomical observations made at Philadelphia, containing an account of the eclipse of the Moon on the 2d of November 1789.

An account of the transit of Mercury over the Sun's disk, on the 5th of November 1789.

An account of the eclipse of the Sun, on the 6th of November 1790, with an account of corresponding observations, made at the University of William and Mary, in Virginia, by Dr. J. Madison, and at Washington College, in Maryland, by the Rev. Dr. Smith.

Short and elegant theorems for finding the sum of the several powers of the lines, either to a radius of unity, or any other; in a letter to Mr. Robert Patterson.

Besides these publications, our society is in possession of the following communications from Mr. Rittenhouse, which are now in the press and will be speedily published in the fourth volume of our transactions.

A method of determining the true plane of a planet in an eliptical form by converging series, directly from the mean anomaly.

A new and easy method of calculating logarithms; in a letter to Mr. Robert Patterson.

A description of an improvement on pendulum clocks, by which the error arising from the different density, or resistance of the medium in which the pendulum vibrates, is effectually obviated.

Lastly, experiments on the expansion of wood by heat.

Talents so splendid, and knowledge so practical in mathematicks, are like mines of precious metals. They become public property by universal consent. The State of Pennsylvania was not insensible of the wealth she possessed in the mind of Mr. Rittenhouse. She claimed him as her own, and employed him in business of the most important nature.

In the year 1779 he was appointed by the legislature of Pennsylvania, one of the commissioners for adjusting a territorial dispute between Pennsylvania and Virginia, and to his talents, moderation and firmness, were ascribed in a great degree, the satisfactory termination, of that once alarming controversy in the year 1785.

In the year 1784 he assisted in determining the length of five degrees of longitude from a point on the Delaware, in order to fix the western limits of Pennsylvania.

In 1786, he was employed in fixing the northern line which divides Pennsylvania fron New-York.

But the application of his talents and knowledge to the settlement of territorial disputes, was not confined to his native state. In the year 1769, he was employed in settling the limits between New-Jersey and New-York, and in 1787 he was called upon to assist in fixing the boundary line between the States and Massachusetts and New-York. This last business, which was executed with his usual precision and integrity, was his farewell peace offering to the union and happiness of his country.

In his excursions through the wilderness, he carried with him his habits of inquiry and observation. Nothing in our mountains, soils, rivers, and springs escaped his notice. It is to be lamented that his private letters, and the memories of his friends, are the only records of what he collected upon these occasions. Philosophers, or naturalist, whosoever thou art! that shalt hereafter traverse the unfrequented woods of our state, forget not to respect the paths, first marked by the feet of this ingenious and faithful servant of the public. Honour the fountains consecrated to science by his skilful hand, and inhale with double pleasure the pure atmosphere of the mountains, on which he renewed his acquaintance with the canopy of heaven, after passing whole weeks in forests so shady, as to conceal from him the rays of the sun. And citizens of Pennsylvania, friends and patrons of literature, be grateful for his services. Let the remembrance of them be dear to the present generation, and let a part of the state distinguished in a more especial manner for its resources in natural knowledge, bear his name with honor to the latest posterity.

In the year 1791, he was chosen successor to Dr. Franklin in the chair of our society. In this elevated station, the highest that philosophy can confer in our country, his conduct was marked by its usual line of propiety and dignity. Never did the artificial pomp of station command half the respect, which followed his unassuming manners in the discharge of the public duties of this office. You will often recollect, gentlemen, with a mixture of pleasure and pain, the delightful evenings you passed in the society, every time he presided in your meeting. They were uniformly characterized by ardor in the pursuits of science, urbanity and brotherly kindness. His attachment to the interests of the society was evinced soon after he accepted the President's chair, by a donation of three hundred pounds.

But his talents and knowledge were not limited to mathmatical or material subjects; his mind was a repository of the knowledge of all ages and countries. He had early and deeply studied most of the different systems of theology. He was well acquainted with practical metaphysicks. In reading travels he took great delight. From them, he drew a large fund of his knowledge of the natural history of our globe. He possessed talents for music and poetry, but the more serious and necessary pursuits of his life, prevented his devoting much time to the cultivation of them. He read the English poets with great pleasure. The muse of Thomson charmed him most. He admired his elegant combination of philosophy and poetry.

However opposed these studies may appear, they alike derive their perfections from extensive and accurate observations of the works of nature. He was intimately acquainted with the French, German and Dutch languages, the two former of which he acquired without the assistance of a master. They served the valuable purpose of conveying to him the discoveries of foreign nations, and thereby enabled him to prosecute his studies with more advantage, in his native language.

In speaking of Mr. Rittenhouse, it has been common to lament his want of what is called a liberal education.—Were education what it should be, in our public seminaries, this would have been a misfortune, but conducted as it is at present, agreeably to the systems adopted in Europe in the sixteenth century, I am disposed to believe that his extensive knowledge, and splendid character are to be ascribed chiefly to his having escaped the pernicious influence of monkish learning upon his mind in early life. Had the usual forms of a public education in the United Stated been imposed upon him; instead of revolving through life in a planetary orbit, he would probably have consumed the force of his genius by fluttering around the blaze of an evening taper. Rittenhouse the philosopher, and one of the luminaries of the eighteenth century, might have spent his hours of study in composing syllogism, or in measuring the feet of Greek and Latin poetry.

It will be honourable to the citizens of the United States, to add, that they were not insensible of the merit of our philosopher. Inventions and improvements in every art and science, were frequently submitted to his examination, and were afterwards patronised by the public, according as they were appproved by him. Wherever he went, he met with public respect, and private attentions. But his reputation was not confined to his native country. His name was known and admired in every region of the earth, where science and genius are cultivated and respected.[1]

---

[1] The degree of master of Arts was conferred upon him by the College of Philadelphia, in 1768. The same degree was conferred upon him by the College of William and Mary, in Virginia, in 1784. In the year 1789, he received the degree of Doctor of Laws from the College of New-Jersey. He was elected a Member of the American Academy of Arts and Sciences at Boston in 1782, and of the Royal Society in London in 1795.

Such were the talents and knowledge, and such the fame, of our departed President! His virtues now demand our tribute of praise.— And here, I am less at a loss to know what to say, than what to leave unsaid. We have hitherto beheld him as a philosopher, soaring like the eagle, until our eyes have been dazzled by his near approaches to the sun. We shall now contemplate him at a less distance, and behold him in the familiar character of a man, fulfilling his various duties in their utmost extent. If any thing has been said of his talents and knowledge that has excited attention, or kindled desires in the younger members of our society, to pursue him in his path of honor, let me request them not to forsake me here. Come, and learn by his example, to be good, as well as great.—His virtues furnish the most shining models for your imitation, for they were never obscured in any situation or stage of his life, by a single cloud of weakness or vice. As the source of these virtues, whether of a public or private nature, I shall first mention his exalted sense of moral obligation, founded upon the revelation of the perfections of the Supreme Being. This appears from many passages in his oration, and from his private letters to his friends. In his oration we find the following pious sentiment. "Should it please that Almighty Power who hath placed us in a world in which we are only permitted 'to look about us and to die,' to indulge us with existence throughout that half of eternity which still remains unspent, and to conduct us through the several stages of his works, *here* (meaning in the study of astronomy) is ample provision made for employing every faculty of the mind, even allowing its powers to be enlarged through an endless repetition of ages. Let us not complain of the vanity of this world, and that there is nothing in it capable of satisfying us. Happy in those wants—happy in those desires, forever in succession to be gratified—happy in a continual approach to the Deity."

"I must confess that I am not one of those sanguine spirits who seem to think that when the withered hand of death has drawn up the curtain of eternity, all distance between the creature and the Creator, and between finite and infinite, will be annihilated. Every enlargement of our faculties—every new happiness conferred upon us, every step we advanced towards the Divinity, will very probably render us more and more sensible of his inexhaustible stores of communicable bliss, and of his inaccessible perfections."

There appears to be a natural connection between a knowledge of the works of nature and just ideas of the divine perfections; and if philosophers have not in all ages been equally devout with our President, it becomes us to acquire how far the beneficial influence of philosophy upon religion, may have been prevented by their minds being pre-occupied in early life with the fictions of ancient poets, and the vices of the heathen gods. It remains yet to be determined, whether all the moral as well as natural attributes of the Deity may not be discovered in the form, and economy of the material world, and whether that righteousness which descended from heaven near eighteen hundred years ago, may not wait for philosophical truth to spring up from the earth, in order by uniting with it, to command universal belief and obedience. This opinion as far as it relates to one of the moral attributes of the Deity, seems to have been admitted by our philosopher in the following elegant and pious extract from a letter to one of his friends "give me leave (says he) to mention two or three proofs of infinite goodness in the works of creation. The first is, possessing goodness in ourselves. Now it is inconsistent with all just reasoning to suppose, that there is any thing good, lovely, or praise-worthy in us, which is not possessed in an infinitely higher degree by that Being who first called us into existence. In the next place I reckon the exquisite and innocent delight that many things around us are calculated to afford us. In this light the beauty and fragrance of a single rose is a better argument for divine goodness than a luxuriant field of wheat. For if we can suppose that we are created by a malevolent Being with a design to torment us for his amusement, he must have furnished us with the means of subsistence, and either have made our condition tolerable, or not have left the means of quitting it at pleasure, in our own power. Such being my opinions, you will not wonder at my fondness for what Mr. Addison calls 'the pleasures of the imagination.' They are all to me, so many demonstration of infinite goodness."

If such be the pious fruits of an attentive examination of the works of the Creator, cease ye ministers of the gospel to defeat the design of your benevolent labors, by interposing the common studies of the schools between our globe, and the minds of young people. Let their first ideas be those which are obtruded upon their senses, by the hand of nature. Permit the firmament of heaven, and the animal, vegetable and mineral productions of the earth, to instruct them in the wisdom and goodness of the Creator, and let the effects of physical evil upon general happiness, vindicate the divine government, in permitting the existence of moral evil in our world. Thus the perverse passions of man, may be made to unite with storms and tempests, in furnishing proofs of the goodness of the Creator of the Universe.

But the religion of Mr. Rittenhouse, was not derived wholly from his knowledge and admiration of the material world. He believed in the Christian revelation. Of this, he gave many proofs, not only in the conformity of his life, to the precepts of the gospel, but in his letters and conversation. I well recollect in speaking to me of the truth and excellency of the Christian religion, he mentioned as an evidence of its divine origin, that the miracles of our Saviour differed from all other miracles, in being entirely of a kind and benevolent nature. It is no small triumph to the friends of Revelation to observe, in this age of infidelity, that our religion has been admitted and even defended by men of the most exalted understanding, and of the strongest reasoning powers. The single testimony of David Rittenhouse in its favor, outweighs the declamations of whole nations against it.[2]

As the natural effect of his belief in the relation of the whole human race to each other in a common Father and Redeemer, he embraced the whole family of mankind in the arms of his benevolence. The force and extent of this virtue in his heart, will

---

[2] Since the publication of the Eulogium in a pamphlet, I have received the following account of Mr. Rittenhouse's religious principles, in a letter from his widow, dated August 20th, 1797. "That you were sufficiently authorized to assert what you did respecting Mr. Rittenhouse's religious principles, I now add my testimony to what you have said, for well I know the great truths of religion engaged much of his attention, and indeed were interwoven with almost every important concern of his life. I do not recollect, if in any of the conversations I have had with you, I informed you, what I now do, that Dr. Price's opinions respecting Christianity were more in unison with his own, than any others of the divines; that Dr. Price's sermons was the last book he requested me to read to him, and that the last morning of his life, he reminded me that I had not finished one of the Doctor's discourses which I had began the preceeding evening."

appear from my reading one more extract from his oration. I am aware how much I suffer by introducing quotations from that eloquent performance, for they will cast a shade upon all I have said, or shall say upon this occasion.

"How far, (says our philosopher) the inhabitants of the other planets may resemble men, we cannot pretend to say. If like them they were created liable to fall, yet some, if not all of them may still retain their original rectitude. We will hope they do; the thought is comfortable.—Cease then Galileo to improve thy optic tube, and thou great Newton, forbear thy ardent search, into the mysteries of nature, lest ye make unwelcome discoveries. Deprive us not of the pleasure of believing that younder orbs, traversing in silent majesty the etherial regions, are the peaceful seats of innocence and bliss, where neither natural or moral evil has ever intruded, and where to enjoy with gratitude and adoration the Creator's bounty, is the business of existence. If their inhabitants resemble man in their faculties and affections, let us suppose that they are wise enough to govern themselves according to the dictates of that reason, God has given in such a manner, as to consult their own, and each other's happiness upon all occasions. But if on the contrary, they have found it necessary to erect artificial fabrics of government, let us not suppose they have done it with so little skill, and at such an enormous expense, as to render them a misfortune, instead of a blessing.—We will hope that their statesmen are patriots, and that their kings (if that order of beings has found admittance there) have the feelings of humanity. Happy people!—and perhaps more happy still, that all communication with us is denied. We have neither corrupted you with our vices, nor injured you by violence. None of your sons and daughters have been degraded from their native dignity, and doomed to endless slavery in America, merely because their bodies may be disposed to reflect, or absorb the rays of light, different from ours. Even you, inhabitants of the Moon, situated in our very neighbourhood, are effectually secured from the rapacious hands of the oppressors of our globe. And the utmost efforts of the mighty Frederick, the tyrant of the North, and scourge of mankind, if aimed to disturb your peace, becomes inconceivably ridiculous and impotent."

"Pardon these reflections. They arise not from the gloomy spirit of misanthropy. That Being, before whose piercing eye all the intricate foldings of the human heart, become expanded, and illuminated, is my witness with what sincerity, with what ardor—I wish for the happiness of the whole race of mankind.—How much I admire that disposition of lands and seas which affords a communication between distant regions, and a mutual exchange of benefits—How sincerely I approve of those social refinements, which add to our happiness, and induce us with gratitude to acknowledge our Creator's goodness, and how much I delight in a participation of the discoveries made from time to time in nature's works, by our philosophical brethren in Europe. But (adds our philosopher) when I consider that luxury, and her constant follower tyranny, which have long since laid the glories of Asia in the dust, are now advancing like a torrent, irresistible, and have nearly completed their conquest over Europe—I am ready to wish—vain wish! that nature would raise her everlasting bars between the new and the old world, and make a voyage to Europe as impracticable as one to the moon."

As when a traveller in passing through a wilderness, slackens his pace to prolong the pleasure of a sudden and unexpected prospect of a majestic river pouring its waters down the declivity of a cloud-cap't mountain, and spreading fertility and verdure throughout the adjacent vallies, so we feel disposed to pause, and feast upon the sublime sentiments contained in the passage which I have read. Citizens of the United Staes, receive and cherish them as a legacy from a friend, or a brother. Be just, and loose the bands of the African slave. Be wise, and render war odius in our country. Be free, by assuming a national character and name, and be greatly happy, by erecting a barrier against the corruptions in morals, government, and religion, which now pervade all the nations of Europe.[3]

---

[3] Mr. William Barton, nephew to Mr. Rittenhouse, has favoured me with the following extract of a letter in September, 1755, to his brother-in-law, the Rev. Mr. Barton, who was the friend and correspondent of his youth, which shews how early and deeply the principles of universal benevolence were fixed in his mind.

"I would sooner give up my interest in a future state, than be divested of humanity;—I mean that good will I have to the species, although one half of them are said to be fools, and almost the other half knaves. Indeed I am firmly persuaded, that

But the philanthropy of Mr. Rittenhouse did not consist simply in wishes for the happiness of mankind. He reduced this divine principle to practice by a series of faithful and disinterested services to that part of his fellow creatures, to which the usefulness of good men is chiefly confined. His country, his beloved country, was the object of the strongest affections of his heart. For her, he thought,— for her, he laboured,—and for her in the hours of her difficulties and danger, he wept,—in every stage of the American revolution. Patriots of 1776, you will acquit me of exaggeration here, for you feel in the recollection of what passed in your own bosom, a witness of the truth of each of these assertions. The year of the declaration of Independence, which changed our royal governments into Republics, produced no change in his political principles for he had been educated a Republican by his father. I can never forget the pleasure with which he avowed his early but secret attachment to an elective and representative form of government. Often have I heard him above twenty years, ago, predict the immense encrease of talents and knowledge which has been produced by the strength and activity that have been infused into the American mind, by our republican constitutions. Often, likewise, at the same remote period of time, have I heard him anticipate with delight, the effects of our revolution in sowing the seeds of a new order of things in other parts of the world. He believed political, as well as moral evil to be intruders into the society of man—that general happiness was the original design, an ultimate end of the divine government, and that a time would come, when every part of our globe, would echo back the heavenly proclamation of universal peace on earth, and good will to man.

Let it not be said, that he departed from the duties of a Philosopher, by devoting a part of his time and talents to the safety and happiness of his country. It belongs to monarchies, to limit the business of government to a privileged order of man, and it is from the remains of a monarchical spirit in our country, that we com-

---

we are not at the disposal of a Being who has the least tincture of ill-nature, or requires any in us.—You will laugh at this grave philosophy, or my writing to you on a subject which you have thought of a thousand times: but, can any thing that is serious, be ridiculous?—Shall we suppose Gabriel smiling at Newton, for labouring to demonstrate whether the earth be at rest or not, because the former plainly sees it move!"

plain when clergymen, physicians, philosophers and mechanics, take an active part in civil affairs. The obligations of patriotism are as universal and binding, as those of justice and benevolence, and the virtuous propensities of the human heart are as much resisted by every individual who neglects the business of his country, as they are by the extinction of the domestic affections in a cell. Man was made for a republic, and a republic was made for men, otherwise Divine power and goodness have been wasted, in the creation and gift of his public affections.—Our philosopher adopted this truth from the evidence of his feelings, in common with the rest of mankind, but it was strongly reinforced in his mind by numerous analogies of nature. How was it possible for him to contemplate light and air as the common and equal portions of every man, and not acknowledge that heaven intended liberty to be distributed in the same manner among the whole human race! Or how could he behold the beauty and harmony of the universe, as the result of universal and mutual dependence, and not admit that heaven intended rulers to be dependent upon those, for whose benefit alone, all government should exist. To suppose the contrary, would be to deny unity and system in the plans of the great creator of all things.

I shall make no apology for these sentiments. They are not foreign to the solemnity of this discourse. Had I said less of the political principles and conduct of our enlightened President, hundreds and thousands of my fellow-citizens would have accused me, of an act of treachery to his memory. May the time never come, in which the praises of our republican governments, shall not be acceptable to the ears of an American audience!

In the more limited circles of private life, Mr. Rittenhouse commanded esteem and affection. As a neighbour he was kind and charitable. His sympathy extended in a certain degree to distress of every kind, but it was excited with the most force, and the kindest effects, to the weakness, pain and poverty of old age.—As a friend he was sincere, ardent, and disinterested. As a companion, he instructed upon all subjects. To his happy communicative disposition, I beg leave to express my obligations in this public manner. I can truly say, after an acquaintance with him for six-and-twenty years, that I never went into his company, without learning something. With pleasure have I looked beyond my present labours to a time, when his society should constitute one of the principal enjoyments of the evening of my life.—But alas! that time, so often anticipated, and so delightful in prospect—will never—come. I hope it will not be thought that I tread too closely upon his footsteps, when I presume to lift the latch of his door, and to exhibit him in the domestic relations of a husband and father. It was the practice of the philosophers of former ages, to pass their lives in their closets, and to maintain a formal and distant intercourse with their families! but our philosopher was a stranger to pride and imposture in every thing. His family constituted his chief society, and the most intimate circle of his friends. When the declining state of his health, rendered the solitude of his study, less agreeable than in former years, he passed whole evenings in reading or conversing, with his wife and daughters. Happy family! so much and so long blessed with such a head! and happier still, to have possessed dispositions and knowledge to discern and love his exalted character, and to enjoy his instructing conversation!—Thus Sir Thomas Moore lived with his accomplished wife and daughters;—Thus Cicero educated his beloved Tullia; and in this way only, can the female sex be elevated to that dignity, and usefulness in society, for which they were formed, and by which from their influence upon manners, a new era would be created in the history of mankind.

The house and manner of living of our president, exhibited the taste of a philosopher, the simplicity of a republican, and the temper of a Christian. He was independent, and contented with an estate, small in the estimation of ambition and avarice, but amply suited to all his wants and desires. He held the office of treasurer of Pennsylvania, by an annual and unanimous vote of the legislature, between the years 1777, and 1789. During this period, he declined purchasing the smallest portion of the public debt of the state, thereby manifesting a delicacy of integrity, which is known and felt only by pure and elevated minds.

In the year 1792, he was persuaded to accept of the office of Director of the mint of the United States. His want of health, obliged him to resign it in 1795. Here his conduct was likewise above suspicion, for I have been informed by his colleague in office,[4] that

---

[4] Dr. Way.

in several instances, he paid for work done at the mint out of his salary, where he thought the charges for it would be deemed extravagant by the United States.

His economy extended to a wise and profitable use of his time. No man ever found him unemployed. As an apology for detaining a friend a few minutes, while he arranged some papers he had been examining, he said, "that he had once thought health, the greatest blessing in the world, but that he now thought there was one thing of much greater value, and that was time." The propriety of this remark will appear when we consider, that Providence, so liberal in other gifts, bestows this, in a sparing manner. He never gives a second moment, until he has withdrawn the first, and still reserves the third in his own hand.

The countenance of Mr. Rittenhouse, was too remarkable to be unnoticed upon this occasion. It displayed such a mixture of contemplation, benignity, and innocence, that it was easy to distinguish his person in the largest company, by a previous knowledge of his character. His manners were civil, and engaging to such a degree, that he seldom passed an hour, even in a public house, in travelling through our country without being followed by the good wishes of all who attended upon him. There was no affectation of singularity, in any thing he said or did: even his hand writing, in which this weakness so frequently discovers itself, was simple and intelligible at first sight to all who saw it.

Here I expected to have finished the detail of his virtues, but in the neighbourhood of that galaxy created by their connected lustre, I behold a virtue of inestimable value, twinkling like a rare, and solitary star. It is his superlative modesty. This heaven born virtue was so conspicuous in every part of his conduct, that he appeared not so much to conceal as to be ignorant of his superiority as a philosopher and a man, over the greatest part of his fellow creatures.

In reviewing the intellectual endowments and moral excellency of Mr. Rittenhouse, and our late intimate connection with him, we are led to rejoice in being men.

We proceed now to the closing scenes of his life.

His constitution was naturally feeble, but it was rendered still more so, by sedentary labor, and midnight studies. He was afflicted for many years with a weak breast, which, upon unusual exertions of body or mind, or sudden changes in the weather, became the seat of a painful and harrassing disorder. This constitutional infirmity was not without its uses. It contributed much to the perfection of his virtue, by producing habitual patience and resignation to the will of heaven and a constant eye to the hour of his dissolution. It was a window through which he often looked with pleasure towards a place of existence, where from the encrease and perfection of his intuitive faculties, he would probably acquire more knowledge in an hour, than he had acquired in his whole life, by the slow operations of reason; and where, from the greater magnitude and extent of the objects of his contemplation, his native globe, would appear like his cradle, and all the events of time, like the amusements of his infant years.

On the 26th of June, of the present year, the long expected messenger of death, disclosed his commission. In his last illness, which was acute and short, he retained the usual patience and benevolence of his temper. Upon being told that some of his friends had called at his door to enquire how he was; he asked why they were not invited into his chamber to see him. "Because (said his wife) you are too weak to speak to them." "Yes (said he) that is true, but I could still have squeezed their hands,"—Thus with a heart overflowing with love to his family, friends, country, and to the whole world, he peacefully resigned his spirit into the hands of his God. Let the day of his death be recorded in the annals of our society, and let its annual return be marked by some public act, which shall characterise his services and our grief, and thereby animate us and our successors, to imitate his illustrious example!

It has been the fashion of late years, to say of persons who had been distinguished in life, when they left the world in a state of indifference to every thing, and believing, and hoping in nothing, that they died like philosophers. Very different was the latter end of our excellent president. He died like a christian, interested in the welfare of all around him—believing in the resurrection, and the life to come, and hoping for happiness from every attribute of the Deity.

Agreeably to his request, his body was interred in his observatory near his dwelling house, in the presence of a numerous concourse of his fellow-citizens. It was natural for him in the near prospect of appearing in the presence of his Maker, to feel an attachment to that spot in which he had cultivated a knowledge of his perfections, and held communion with him through the medium of his works. Hereafter it shall become one of the objects of curiosity in our city. Thither shall the philosophers of future ages resort to do homage to his tomb, and children yet unborn, shall point to the dome which covers it, and exultingly say, "there lies our Rittenhouse."

Let us my respected colleagues, repair for a few minutes to that awful spot.—In entering it—we behold the telescope, dear instrument of his discoveries, turned upon its axis, and pointed to the earth, which has closed its master's eyes.—How artless—the inscription upon his tombstone!—It contains nothing but his name, and the simple record of the days and years of his birth and death.—Very different would have been the monument of his worth and fame, had not the gratitude and affection of his friends been controuled by his dying request. His head would have reclined in marble, upon the lap of religion. At his feet, science would have sat—bathed in tears; while the genius of republican liberty, in the figure of a venerable hermit, bending over his grave, would have deplored the loss of his favourite son.—Alas!—too—too soon has our beloved president been torn from the chair of our society!—Too soon has he laid aside his robes of office, and ceased to minister for us day and night at the alter of science!—Ah! who now will elevate his telescope, and again direct it towards yonder heavens? Who now will observe the transit of the planets? Who now will awaken our nation to view the trackless and stupendous comet? Who now will measure the courses of our rivers, in order to convey their streams into our city, for the purposes of health and commerce?—Nature is dumb;—for the voice of her chief interpreter is hushed in death.—In this hour of our bereavment, to whom shall we look?—but to THEE, FATHER of life and light:—thou author of great and good gifts to man. O! let not thy Sun, thy Moon, and thy Stars now shine unobserved among us! may the genius of our departed president, like the mantle of thy prophet of old, descend upon some member of our society, who shall, as he did, explain to us the misteries of thy works, and lead us step by step, to THYSELF, the great overflowing fountain of wisdom, goodness and mercy, to the children of men!

FINIS